REFLECTIVE HISTORY SERIES

Barbara Finkelstein and William J. Reese, Series Editors

Curriculum & Consequence:
Herbert M. Kliebard and the Promise of Schooling
BARRY FRANKLIN, EDITOR

Schooled to Work:
Vocationalism and the American Curriculum,
1876–1946
HERBERT M. KLIEBARD

Moral Education in America:
Schools and the Shaping of Character
from Colonial Times to the Present
B. EDWARD MCCLELLAN

The Failed Promise of the
American High School, 1890–1995
DAVID L. ANGUS & JEFFREY E. MIREL

HERBERT M. KLIEBARD

Photo by Jeff Miller

CURRICULUM
&
CONSEQUENCE

Herbert M. Kliebard
and the Promise of Schooling

Edited by
BARRY M. FRANKLIN

FOREWORD BY ARNO BELLACK

Teachers College, Columbia University
New York and London

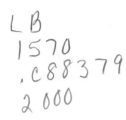
Published by Teachers College Press, 1234 Amsterdam Avenue, New York, NY 10027

Library of Congress Cataloging-in-Publication Data

Curriculum and consequence : Herbert M. Kliebard and the promise of schooling / edited by Barry M. Franklin.
    p. cm. — (Reflective history series)
   Includes bibliographical references and index.
   ISBN 0-8077-3951-0 (alk. paper) — ISBN 0-8077-3950-2 (pbk. : alk paper)
    1. Education—United States—Curricula—History. 2. Curriculum planning—United States—History. 3. Education—United States—Philosophy—History. 4. Kliebard, Herbert M.   I. Kliebard, Herbert M.
II. Franklin, Barry M. III. Series.
LB1570.C88379 2000
375'.001'0973—dc21   00-020248

ISBN 0-8077-3950-2 (paper)
ISBN 0-8077-3951-0 (cloth)

Contents

PART III
CURRICULUM DIFFERENTIATION

PART IV
LIBERAL EDUCATION AND THE CURRICULUM

Foreword

The curriculum as a field of professional study in American education emerged in the early decades of this century. It wasn't until the 1950s and 1960s, however, that the history of curriculum development came to be viewed as an important area for scholarship and research. The first review essay dealing with the history of curriculum thought and practice in the *Review of Educational Research* series, published by the American Educational Research Association, appeared in 1969, and in 1977 the Society for the Study of Curriculum History was founded.

Dawning interest in historical studies of curriculum was occasioned in large part by the continuing debates about education in the United States that had proceeded without interruption since the end of World War II. All aspects of the school's operation came under scrutiny by critics, but the curriculum, particularly, found itself in direct line of fire from individuals and groups representing widely divergent views about what should be taught in the schools. As a result, curriculum specialists found themselves engaged in a great deal of soul searching and self-criticism. One of the most telling charges against the curriculum field from within its own ranks was that it had lost historical perspective and that a preoccupation with current problems had led it to ignore the historical roots out of which these problems had arisen.

Among the internal critics was Herbert Kliebard who early in his career had called attention to the curious fact that in the curriculum field "each generation is left to discover anew the persistent and perplexing problems that characterize the field." Already in his doctoral studies he had developed an interest in curriculum history, but it was after he joined the University of Wisconsin faculty in the mid-1960s that he concentrated his research efforts on historical studies of the curriculum.

Through his writing and research Herb has been singularly influential in reorienting the curriculum field to include historical studies in its research agenda. His most influential work, *The Struggle for the American Curriculum, 1893–1958*, stands at the heart of his approach to curriculum history. It is an absorbing exposition of his thesis that "by the 1890s the forces for control of the American curriculum were in place, and the early part of the twentieth century became the battleground for that struggle." Specifically, it is the history of the continuing battle for control of the curriculum among competing groups, identified as humanists, developmentalists, social efficiency educators, and social meliorists. Each group proposed its distinctive ideological answer to the basic curriculum question of what knowledge available in our culture lays legitimate claim to a place in the instructional program of the schools. The outcome of this struggle was "an undeclared, almost unconscious, detente" among the contesting groups. "What became the American curriculum," Herb contends, "was not the result of any decisive victory by any one of the contending parties, but a loose, largely unarticulated and very untidy compromise." Through meticulous research Herb thus offers a persuasive interpretation of reform efforts during the first half century, not as a unitary movement labeled "Progressive Education," but as several reform movements each with its unique agenda for curriculum change.

Herb's influence in bringing curriculum history to prominence came not only through his writing and research but also through his role as Professor of Education at the University of Wisconsin, as two of his colleagues, Thomas Popkewitz and Michael Apple, testify in essays included in this volume. They point to Herb's curriculum courses that provided graduate students with historical perspective in a field traditionally lacking a sense of history and to his success in advising doctoral candidates, many of whom selected dissertation topics in curriculum history. Above all, they point to the admirable collegial relationships Herb enjoyed with students and faculty and cite as examples the influence Herb's work had, and continues to have, on their own work.

In recognition of Herb's exemplary achievements in both scholarship and teaching, the School of Education at the University of Wisconsin honored him with its Distinguished Faculty Award, and Columbia's Teachers College presented him with its Distinguished Alumni Award.

I would like to add a personal word. I have known Herb as a friend and colleague for almost 40 years. Our association goes back to Herb's graduate studies at Teachers College when he was a valued member of a research staff studying classroom teaching. In that capacity he demonstrated competence in empirical research that equaled the high competence he now displays in historical research. Over the years we have kept in close touch, occasionally collaborating on projects and always ready to confer and correspond about educational matters, frequently trying out ideas not yet fully developed. Also, I have enjoyed getting to know Herb's family, and I have appreciated the generous hospitality of Herb and his wife Bernice during my occasional visits to Madison.

I join the authors of this volume in extending congratulations to Herb on his retirement after a long and successful career.

Arno Bellack
New York City, New York

Introduction

Herbert M. Kliebard's Intellectual Legacy

Barry M. Franklin

Nothing has come closer to the mark in singling out the core of Herbert Kliebard's scholarly enterprise than did the remarks of one reviewer of *Forging the American Curriculum* who noted that in every chapter in this important book Kliebard asks "where and why did theorizing about the American curriculum go wrong" (Ramsay, 1993, p. 460). For Kliebard, throughout his 36 years on the faculty of the University of Wisconsin-Madison, this question of why and how twentieth-century curriculum theorists have gone astray has been a persistent theme that he has returned to again and again in 7 books, almost 80 essays and articles and numerous conference papers and presentations.

This volume helps to commemorate, at the time of his retirement from the University of Wisconsin, the career and legacy of Herbert Kliebard. It brings together essays written by colleagues and former students that explore issues in which Kliebard pioneered. These authors try to extend the discussion to new intellectual terrain and, like Kliebard, seek to answer the question of what went wrong.

Early in his career Kliebard chose history as the best vehicle for uncovering the errors and misconceptions of the curriculum field. This was understandable since his doctoral adviser at Columbia University's Teachers College, Arno Bellack, had a strong interest in the history of the curriculum and later wrote the key essay that defined curriculum history as a field of study (Bellack, 1969). Although Kliebard's first book and his earliest articles explored topics of classroom discourse and teaching, and many of his publications were efforts to explore curriculum theory, his historical scholarship became the most widely known and read. Clearly, no contemporary scholar has done more to make curriculum history a recognized field of inquiry than has Kliebard. In his foreword to Kliebard's most recent book, *Schooled to Work*, William J. Reese (1999) labeled him "the leading historian of curriculum of his generation" (p. x).

Two interrelated themes have been especially important in Kliebard's historical and theoretical work (see Kliebard, 1992). One is the issue of *democracy*. Kliebard, not unlike his intellectual hero, John Dewey, has devoted himself to examining what he sees as the misdirected efforts of many twentieth-century educators to sacrifice principles of democracy and equality in the search for supposedly more efficient and utilitarian ways of selecting, organizing, and distributing school knowledge. The underlying message in this work, as it was in Dewey's, is that schools and their curricula should serve to cultivate a democratic citizenry and promote a sense of the common good.

The second theme is that of *liberal education*. To Kliebard's way of thinking, one of the most grievous errors of those who have worked in the curriculum field during this century has been their abandonment of liberal education in favor of curricular schemes that justify schooling for its external and functional ends and not for its intrinsic values. Two issues on this score have been particularly troubling to him. One has been the efforts of American school reformers throughout this century to vocationalize the school curriculum, thereby narrowing the goal of schooling to occupational preparation. The other has been the apparent willingness of twentieth-century curriculum leaders to sacrifice a commitment to the cultivation of intelligence, which for Kliebard stands at the heart of liberal education, in favor of curricular programs that are thought to meet the immediate concerns and interests of youth. It is in examining these two themes that Kliebard has, throughout his writings, explored both the consequences that have accompanied our curriculum thought and practice, and the promise that schooling holds out for our citizenry and polity.

Although perhaps analytically distinct, these two themes appear together in Kliebard's writings. From his vantage point, attempts to substitute a more directly functional curriculum for liberal education have most threatened the democratic purposes to which American public schooling should aspire. Thus Kliebard looks to Dewey for his vision of liberal education and for his critique of efforts to stray from it. As Kliebard (1995) himself has noted, he has often used Dewey's voice as a way of offering his own comments on the state of the American curriculum.

Herbert Kliebard was born in New York City in 1930, attended New York City public schools, and graduated from City College of New York in 1952 with a bachelor's degree in English. He began teaching English at Bronx Vocational High School while working on a master's degree at

City College. He completed his degree during the Korean War and in 1953 was drafted into the U.S. Army. Following two years of military service, Kliebard returned to Bronx Vocational for a year and then assumed a position as a reading specialist in the Nyack, New York, Public Schools.

While teaching in Nyack, Kliebard began graduate study in reading at Teachers College. Although he enjoyed graduate study, he did not find his course work in reading to be particularly stimulating. Consequently, after receiving his educational specialist degree, he switched to the field of curriculum and began doctoral work with Arno Bellack as his adviser. While completing his doctorate, he served as Bellack's research associate for the project that would result in the publication of his first book, *The Language of the Classroom,* which he coauthored with Bellack, Ronald Hyman, and Frank Smith, Jr. (1966). In 1963, Kliebard received his Ed.D. in curriculum and joined the faculty of the University of Wisconsin-Madison where he remained for the next 36 years.

During his early years at Wisconsin, Kliebard did try to incorporate curriculum history into some of the courses that he was teaching. His attraction to this subject was, in his words, "somewhat instinctual" and represented his lens for interpreting curriculum issues. Yet, curriculum history was not the focus of his teaching or scholarship. In fact, at this point in his career he was teaching the course entitled the Nature of Instruction and was publishing essays on classroom discourse and teaching. Sometime in 1966 or 1967, as he recalls, he was invited back to Teachers College to give a lecture on a topic of his choice. He selected curriculum history as his theme. The lecture and subsequent article, "The Curriculum Field in Retrospect" (1968), was his first publication that was explicitly devoted to curriculum history. Thereafter, he explored curriculum history in a more self-conscious way, making it the focus of his teaching and scholarship. (The biographical information in the last three paragraphs is from H. Kliebard, personal communication, June 16, 1998.)

My first encounter with Herbert Kliebard was somewhat serendipitous. I arrived at the University of Wisconsin-Madison in the fall of 1970 a year after completing a master's degree in the teaching of history from another university. Because of a lack of available positions for secondary social studies teachers, I had spent the intervening year as an administrator for the Human Resources Administration of the City of New York working on a curriculum development project in the area of manpower training. Hoping this time to avoid the perils of an obviously tight job market for both social studies teachers and historians, I decided to embark on a doctoral program in curriculum.

As it turned out, the faculty member who served as my temporary adviser during my first year at Wisconsin had a practice of assigning his graduate students to the courses that they were to take. For reasons that I never quite figured out, he often assigned students who had the same research interests to very different courses. It was fortuitous that I was the first of his new graduate students to meet with him; among the courses he selected for me for my first semester of work was Curriculum Planning with Herbert Kliebard. If I had come later, I could have just as easily been assigned to any of a number of other courses to which he directed his new graduate students, such as statistics, educational research methods, or the social psychology of education. More than anything, it was that first course with Herb that reminded me again of my abiding interest in history and offered me a view of how that interest could serve as an important lens for interpreting issues of curriculum. It was, in fact, my ongoing contact with Professor Kliebard during the ensuing four years that led me to focus my doctoral study on curriculum history, to select a historical topic for my dissertation, and to make curriculum history my research specialty as I embarked on my own career in higher education.

As I developed ideas for the research paper that was required in Curriculum Planning, I had call on numerous occasions to visit Herb during his office hours. I would typically arrive at his door, which was always open, and leave two or three hours later, having talked in collegial fashion about my prospective paper, the educational world in general, and almost everything and anything in between. Nothing that occurred during my first year as a graduate student at Wisconsin did more to give me a sense of intellectual confidence concerning my abilities to complete my doctorate than did these opportunities to be able to share ideas on an equal footing with such a well-known scholar as Herbert Kliebard. Later I was to learn that this kind of accessibility was a hallmark of Herb's presence at the University of Wisconsin.

The most memorable times of my relationship with Herbert Kliebard have been the two occasions when he asked me to coauthor essays with him. Herb does not often write with others and I took it as a distinct honor to be invited to be his coauthor, once early in my career and again during the last two years. In both instances it was a joy to work with Herb. He is a wonderful model of careful research, thoughtful deliberation, and masterful prose. What I remember most from these two experiences is the concern that he had for ensuring that the project was truly a collaboration. As we exchanged computer disks or, in the case of the first essay, written drafts, I was continually struck by his concern that what was in the text was a reflection of the thinking of both of us and by the efforts he took to ensure that our work relationship was not that of an apprentice and his master but a true partnership. In my own collaborative research efforts, I have turned to my work with Herbert Kliebard for my model.

The eight essays that make up this volume are quite diverse in their content and approach. In some instances, the authors are exploring issues about which Kliebard himself has written. In other cases, the issues are different although related to concerns which guided his work. As I noted earlier, two characteristics bind these essays together: (a) They all address and often extend treatment of subjects that Kliebard was one of the first, if not the first, to explore, and (b) their impetus is to figure out how and why our theorizing about these curricular matters went wrong and to examine the resulting consequences.

I have already pointed out that the ideas of John Dewey have always played a major role in Kliebard's scholarship; his own viewpoint on matters educational and social is clearly very Deweyan. In addition, Kliebard has been an important interpreter of Dewey's educational philosophy. His examination of the curriculum at the University of Chicago Laboratory School in *The Struggle for the American Curriculum* (1995) is one of the best and clearest expositions of what Dewey meant by the progressive organization of subject matter and how that view was applied to the creation of an actual course of study.

The first two essays in the volume, one by Daniel Pekarsky and the other by José Rosario, also take their cues from Dewey. In Chapter 1 Pekarsky revisits what has been a key concern of Herbert Kliebard's, the place of educational objectives in the process of curriculum planning. Like Kliebard, Pekarsky examines Dewey's treatment of ends or aims and their relationship to human action. He argues that Kliebard was correct in his critique of the Tyler Rationale in warning us against the belief that curriculum planning cannot take place without external objectives. Pekarsky goes on to say, however, that such a belief is misguided if, taken too far, it becomes a rejection of any reliance on external objectives in educational planning. What is called for, he maintains, is a nuanced understanding of the value of considering the ends of action, one that leads to a notion of "guiding visions." Pekarsky concludes by arguing that invoking these guiding visions in our curriculum planning is consistent with Dewey's warning about a slavish concern for the future while helping us to clarify and to provide a rationale for our educational practice.

José Rosario's essay is one of two in this collection that carries on the kind of tradition of classroom research that marked Kliebard's early scholarship. In Chapter 2 Rosario examines what he believes to be the longstanding but futile quest of American school reformers to reconstitute schools as communities. His starting point is Dewey's notion of community, which he interprets through a communitarian lens. What defines a community for Dewey, Rosario argues, is its cultivation of character, virtue, and civic mindedness. Dewey's notion of community, in other words, sees the school or any other communitarian setting as a venue for moral education. Rosario then turns to his own ethnographic studies of two urban middle schools, which he names Rosebush and Owen, that explicitly sought to restructure themselves as communities. In both instances Rosario judged the efforts were failures because personnel of both schools, particularly the principals, invoked the notion of community to describe what were managerial strategies designed for accountability and control, not for the cultivation of character, virtue, and civic mindedness.

What has troubled Kliebard about the impact of efficiency-oriented thinking on the curriculum has been its penchant for standardization and uniformity. For Kliebard (1971) this has been clearly an antidemocratic impetus that threatens the sense of adventure and intellectual satisfaction that should accompany educational activity and reduces it to a process of regimentation. In this vein, he has been particularly critical in his writings of efforts throughout this century to use the schools as instruments of social control for perpetuating existing social-class arrangements and the social inequality that they brought (1995). The chapters by Michael Apple and Thomas Popkewitz extend Kliebard's treatment of the notion of social control in insightful and interesting ways.

In Chapter 3 Michael Apple explores the politics surrounding both recent neoliberal, market-oriented reforms, such as vouchers and choice programs, and neoconservative reforms, such as state and national curriculum standards and student performance testing. As Apple sees it, these reforms are part of a larger movement, which he labels the "conservative restoration," whose stated goal is to dominate not only education but, in his words, "all things social." The impetus for this effort, according to Apple, is clearly rightist in orientation and claims to seek a return to a supposed, albeit romanticized, past of hierarchy, order, and stability. Drawing, however, on the work of a number of scholars associated with the new sociology of education, including Pierre Bourdieu and Basil Bernstein, Apple shows how such neoliberal efforts to promote vouchers and choice programs square with the neoconservative and authoritarian goals of its restoration partners.

Apple concludes his essay by suggesting how progressive-minded educators can counter this trend.

During the last several years, Kliebard has himself offered an innovative approach to the issue of social control by exploring the symbolic impact of such curriculum movements as vocational education. Efforts to vocationalize the curriculum, he argues, never lived up to the promise of preparing students to enter the workforce or of improving the competitiveness of the American economy. The great regulative success of the proponents of vocational education, according to Kliebard (1990, 1999), was their ability to manipulate the language of vocationalism to create certain beliefs about work, schooling, and the duties of citizenship.

In pursuing this line of argument, Kliebard is in effect talking about the language in which we frame curriculum proposals and theories, or what postmodern curriculum scholars refer to as "curriculum discourse." Chapter 4, by Thomas Popkewitz, is in this postmodern tradition and historically explores what he sees as the regulative, or governing, role of the curriculum. The history of curriculum, Popkewitz argues, is an account of changes in the knowledge (rules of classifications and categories) that organizes school subjects, teaching, and childhood. This approach to curriculum studies draws on the tradition of the sociology of knowledge and elements of postmodern social theory that Popkewitz refers to as "social epistemology." Central to his discussion is a method for considering the distinctions about school subjects and children in the curriculum as related to each other and as social practices. Popkewitz's concerns are (a) how the knowledge of schooling embodies social and cultural distinctions about the moral conduct of the individual, and (b) how the curriculum as a theoretical problem of knowledge functions to qualify and disqualify individuals for action and participation. In exploring these issues, Popkewitz's understanding of curriculum history goes beyond more traditional accounts that liken the regulative role of the curriculum to the state building required to provide for new administrative capacity or to the social control arguments of "hidden curriculum" studies. Far more important, he argues, is how the distinctions and divisions in school knowledge change over time to discipline, construct, and divide the individuality of the teacher and child.

The principal mechanism whereby schools perpetuate class privilege and inequality for Kliebard has been curriculum differentiation (1971). He has written extensively on the successful efforts of early twentieth-century social efficiency-oriented school reformers to institutionalize the practice of channeling students to different educational and life destinies on the basis of often erroneous judgments about their abilities and their supposed citizenship and occupational roles (1975). In this regard, he has given special attention to the place of vocational education and the broader idea of vocationalism in American schooling (1992, 1999; Kliebard & Franklin, in press). Reba Page's essay as well my own offer different twists on this theme in Kliebard's scholarship.

Chapter 5 is the second chapter drawn in part from an ethnographic case study. Like Rosario, Page has expanded and further developed the kind of classroom research that marked Kliebard's early career. In her essay, she explores how Americans during this century have thought about the practice of curriculum tracking. Her starting point is the often inconclusive debate between its supporters and opponents. Page then turns to a case study of tracking-in-practice to illustrate how the "tracking show" goes beyond symbolic action and has real world consequences for students, teachers, and schooling. Finally, Page raises questions about the kind of educational equality people expect from schools and suggests that examining school practices may prove instructive in helping them move past the abstract and seemingly intractable debate between the promoters and opponents of tracking.

My own essay in Chapter 6 examines efforts of classroom teachers from the turn of the twentieth century until the late 1960s to provide for low-achieving children. Despite the pervasive and persistent nature of this problem, we still lack a historical account of this effort. The essay fills this lacuna by using a series of portraits depicting encounters between low-achieving children and classroom teachers during the first 70 years of this century. For the most part, teachers relied on such forms of curriculum differentiation as special classes, curriculum modification, remedial programs, and compensatory education to accommodate these students. Yet, despite the prevalence of these practices, I identify teachers who undertook informal initiatives within their regular classes to provide for low achievers. One such teacher, for example, was Herbert Kliebard during his years in Nyack, New York. I conclude by considering what this historical account tells us about some of today's unresolved issues surrounding the education of low-achieving children, particularly the question of curriculum differentiation.

Taken as a whole, the body of scholarship that Kliebard has produced over his long and incredibly productive career tells an important story. It recounts how American educators during the course of this century abandoned liberal education for a more functional type of schooling and what negative consequences for our children and our culture resulted from such education (Kliebard, 1984, 1988). Kliebard does not provide his readers with a specific curriculum remedy to address this problem. If, however, we listen for the voice of Dewey in his work, we get the sense that Kliebard's brand of liberal education, too, is one that seeks to find a common ground where the natural, almost endless curiosity of children and their yearning for mastery intersect with the disciplines of knowledge (Kliebard, 1977). The last two essays in this volume address the question of liberal education.

Chapter 7, by William Reese, examines the career of America's most important late-nineteenth-century educational leader and defender of liberal education, William T. Harris. Reese's intent is to explain why this important figure in the educational world of his day—superintendent of the St. Louis Public Schools, president of the National Educational Association, and longtime U.S. Commissioner of Education—became in his own lifetime an anachronism with little influence and few supporters. Although he championed a number of educational innovations, what offset these accomplishments and doomed Harris's standing and prestige, Reese speculates, was his support of common schools and an academic curriculum and his opposition to the introduction of vocational education in the public schools. Ultimately, his vision of liberal education was undermined by the modern educational ideology of testing, differentiation, and vocationalism.

In Chapter 8 Kathleen Cruikshank uses the 1936 National Council of Teachers of English (NCTE) report, *A Correlated Curriculum*, to explore the efforts of curriculum reformers during this century to locate an alternative to the traditional disciplines of knowledge as the organizing element for the school curriculum. Her focus is the work during the 1930s of NCTE's Curriculum Commission and the role in that group assumed by the organization's president, Ruth Mary Weeks. Weeks, according to Cruikshank, is representative of those educators who, though sympathetic to the idea of curriculum integration, did not simply embrace the efficiency-oriented thinking about the necessity of rendering the school program more utilitarian. What these reformers sought was a means of changing the curriculum in line with the best progressive thinking, while maintaining the value that traditional disciplines gave to the cultivation of the intellect. Cruikshank ends her essay by considering the importance of this viewpoint in the history of the American school curriculum.

As all of the essays in this volume attest, Herbert Kliebard has inspired students and colleagues to examine the curriculum in novel ways. But his own prodigious scholarship is the real testimony to his importance as a researcher. More than anyone else's, Kliebard's writings have defined and shaped curriculum history as a recognized area of inquiry within both curriculum studies and the history of education. His focus on two important tendencies in twentieth-century educational thought— the sacrifice of democratic principles in the name of efficiency and the retreat from liberal education—has yielded a conceptually rich and critically informed body of research. Kliebard's brand of scholarship offers a context for interpreting curriculum work that looks beyond its technical dimensions to consider its broader cultural and political influences. In doing so, his scholarship has helped connect curriculum studies with a larger body of foundational and policy scholarship that augments our broader understanding of the curriculum. In particular, he has advanced the field of Dewey studies by providing what is probably the best treatment of Dewey's thinking about the curriculum. As I pointed out early in the chapter, Kliebard uses Dewey's voice as part of his own authorial expression to provide a sense of how one might employ a Deweyan perspective for interpreting educational issues and problems, both historical and contemporary.

As important as Kliebard's research has been in cementing his legacy, so, too, has been his impact on the work of other scholars and the many hundreds of students he has taught over his long and distinguished career. As the essays in this volume suggest, Kliebard's scholarship has been influential in directing the attention of colleagues, students, and others to significant but often neglected lines of inquiry. His historical account of the development of the American curriculum has uncovered a cast of characters and events that has spurred forward the research and writing of other scholars, both in curriculum studies and in educational history. In the latter area of study, he has played a major role in opening up the curriculum as a legitimate field of inquiry for educational historians.

Kliebard's research on Dewey has been vital in drawing attention to what Dewey has had to say about such perennial curriculum problems as the place of educational objectives and the link between schooling and community. In addition, his extensive work on efficiency-oriented curriculum reform, particularly his research on vocational education, has been instrumental in directing researchers toward further explorations of the regulative role of the curriculum, not only in the United States but internationally. As a result of his continuing search to find out what has gone wrong in the theorizing about the curriculum, Herbert M. Kliebard has bequeathed to scholars in curriculum studies and educational history a terrain in which to work that is far more interesting than it was 36 years ago when he joined the faculty of the University of Wisconsin. The contributors to this volume thus take pride in honoring this man of enormous achievement and great modesty.

REFERENCES

Bellack, A. A. (1969). History of curriculum thought and practice. *Review of Educational Research, 39*, 283–292.

Bellack, A. A., Kliebard, H. M., Hyman, R. T., & Smith, F. L., Jr. (1966). *The language of the classroom*. New York: Teachers College Press.

Kliebard, H. M. (1968). The curriculum field in retrospect. In P. W. F. Witt (Ed.), *Technology and the curriculum* (pp. 69–84). New York: Teachers College Press.

Kliebard, H. M. (1971). Bureaucracy and curriculum theory. In V. F. Haubrich (Ed.), *Freedom, bureaucracy, and schooling* (pp. 74–93). Washington, DC: Association for Supervision and Curriculum Development.

Kliebard, H. M. (1975). The rise of scientific curriculum-making and its aftermath. *Curriculum Theory Network, 5*, 27–38.

Kliebard, H. M. (1977). Curriculum theory: Give me a "for instance." *Curriculum Inquiry, 6*, 257–282.

Kliebard, H. M. (1984). The decline of humanistic studies in the American school curriculum. In B. Ladner (Ed.), *The humanities in precollegiate education* (The eighty-third Yearbook, pt. 2, pp. 7–30). Chicago: National Society for the Study of Education: Distributed by the University of Chicago Press.

Kliebard, H. M. (1988). The liberal arts curriculum and its enemies: The effort to redefine general education. In I. Westbury & A. C. Purves (Eds.), *Cultural literacy and the idea of general education* (The eighty-seventh Yearbook, pt. 2, pp. 29–51). Chicago: National Society for the Study of Education: Distributed by the University of Chicago Press.

Kliebard, H. M. (1990). Vocational education as symbolic action: Connecting schooling with the workplace. *American Educational Research Journal, 27*, 9–28.

Kliebard, H. M. (1992). *Forging the American curriculum: Essays in curriculum history and theory*. New York: Routledge.

Kliebard, H. M. (1995). *The struggle for the American curriculum, 1893–1958* (2nd ed.). New York: Routledge.

Kliebard, H. M. (1999). *Schooled to work: Vocationalism and the American curriculum, 1876–1946*. New York: Teachers College Press.

Kliebard, H. M., & Franklin, B. M. (in press). The ascendance of practical and vocational mathematics, 1893–1945: Academic mathematics under siege. In G. M. A. Stanic & J. Kilpatrick (Eds.), *A recent history of mathematics education*. Reston, VA: National Council of Teachers of Mathematics.

Ramsay, J. G. (1993). [Review of the book *Forging the American curriculum: Essays in curriculum history and theory*]. *History of Education Quarterly, 33,* 459–461.

Reese, W. J. (1999). Foreword. In H. M. Kliebard, *Schooled to work: Vocationalism and the American curriculum, 1876–1946* (pp. ix–xi). New York: Teachers College Press.

PART I
THE DEWEY LEGACY

Chapter 1

Guiding Visions and Educational Planning

Daniel Pekarsky

Responding to an analysis of his earlier critique of the Tyler Rationale (Kliebard, 1970), Herbert M. Kliebard (1995) makes clear his rejection of the view that the process of curriculum planning requires a statement of objectives as an indispensable prerequisite. Identifying his own view with that of Dewey, Kliebard writes:

> With remarkable insight, Dewey . . . once observed that "men have constructed a strange dream-world when they have supposed that without a fixed ideal of a remote good to inspire them, they have no inducement to get relief from present troubles, no desire for liberation from what oppresses and for clearing up what confuses present action." Obviously, Dewey is speaking here not about the curriculum or even of education in a broad sense but about a bizarre human tendency that assumes it is necessary to imagine an idealized state as an impetus for taking action generally. That misguided human tendency is nowhere more evident than in the almost universal belief that objectives are an indispensable ingredient in the curriculum planning process. The rationale is merely the most visible manifestation of that popular delusion. (p. 87)

Although Kliebard's warning against the belief that educational planning and practice cannot proceed meaningfully in the absence of external objectives is very sound, this warning is misguided if it is taken as an injunction to avoid any reliance on external objectives in educational planning. In this essay I will argue that, properly conceived and used, imagined end states have a valuable role to play in guiding educational planning and practice.

As background to the discussion, it will be important to distinguish between different kinds of end states. One can speak about the objectives of any particular learning episode or of an entire curriculum or course. At a broader level, one can speak of the overarching purposes, goals, or vision that inform an educational process or institution—something that addresses the question: What kind of person, possessed of what kinds of skills, understandings, and dispositions, is one hoping to nurture? I will be using the term *guiding vision* to identify this kind of end state. Though questions concerning the desirability of, or need for, articulated end states as guides to educational planning can be raised meaningfully at all of these levels, in this chapter I am interested primarily, but not exclusively, in what I have just characterized as guiding visions and the general educational goals that flow from them.

CRITIQUE OF THE OBJECTIVES DOGMA

I will begin by expressly agreeing with Kliebard's denial that the identification of objectives is indispensable to good teaching and curriculum planning. That this is the case will be readily understood the moment one identifies, as one easily can, instances of great teaching and superb curricula that have not been guided by explicitly articulated objectives. Many of us have met up with educators who have a sure, but very intuitive, sense of what they should be doing with students without ever articulating it systematically to others or even to themselves; in fact, when they do try to articulate what they are doing, they may prove utterly inadequate to the task of explaining what they are doing, why they are doing it, what they are actually accomplishing, or how what they are accomplishing is connected to what they are doing.

Moreover, not only is the identification of objectives not an indispensable guide to the development of excellent teaching and curricula, there are times when it may be seriously destructive to the process of education. Consider, for example, the hypothetical case of an intuitive teacher who is widely recognized as very effective, but who, after encountering the gospel of objectives, determines to become even more effective by systematically identifying his or her objectives and then shaping his or her teaching practice in their light. It is entirely possible that the effort to identify appropriate objectives to guide his or her future activity will fail to capture all, and perhaps even the most important, of the outcomes that his or her traditional practice has been achieving. It is conceivable that if this educator is true to the resolve to redesign his or her teaching practice with systematic attention to these articulated objectives, much of what made this person's teaching most significant will be lost. How powerful one finds this last point will depend on the extent to which one believes there is "a wisdom of practice" that goes significantly beyond what can be articulated, a matter on which Burkeian conservatives and political-educational liberals are likely to disagree; but few would deny that there is at least some merit in this objection to an engineering approach to education (see Atkin, 1970; Oakeshott, 1962).

Dewey's Objections to "Preparation for the Future"

A related but different set of objections to the idea of determining learning experiences in the present based on objectives grounded in a conception of what the child will need to live well down the road is developed by John Dewey. Because of its power, and because it is the view that Kliebard seems to have in mind when he critiques the education-by-objectives approach to curriculum planning, it will be instructive to look carefully at Dewey's position. Dewey (1938/1963) writes:

> When preparation is made the controlling end, then the potentialities of the present are sacrificed to a suppositious future. When this happens, the actual preparation for the future is missed or distorted. The ideal of using the present simply to get ready for the future contradicts itself. It omits, and even shuts out, the very conditions by which a person can be prepared for the future. We always live at the time we live and not at some other time, and only by extracting at each present time the full meaning of each present experience are we prepared for doing the same thing in the future. This is the only preparation which in the long run amounts to anything. (p. 49)

Imagining an approach to education in which the educator's only concern is to nurture characteristics now that will supposedly prove valuable down the road, in this passage Dewey succinctly and suggestively intimates a number of powerful criticisms.

One is that the anticipated future is at best "suppositious." Though what Dewey has in mind by this observation is left vague, his words suggest some powerful points. In the first place, the future is suppositious in that what our own physical, social, and psychological state of being will be down the road is in fact very hard to predict. Indeed, our very existence at some time in the future is mere supposition, a point that figured prominently in Rousseau's (1762/1911) eloquent argumentation against hurtful interventions in the present that are designed to assure the child's future welfare:

What is to be thought, therefore, of that cruel education which sacrifices the present to an uncertain future, that burdens a child with all sorts of restrictions and begins by making him miserable, in order to prepare him for some far-off future which he may never enjoy? . . . Fathers, can you tell when death will call your children to him? Do not lay up sorrows for yourselves by robbing them of the short span which nature has allotted to them. (pp. 42–43)

Another criticism of "preparation for the future" that seems embedded in Dewey's comments is that, life being what it is, the state of the world—the social, technological, and economic circumstances— for which educators are trying to prepare the child may turn out to be wildly different from anything they anticipate at the time. This is particularly likely in a world in which technology changes so rapidly: to focus educational efforts in childhood on the attainment of technological know-how that is likely to prove outdated by the time the children reach adulthood is to proceed foolishly.

Not only is it high risk to adopt an approach to education that empties the present of all meaning save that of getting ready for a future in which what is learned will be usable, it is also high cost; it is, Dewey suggests, dangerous to approach the present simply as a way of getting ready for the future, ignoring all of its potentialities and resources save those that will contribute to that imagined future. Two considerations, one narrow and the other more general, are at work in this judgment.

The narrow reason is that skills acquired in isolation from the contexts in which they enter meaningfully into the individual's life projects and at the cost of doing violence to the child's living concerns and energies are unlikely to be learned well. In particular, they are unlikely to be learned in a way that will render them usable under the actual conditions of life:

But it is a mistake to suppose that the mere acquisition of a certain amount of arithmetic, geography, history, etc. which is taught and studied because it may be useful at some time in the future, has this effect, and it is a mistake to suppose that acquisition of skills in reading and figuring will automatically constitute preparation for their right and effective use under conditions very unlike those in which they are acquired. Almost everyone has had occasion to look back upon his school days and wonder what has become of the knowledge he was supposed to have amassed during his years of schooling, and why it is that the technical skills he acquired have to be learned over again . . . It was segregated when it was acquired and hence is so disconnected from the rest of experience that it is unavailable under the actual conditions of life. It is contrary to the laws of experience that learning of this kind, no matter how thoroughly engrained at the time, should give genuine preparation. (Dewey, 1938/ 1963, pp. 47–48)

The more general reason is that such experiences are ultimately very destructive; to use Dewey's language, they are "miseducative." For instead of teaching the child the important lesson of how to get the very most out of his or her experience, they teach the very opposite; that is, they nurture dispositions which undermine the possibility of making the most of one's experience. Though profoundly important, what Dewey (1938/1963) has in mind may require explanation. It can usefully be broken down into the following claims.

First, human beings make the most of their experience on this earth by being true to each moment of life. We live fully not by deferring richly meaningful experiences to some future point in time for which the present is mere preparation, but by being fully and meaningfully engaged during each present moment.

Second, the disposition and capacity to make each moment rich with meaning is not innate but is itself an achievement that requires nurture. At any given moment, the interaction between the individual and environment is characterized by a multitude of energies, impulses, resources, and constraints; to turn this constellation of "stuff" into a coherent and immediately meaningful plan of action requires careful observation, intelligence, ingenuity, and patience of a high order. These and other characteristics that enter into the disposition and capacity to make the most of each moment are unlikely to arise in the absence of sustained cultivation.

Third, the way to nurture the requisite dispositions and capacities is through experience—that is, through repeated opportunities, initially under the guidance of an educator, to weave present impulses, resources, and constraints into a coherent plan of action that facilitates engaged present activity. In other words, the best way to prepare the child for a future in which he or she is to make the most of every present moment is to encourage and help the child right now in the present to make the most of every present moment. To use an analogy of Dewey's that calls to mind Aristotle's (trans. 1962) account of the genesis of moral virtues: just as it is through swimming that one becomes a good swimmer, it is only by having repeated opportunities to make the most of every present moment that one develops the capacity and disposition to make the most of every moment.

It follows from this that educational arrangements that require the child to subordinate present interest and engagement to the needs of some future end state nurture precisely the wrong dispositions in the child. They nurture not a tendency to make the most of every present moment, but the opposite—the tendency to live without meaning in the present on a bet that some day a meaningful future will accrue. Such a tendency, Dewey suggests, becomes in effect a basic structure of being. Thus Dewey (1922/1957) writes of "the practical man":

> In his utopian search for a future good he neglects the only place where good can be found. He empties present activity of meaning by making it a mere instrumentality. When the future arrives it is only after all another despised present. By habit as well as by definition it is still a means to something which has yet to come. (p. 252)

ON NOT THROWING THE BABY OUT WITH THE BATH WATER

Although there is much that I agree with in the ideas that stand behind the view that attention to objectives and distant ends can and often does have the effect of contaminating rather than aiding educational deliberation and practice, this position warrants scrutiny. Not only is this position problematic, it is even inadequate as a reflection of Dewey's overall position.

Before turning my attention to Dewey, however, I want to comment briefly on the more general view, cited above and associated with certain brands of conservatism, according to which the move from prereflective practice to practice informed by consciously identified objectives carries the risk of losing valuable achievements that, though unrecognized by the participants, are consequences of traditional practice. Although this risk is real, it is doubtful that it should be accorded decisive weight. Whatever the merits of remaining true to traditional practice during historical periods when this practice seems adequate to the needs of the community ("If it ain't broke, don't fix it!"), there is good reason to think systematically about the rationale for and purposes of our practices when they seem to many observers to be purposeless, if not counterproductive. Under such circumstances, the conservative insight that there is often an unrecognized wisdom in traditional practice dictates caution; but it hardly warrants avoiding either careful reflection concerning the whys and wherefores of our practice or the conscious effort to shape practice in the light of our educational aspirations.

Toward a Balanced Deweyan Perspective

I turn now to an assessment of the Deweyan critique of using images of a remote human good to guide educational practice in the present. Note, first, that to the extent that Dewey's argument against using the present to get ready for the future depends on the suppositious character of the future, its strength depends on how suppositious the future actually is. While there is a sense in which *my* future and *the* future are always suppositious, some aspects of the future are much less suppositious than are others. Thus, this particular argument against subordinating the present to the future is fairly strong if the future for which the child is being prepared is defined by certain technological circumstances which are very likely to change. But this is not true of all skills and dispositions that we think the child will need in the future. It is, for example, fairly likely that English proficiency will be a valuable tool for Americans growing up at the end of the twentieth century, and it would be hard to argue against making its acquisition (e.g., by non-English speakers) an objective of educational practice on the ground that its utility down the road is mere supposition. Similarly, we can readily identify certain general dispositions, skills, and attitudes that have a very strong likelihood of being valuable in the distant future, no matter how the future is likely to be different from our imaginings of it; and it would be difficult to assault an intervention designed to cultivate them on the grounds that the future is suppositious.

A very different consideration is this: to prepare the child to become a certain kind of adult has been at the heart of many a parent's educational aspirations for time immemorial; certainly, many parents believe that their job as educators is to lead their children towards a way of life thought by them to be desirable. If Dewey's attack on "preparation for the future" carries the implication that such an approach to child rearing is inherently unwise, I would suggest that this departure from common sense across the ages would cast a measure of doubt on his general position.

It is, of course, possible that Dewey intends this kind of radical departure from age-old beliefs about the nature and aims of education and that this is part of what makes him one of the most revolutionary and interesting educational philosophers of all time. I will argue below, however, that in assaulting the idea of education as preparation Dewey is not objecting to using a vision of human well-being to guide our efforts at education; his view, I will suggest, is considerably more nuanced.

In an effort to develop a balanced account of Dewey's view, I will begin by observing that Dewey's insistence that the present not be sacrificed to the future decidedly does not carry the implication that human beings in general or educators in particular should refrain from thinking about the future as they deliberate about what to do in the present. On the contrary, attention to the future is very important; but its importance does not, in his view, reflect the belief that meaning resides in some future state of affairs to which the present is a subservient means. Rather, as Dewey writes in *Human Nature and Conduct* (1922/1957), attention to the future is warranted for two other reasons.

First, Dewey suggests, attention to a desired future state of affairs potentially attainable through our efforts can give direction and meaning to our present activity. Indeed, a principal criterion of a good aim is its capacity adequately to organize the competing, or in any case disintegrated, impulses found in the present. Note that here Dewey turns on its head a conventional view of the relationship between present and future. The present is not to be understood as a means to some desirable future. Rather, having in mind some desirable future, an end-in-view, is itself a means of making the present meaningful.

Dewey's second reason for urging attention to the future is that, like it or not and for better or for worse, what happens in the present will affect the future. True, our ability to shape the future is very limited, but even a small measure of control is worth a lot, and such control requires us to think carefully about the tendency of possible present activities to bring about certain outcomes.

But this second reason brings an important question into focus: by what standard are we to distinguish between desirable and undesirable future outcomes? It is a question to which Dewey has a resounding response: for an experience to qualify as educative, it must contribute to the agent's growth, helping him or her acquire the skills and habits of mind and heart that will make possible a life of growth (Pekarsky, 1990). This reference to growth points to a powerful reason for believing that Dewey is not arguing against using a vision of human well-being to inform educational planning: namely, he himself relies on such a vision in his educational thinking. For a life of growth, as Dewey understands it, is anything but a nondescript, morally neutral life. On the contrary, it requires an elaborate set of skills, attitudes, and dispositions—specifically, the skills, attitudes, and dispositions that make possible the exercise of intelligence in all aspects of life and enthusiastic participation in a democratic community. It is a vision of human flourishing that also speaks to the question of where and how meaning is to be found in a flourishing life, a vision that emphasizes that life at its best is a process of being fully engaged in the present in ways that contribute to one's continuing growth (Pekarsky, 1990). Aims that emerge out of the life process as means of giving order to otherwise inchoate and competing impulses are to be applauded; on the other hand, the adoption of external goals whose achievement does violence to the energies and impulses at work in the present in the name of a distant future are unacceptable. And what makes them unacceptable is that they violate Dewey's understanding of what it means to live well.

A significant proof, if one is needed, that Dewey's view does not represent a morally neutral vision of human well-being lies in the fact that many will not find this vision at all congenial. Not everyone believes, after all, that human well-being requires continuing growth in Dewey's sense or an unwillingness to sacrifice the present on the altar of the future. A community that holds that the good life consists in not veering from authoritative beliefs and practices ordained by God or a tradition, or that the exercise of intelligence stands in the way of spontaneous enjoyment of life, or that the capacity to delay gratification indefinitely is a sign of moral worthiness will not look favorably on Dewey's espousal of growth; it will rightly see Dewey as recommending a particular—and in their view unacceptable—conception of the good life.

It is, of course, conceivable that although Dewey espouses a vision of human well-being, he fails to recognize that it is deeply intertwined with his approach to education, and that he thinks that educational planning and practice can proceed adequately without reference to any larger vision of human existence. If, in fact, this is Dewey's belief, then he is, I submit, mistaken. However, not only does his approach to education favor the development of those attitudes, dispositions, and understandings that are at the heart of his vision of a flourishing life in its social and individual dimensions, but one could justly say that such a vision is implicit in the way he understands the challenges of intelligent pedagogy and curriculum design. As an example, an approach to educational planning that insists on the importance of letting aims grow out of the present situation and that emphasizes the value of reconciling the disparate energies to be found in the present situation may well be ideally suited to the cultivation of human beings who throughout their lives will, as Dewey hopes they will, approach each present moment in this way.

If Dewey failed to recognize the extent to which his approach to education is tied to his vision of human well-being, this would not be the first or the last instance of such a failure among educational thinkers. But in Dewey's case, it is highly doubtful that he is unaware that he has a vision of the good life and that in a deep and organic way it informs his approach to educational planning and practice. And if this is the case, we are left to ponder what upsets him in the tendency to rely on imagined future states of human flourishing to guide education in the present. I believe that two different concerns are at work in his view. I will argue that Dewey's real complaint is not against using a vision of human well-being to guide our efforts at education, but against (a) reliance on inadequate visions and (b) the ways in which such visions, even adequate ones, typically figure in educational planning. I will briefly consider each of these points in turn.

The first concern pertains to the kinds of visions of human well-being that typically inform educational planning. Surrounded by and responding to prominent educational thinkers associated with the Social Efficiency movement, Dewey is deeply troubled by the narrowly conceived, highly specialized future roles that they believe should guide the education of children growing up in American society. Reliance on visions of human well-being that offer overly narrow, pigeonholed roles for the developing members of the community and that are tied to changeable social and technological circumstances is shortsighted and destructive. But it does not follow from this—nor, I submit, does Dewey believe—that we should do away with all visions; rather, the challenge is to identify—as Dewey believes he has—a vision of human good that incorporates liberally conceived dispositions and abilities that have promise of contributing to the quality of life across a wide range of social circumstances.

There is, however, more to Dewey's objection to educational planning that is dominated by a vision of a temporally remote human good, and this brings me to his second concern. Though he is troubled by the kinds of visions that often inform educational planning, he is, I suggest, as concerned, if not more concerned, with the ways that visions of human well-being (even generously conceived visions) figure in educational planning. More concretely, what troubles him is the idea that the way to actualize a vision of human flourishing is to regard the process of education as a sequence of steps, each of which is preassigned a particular function in the achievement of the overall vision (in the same way as one might build a car by assigning each individual on the assembly line a discrete task). The problem with such an approach is not that a vision of human well-being informs the process, but that this way of using the vision to guide the child's growth is essentially counterproductive. As noted earlier in this essay, the attempt to teach the skills and attitudes associated with this vision in isolation from one another and from real-life engagement will prove ineffective.

But the fact that this unintelligent use of a guiding vision should be rejected does not mean that it is impossible to identify an intelligent approach to the employment of a vision to inform educational planning and practice. And, indeed, I suggest, it is precisely such an approach that Dewey is recommending. That is, Dewey's critique of education as preparation for the future is most forceful and credible if it is understood not as an argument against referring to distant visions of future human good in determining educational arrangements but as primarily a critique of the unintelligent use of such visions. Put differently, the challenge is to be thoughtful and intelligent in using a vision of the ideal graduate or community of graduates as a guide to present conduct, rather than turning childhood into a series of steps, each of which is assigned a particular body of knowledge or attribute of personality or intellect associated with the ideal.

But just what does it mean to be thoughtful and intelligent in using a vision as a guide to practice? For one thing, it may require taking seriously Dewey's notion that we ought never to turn the present into a mere means in the service of some distant future state of being: The needs of the present must always be given their due, and this means that the educator must always help the students make the most of any given present situation. But how, one might ask, is this compatible with the idea that present practice should also be informed by some vision of the kind of person or community that is to be brought into being through education? A credible answer might grow out of the following insight: Since the present can be rendered meaningful in a multitude of ways, having a guiding vision can help the educator to choose, from among different ways of rendering present experience meaningful, those which show promise of leading the child in the direction of the desired ideal.

The point here is analogous and close to Dewey's own comments in *The Child and the Curriculum* (1902), where he speaks of the way to use the mature outlook of civilization in educational decision making. Knowledge of this mature outlook is not to be used as a basis for dividing up the wealth of civilization into skills and understandings that will be sequentially spread across *x* number of years of school. Rather, this outlook makes it possible for the educator better to interpret and see the possible significance of the child's present interests, tendencies to action, and capacities, and to judge how, suitably nurtured, they may lead towards understandings, dispositions, and capacities that will allow for fruitful and mature integration into the larger civilization into which he or she has been born. Dewey (1902) stated it this way:

> Now, the value of the formulated wealth of knowledge that makes up the course of study is that it may enable the educator *to determine the environment of the child*, and thus by indirection to direct. Its primary value, its primary indication, is for the teacher, not for the child. It says to the teacher: Such and such are the capacities, the fulfillments, in truth and beauty and behavior, open to these children. Now see to it that day by day the conditions are such that *their own activities* move inevitably in this direction, toward such culmination of themselves. Let the child's nature fulfill its destiny, revealed to you in whatever of science and art and industry the world now holds as its own. (p. 31)

Thus, a Deweyan approach to educational planning would require the educator to view the living reality that the child represents through the interpretive lenses and the images of what-might-be-possible-for-this-child afforded by the culture. Liberally informed by such perspectives and by the ideal of growth, the educator is to develop a deep understanding of the learner's energies, interests, capacities, skills, understandings, and potentialities, as well as of the resources available in the environment, in order to identify an activity that meaningfully organizes these situational elements and at the same time shows promise of contributing to the child's growth along one or more dimensions.

Two features of this approach are particularly noteworthy. First, the aim of the activity (the kind of growth that will be encouraged) is not determined in advance but emerges out of careful attention to the various elements in the situation. Second, unlike education defined by preexisting objectives, this approach makes full use of the learner's living energies and interests, thus avoiding the sacrifice of present potentialities to the future. Whereas the traditional pedagogy associated with "preparation for the future" transforms the present into a mere means in the service of some future end state, Dewey insists that even as the present is used to prepare for the future, it must always be treated as an end in itself. Even more strongly, Dewey seems to believe that the vision of human well-being that guides the educator's efforts must already live, in some meaningful form, in the present; and if it does not, it is unlikely that this vision will ever be meaningfully embodied in the learner's life. The example cited earlier is particularly instructive: The only way to prepare the child for an adulthood in which he or she consistently makes the most of the present is to give the child guided opportunities to make the most of the present throughout the growing-up years.

Drawing on the work of social philosophers, one might describe this approach to curriculum design as the equivalent of a side-constraint view in social philosophy, that is, a view that insists that achieving social goods is always to be constrained by certain principles (even if abandoning those principles might contribute to the achievement of a particular good). Analogously, the principle that the design of educational experiences must always make full use of the learner's living energies and interests operates, in Dewey's view, as a side constraint on any efforts to promote any desirable future states of being. There is, however, this significant difference: Whereas the side-constraint perspective in social philosophy holds that it is morally unacceptable to violate certain principles in the service of achieving certain end states, Dewey's view seems to be that such trade-offs will prove ineffective— ultimately, sacrificing present for future good will seriously contaminate the future that is brought into being.

THE POWER OF GUIDING VISIONS

I have acknowledged that reliance on guiding visions of a flourishing human life to be achieved through the educational process is not necessary to effective education and that such reliance is capable of distorting the educational process. However, I have also urged that such distortion is by no means inevitable but arises out of the problematic ways in which such visions are used to guide practice. I have further argued that Dewey himself—a principal critic of the ideal of "preparation for the future" who is sometimes viewed as suspicious of educators' reliance on images of human good to be actualized through education—is himself informed by such a vision in thinking about educational practice. Having cleared the way, I now want to speak in a more positive vein about the power and importance of guiding visions.

This point can be established by considering the way in which having a guiding vision can help to clarify and provide a justification for basic educational goals and emphases. Consider, for example, the case of critical thinking, which is often identified as an educational goal. Because it is open to a variety of interpretations, it is always in danger of sliding into empty rhetoric. The situation changes, however, when it is viewed through the lens of a particular vision of human life. To have an understanding of Dewey's vision of the life of a citizen in a democracy is to have a rich understanding not just of what critical thinking is but of the contexts in which it is desirable and the contributions it can make. As should be clear from this example, understanding this kind of an educational goal through the lens of a particular vision of human well-being serves more than one valuable purpose: Not only does it suggest how to interpret the goal, but it also suggests why and how it is important. Clarity concerning such matters, I would submit, can be invaluable in deciding the content and the design of educational experiences that are appropriate for students. While it is true that educational objectives and visions of human good have often been used in ways that contaminate educational process, as noted above, to dismiss them wholesale is to throw the baby out with the bath water.

Although resistance to identifying images of human good as guides to the educational process can, as in Professor Kliebard's case, spring from healthy anxieties concerning the way such images may contaminate educational planning and practice in the here and now, it may sometimes reflect a troubling phenomenon: namely, an inability or unwillingness to decide what at its heart the process of education should be about, what kind of human being and community we Americans should be trying to cultivate through our educational efforts. And this unwillingness may have the effect of scattering and thereby wasting our limited energies. In this very vein, some very thoughtful critics of American education have argued that our problem today is not that educational institutions are dominated in a pernicious way by some vision of a future for which the young are being prepared, but that, on the contrary, they are informed by no guiding ideal at all. Such is the view of Powell, Farrar, and Cohen who conclude in *The Shopping Mall High School* (1985) that "high schools seem unlikely to make marked progress . . . until there is a much clearer sense of what is most important to teach and learn, and why, and how it can best be done" (pp. 305–306).

According to Powell et al., American secondary school educators have avoided seriously wrestling with the question of the larger purposes that should inform education; and they have done so because they have been unwilling to decide from among the multitude of competing purposes that suggest themselves. The result is an educational system that is adrift, one that lacks a sense of direction that can enlist the enthusiasm of learners, their families, and educators. Unfortunately, Dewey and Kliebard's healthy reminder that we do not always need goals, either proximal or remote, in order for meaningful education to proceed and their warranted concern that such goals, even if reasonable, are prone to being employed in ways that are destructive of meaningful education may be used to legitimize this unhealthy state of affairs. The ideal, I believe, is to remember the wisdom that informs their discomfort over the way visions of future good have sometimes been used to distort educational planning without drawing the conclusion that we should avoid any attempt to use visions of desirable future states of affairs as guides to the present. We should, I submit, be striving for thoughtfully and liberally conceived guiding visions that are employed in ways that enrich rather than deaden present activity.

Acknowledgements. I wish to thank Professor Barry Franklin for his valuable suggestions at various stages of this project. The ideas in the last section of this chapter have been deeply influenced by various writings and lectures of Professor Seymour Fox (e.g., Fox, 1973, 1997), as well as by numerous conversations I have had with him and his colleague Daniel Marom over the years.

REFERENCES

Aristotle (1962). *Nichomachean ethics* (M. Ostwald, Trans.). New York: Library of Liberal Arts.

Atkin, J. M. (1970). Behavioral objectives in curriculum design: A cautionary note. In J. R. Martin (Ed.), *Readings in the philosophy of education: A study of curriculum* (pp. 32–38). Boston: Allyn and Bacon.

Dewey, J. (1902). *The child and the curriculum.* Chicago: University of Chicago Press.

Dewey, J. (1957). *Human nature and conduct.* New York: Modern Library. (Original work published 1922)

Dewey, J. (1963). *Experience and education.* New York: Collier Books. (Original work published 1938)

Fox, S. (1973). Towards a general theory of Jewish education. In D. Sidorsky (Ed.), *The future of the American Jewish community* (pp. 260–271). Philadelphia: Jewish Publication Society.

Fox, S. (with Novak, W.) (1997). *Vision at the heart.* New York and Jerusalem: Council for Initiatives in Jewish Education and the Mandel Institute.

Kliebard, H. (1970). The Tyler rationale. *School Review, 78*(2), 259–272.

Kliebard, H. (1995). The Tyler rationale revisited. *Journal of Curriculum Studies, 27*(1), 81–88.

Oakeshott, M. (1962). *Rationalism in politics.* New York: Basic Books.

Pekarsky, D. (1990). Dewey's conception of growth reconsidered. *Educational Theory, 40*(3), 283–294.

Powell, A., Farrar, E., & Cohen, D. K. (1985). *The shopping mall high school.* Boston: Houghton Mifflin.

Rousseau, J. J. (1911). *Emile* (B. Foxley, Trans.). New York: Everyman's Library. (Original work published 1762)

Chapter 2

Communitarianism and the Moral Order of Schools

José R. Rosario

When I arrived at Mrs. Ennis's fourth-grade classroom as a 10-year-old in early March 1957, I knew nothing about liberalism, democracy, melting pot, or assimilation. I knew even less about communitarianism. But I feel Mrs. Ennis did. As I reflect on those early days in a New York City classroom, I see a caring teacher going out of her way to make me feel as if I belonged in her class. I may have been different, but I also had something in common with her and the rest of her students. She was our teacher, and we were her students. We were to respect one another, treat each other as equals, but never stray too far from the idea that we were first and foremost a class, a community of learning, as we are likely to say now, striving to be the best we could be through cooperation and sharing. In her own unique way, Mrs. Ennis was teaching us something about communitarian sensibility.

Since a term like *communitarian* typically raises eyebrows, and since my sense of community is linked not only to this concept, but to the term *populist* as well, perhaps I should explain before going further. I associate community with the populist and communitarian sensibilities nurtured in agrarian Puerto Rico and Catholicism. Christopher Lasch's (1991) coupling of the words provide the meanings I favor:

> Nineteenth-century populism meant something quite specific, . . . producerism; a defense of endangered crafts (including the craft of farming); opposition to the new class of public creditors and to the whole machinery of modern finance; opposition to wage labor. Populists inherited from earlier political traditions, liberal as well as republican, the principle that property ownership and the personal independence it confers are absolutely essential preconditions of citizenship. (p. 223)

Other values central to populism, in Lasch's sense, include educa-tion, family, religion, and mutual respect. Populists also tend towards communitarianism in Lasch's scheme in that they see the value in community affiliation and the role it plays in the formation of indi-vidual character. (For a discussion of the meaning of populism in the context of Puerto Rico, see Baldridge, 1981, and Berrios, 1993. A more literary and personal account of the phenomenon can be found in Colón, 1961.)

As I came to realize much later, the communitarian sensibility Mrs. Ennis was trying to teach us about was no stranger to my home. My parents, democratic populists that they were, were committed to it as well. But for them, the value of communitarianism was rooted not in politics or liberal humanism, as Mrs. Ennis's seems to have been, but in religion, Catholicism to be precise. We were all deserving of moral standing among equals, they thought, because we were all created in the likeness of God. Belief in individual conscience made us free, and love for the humanity and dignity in others made us civil. This per-spective amounted to a belief that moral identity was prior to any other and community life was essentially about character and living up to one's responsibilities. We were first members of a group, a church, a family, and a neighborhood. Only later, when we were much older and perhaps no longer needed at home, were we to see ourselves as autono-mous individuals. But even then, responsibility and gratitude towards others, particularly the elders, demanded our unquestioned allegiance and obligation.

In my parents' view, identity transcended ethnicity or national origin. They insisted, of course, that we see ourselves as Puerto Ricans, reflecting a passion for national identity they hold even today. But they also encouraged membership in something far greater. It was not enough for them to be Puerto Rican, work hard, and be competent and successful. You also had to have faith in God, trust in your com-munity, and belief in the limits of reason. That explains, I believe, why my brother, three sisters, and I never lasted in an American public school. The year I was to enter the seventh grade, we were all trans-ferred to the local Catholic school.

To be sure, my parents did not turn to Catholic education because they saw no value in public schooling. Had they not, we would have been out much sooner. They chose a Catholic school, rather, for the same reason the parents of Richard Rodriguez (1983) did. "They sent their children to parochial schools because the nuns 'teach better,'" he tells us (p. 53). But my parents also feared what the parents of Esperansa, Sandra Cisneros' (1991) character, feared. "Papa," she recalls, "said nobody went to public school unless you wanted to be bad" (p. 53). My parents lacked trust in the capacity of public schools to integrate children into a moral community capable of fashioning a collective identity. They may have trusted an individual teacher like Mrs. Ennis but not the institution. In Morovis, Puerto Rico, where trust in public education made Catholic schooling, at least for the poor, an unthinkable alternative, the matter seemed different. For my parents, as well as many others, Catholic schooling, at least through the 1970s, was a private option available only to the wealthy of San Juan and other major cities like Mayaguez and Ponce (see Beirne, 1975).

I realize now how justified my parents' mistrust of public education's moral mission in the States was when I think about the efforts of some education reformers, particularly those who see themselves as multiculturalists, to make a fetish of ethnic and cultural identity. I see much good in any practice modeling itself after the kind of care and moral decency I remember Mrs. Ennis displaying. So I see no harm in multiculturalism and the celebration of difference, especially when it aims to guard children against the dehumanization that often results from marginalization. Exposing children to their own history, cultural language, and heritage is surely one way to do this, and I believe the political question of what to emphasize in this connection is not so impossible to resolve. But I fear this liberal practice is a poor substitute for the formation of community and development of character. The practice is more telling of the schools' structural inability to initiate the young into a collective sense of identity than of their mission to advance and preserve, to reproduce, as neo-Marxists have been fond of saying, a liberal order.

To think that opening the school curriculum to new faces and places, new histories and cultures, is sufficient to build community and shape character is, I believe, not just naive; it is also dangerously wrong, if only because identities built on ethnic, national, and cultural grounds alone ultimately lack the power of self-denial, the cornerstone of sacrifice for the good of others. So if the choice is between history, ethnicity, and culture on one hand, and character, civility, and virtue on the other, I would rather sacrifice the former for the latter. None of the Catholic schools I attended ever mentioned my ethnic and cultural background let alone used it to make me achieve. They assumed, quite rightly I think, that moral excellence was far more important than ethnic identity. Their vision of the public into which I was being inducted, they seem to have thought, had more use for virtue and moral and religious convictions than cultural affiliation. They also seem to have believed that I was better off fighting bigotry and discrimination with sound character and cunning reason than with cultural pride or ethnic loyalty. Ethnicity and culture were private markers with no bearing on how we were to act and be treated in public life. It is because I have come to believe they were right that I often feel impatient with the multiculturalist agenda, which seems to place more emphasis on knowledge of culture and self as a guide to conduct than on a sense of moral character. As my parents figured out, the public schools cannot guarantee initiation into community and moral sense, and multiculturalizing the curriculum is no consolation. Thinking that a restructuring of public schools along communitarian lines provides an answer is just as problematic, and I intend to show why in the sections that follow. My starting point is Dewey's notions of character and community. I then move to the resurgence of these ideas in recent years and to an exploration of professionalism as a barrier to what Dewey had in mind.

SCHOOL AS COMMUNITY

In an address to the Rotarians in 1934, John Dewey (1934) raised a very pertinent question that is as relevant today as it was then. "What is the place of the schools," he asked, "in the moral education of the young." The answer he gave is one I have come to share. For Dewey, character was too much of "an inclusive thing" for schools to manage alone.

> If . . . we ask what the schools are doing and can do in forming character, we shall not expect too much from them. We shall realize that at best the schools can be but one agency among the very many that are active in forming character. Compared with other influences that shape desire and purpose, the influence of the school is neither constant nor intense. Moral education of our children is in fact going on all the time, every waking hour of the day and three hundred and sixty-five days a year. Every influence that modifies the disposition and habits, the desires and thoughts of a child is a part of the development of his character. (p. 187)

In giving schools a role in character formation, Dewey placed them last, behind reform of the political economy, increased parental education, and development of recreational outlets for youth. He believed this not because he saw the school "as the least important of factors in moral training but because its success is so much bound up with the operation of the three others" (p. 192). To make them a stronger force, he suggested organizing the school along communitarian and active-learning lines:

> The more the school is organized as a community in which pupils share, the more opportunity there is for this kind of discussion [moral instruction] and the more surely it will lead to the problems of larger social groupings outside the school. . . . The other change is provision of greater opportunity for positive action, with corresponding reduction of the amount of passivity and mere absorption that are still current. (p. 192)

This Deweyan concern that schools be seen as communities and be organized along communitarian lines began to make its way back into educational discourse at about the same time disillusionment with liberalism started to appear in other intellectual quarters. I should point out as well that this concern for community derives from a tradition that runs deep in America. One need only look at the nation's history of religious and social experiments in communal living, as well as its intellectual traditions in literary and political thought, to see just how deep this current flows (Kanter, 1972; McWilliams, 1973; Oved, 1988; Stein, 1992). In fact, when Bill Clinton introduced the languages of social responsibility and covenant into the 1992 political campaign for the American presidency to legitimate his civic-oriented politics, he was reflecting the surfacing of this rich American tradition. Communitarianism had been creeping back into American political discourse since the 1960s as American intellectuals of all political stripes were becoming increasingly disenchanted with the promise of Lockean liberalism, and the doctrines of rights, state neutrality, and autonomous individualism that flow from it.

In education, among the first to show the influence in the 1960s were Fred Newman and Donald Oliver (1972). Newman and Oliver distinguished between two ways of interpreting American society at the time: *missing community* and *great society*. They identified missing community with the "effects of industrialization, urbanization, specialization, and technology that tend to destroy man's sense of relatedness, to disintegrate common bonds, to increase apathy, to depersonalize activities, and to reduce identity and meaning in the human career" (p. 206). In the great society, on the other hand, Newman and Oliver saw "a sturdy optimism in man's progress, a desire to accelerate urbanization, technology, and economic development, on the assumption that such inevitable historical forces can be harnessed to make man more free and more secure to allow him to be more 'human' than ever before" (p. 206).

The two visions were also different in terms of how they construed education. Whereas in the great society view, education meant "raising teacher salaries, building more schools, using computers and audio-visual devices to supply training and meet the manpower needs of the 'national interest,'" in the missing community view, it meant "the creation and nourishment of diverse styles of life which allow for significant choice in the reconstruction of community relationships" (p. 206).

In pushing for education as community, Newman and Oliver were following not only Dewey (1899, 1902, 1916), but also the likes of Emile Durkheim (1961) and Willard Waller (1932/1965), who had been among the first to see value in the proposition that schools are in miniature what societies are in general. In recent years, other reformers have joined the rank to argue that community holds the key to a restructuring of schools (Barth, 1990; Bryk & Driscoll, 1988; Coleman & Hoffer, 1987; Cusick, 1983; Grant, 1988; Lightfoot, 1983; Merz & Furman, 1997; Sergiovanni, 1992, 1994). They point to two general conclusions: (1) that the egalitarian-based reforms of the 1960s brought an erosion in the sense of community in public schools; and (2) that the existence of a communal ethos in schools can make a substantive difference in school effectiveness and performance. Such findings are reflected in reports like *Turning Points* (1989), published by the Carnegie Council on Adolescent Development's Task Force on Education of Young Adolescents, which suggests that students "should, upon entering middle grade school, join a small community in which people—students and adults—get to know each other well to create a climate for intellectual development. Students should feel that they are a part of a community of shared educational purpose" (p. 37).

Behind much of the recent interest to reform American public education along the communitarian lines Dewey suggested is a shift away from two other metaphors available to educators: school as organization and school as culture. The school as organization (or school as factory, in its more pejorative form) took hold at the start of the twentieth century and remains very prevalent today, particularly among school administrators (Tyack, 1974). The metaphor likens schools to a service-oriented bureaucracy, which functions to socialize the young through rationalized activity organized around economic and technical efficiencies, the differentiation of roles, a hierarchical ordering of authority, a division of labor, and a system of procedural rules (Bidwell, 1965). This view also requires that the drama of schooling, its processes as well as its outcomes, be cast in terms of social structure and other related variables (such as class, status, power, race, gender, ethnicity, authority, and role).

In the 1950s, the ethnography of Jules Henry (1963, 1972) did much to counter the supremacy of this metaphor with a view bent on interpreting school functioning in terms of culture. Following Henry's example, Philip Jackson (1968/1990) did much the same in the 1960s, and many others (Spindler, 1982) have followed the pattern since. In the school-as-culture metaphor, sociology gives way to anthropology and narrow socialization replaces broad acculturation as the main function of schooling. Structural variables begin to play weaker roles in explaining how schools mediate order, as the metaphor shifts attention to thicker cultural patterns—broadly conceived as skills, knowledge, attitudes, and conduct—and the ways in which they are learned and reproduced in context through "behavioral regularities" (Sarason, 1971) and meaning-making activity. Such a change has been useful, for much of the social and cultural reproduction that occurs in schools, the metaphor tells us, occurs tacitly through a "hidden curriculum" (Dreeben, 1968; Jackson, 1968/1990) that works independently of formal intentions and aims.

Much of the recent attraction to schools as communities, however, draws its power from comparisons to Catholic education and its concern for the common good. The conventional wisdom among some educators, popularized by the work of James Coleman (Coleman & Hoffer, 1987) and others (Bryk, Lee, & Holland, 1993), is that Catholic schools create a moral milieu or an ethos friendly to scholastic achievement and civic order. I consider that to be true. When I think about my own Catholic training, I often recall the collective sense of intimacy and belonging that the Vincentian priests and the Christian Brothers who taught me built around Catholic tradition and values, as they initiated me into public life through academic learning. Yet, I do not believe, as Anthony Bryk and his colleagues (1993) do, that we can replicate such a communal order, even in secular form if not truly moral, in our public schools. Public schools are fairly constrained to the kind of community they can create, and the sort that Catholic schools typically represent is not one of them. Contrary to what Bryk et al. think, the communal order in Catholic schools is held together not by ideology but by theology. That is what makes it difficult to replicate, as Kenneth Strike (1991) astutely observes. "Different religions have different views of authority and different community structures," he says. "These views are internal to the faith" (p. 470).

THE THINNING OF COMMUNITY

My skepticism toward the capacity of public schools to replicate community in the interest of character development, as Dewey supposed, began to take shape in late spring of 1979, when a colleague and I, while looking for a research site, stumbled onto a middle school that with affection we later christened "Rosebush" (Rosario & Lopes, 1983). Interested at the time in understanding how schools go about the business of reproducing themselves in times of stability and dynamic change, we found a principal, Mr. Thornburg, who was delighted and willing to work with us in any way he could. Since Mr. Thornburg was about to embark on an ambitious project in middle school reform, he had been hoping for someone like us to come around to witness and record the story.

Mr. Thornburg sought to change the moral order of the school by improving the quality of relationships among school members. He believed he could do this along communitarian lines by dividing the school into three smaller units called communities, or houses. Although he labored hard, his vision of a school with a shared sense of goodness and excellence never came to pass. When we left in 1981, the administrators, the teachers, and the parents I had come to know so well were still struggling, with just as much conviction and passion as when I had first met them, to make the school a better place for kids. Two years after I had left, when I called Mr. Thornburg at home to find out how things were going, I learned that many of the friends I had left behind were still struggling to improve the school and that he in particular had been removed from his position for "failing to turn things around." In 1988, when I had occasion to speak to him again, conditions at Rosebush were pretty much the same. Still living within walking distance from the school, in the house he had bought shortly after he had been hired so that he could come to know the community, he could not avoid hearing from parents who were sending their children there about the problems the staff were still facing in trying to make the school a more responsive place for adolescents. During a visit to the school in 1993, I discovered that Mr. Thornburg has retired and now lives in Mexico. But the school, though much quieter and orderly, is not what he longed to see, as a counselor and a teacher who were at the school in 1980 shared with me, as we compared his vision for the school then with the way in which the school still functions now. The closest the school ever came to realizing his views was 10 years after he left when the school was divided into so-called clusters, which resembled in some loose sense the principal's earlier concept of houses. But there was never a sense of or even an appeal to the idea that the school should function as a moral community in the way the principal meant it. The concept of clusters came to be used merely as an organizing tool for smoothing the transition of adolescents to the middle school and ensuring a stable social order.

Unknown to me in 1980 when the Rosebush principal launched his campaign to reorder the moral environment of his school, the school district of Middle City, Indiana, had 7 years earlier inaugurated its shift to a more liberal and progressive education agenda with the opening of its Robert T. Owen Middle School in 1973.[1] At the time, few in the school community saw reason to celebrate. Fearing racial integration, many parents instead protested against sending their children to the school. Then, soon after its doors opened, a building which had been locally and nationally praised for its architecture and progressive mission had turned, by some accounts, into a "zoo." Administrators could not govern, teachers could not teach, students were not behaving, and parents were vigorously complaining. Unable to cope with the social disorganization and ethnic tensions that integration and the open school design produced, parents and teachers began to lose faith, and the Middle City school experiment in progressive education seemed headed toward disaster. Yet, the school managed to recover after some struggle, reverse a vicious cyle of conflict and failure, and save the experiment. What turned the tide? All the signs point to the reorganization of the school into learning communities.

The reorganization of Owen into communities made for a more inclusive approach to education in the school. Unlike its old departmentalized arrangement, for example, the new framework required a fair amount of sacrifice in professional autonomy and subject loyalty. Teachers were expected to broaden their craft, to cooperate among themselves, and to become less subject-centered in their orientation to teaching and learning. Indeed, the attraction of Mr. Gorsich (the school's first principal) to the communal form of school organization was its liberal and progressive appeal to student-centeredness.

> I knew something had to change and I started talking to people about changes and along came this community concept and it fit what I believed in: Groups of teachers responsible for children; someone watching those kids; teachers being counselors for kids and that kind of stuff; kids feeling ownership to something or somebody instead of being lost in this huge building.

Yet, community at Owen was never meant to be taken as anything other than an ordering principle. Community had more to do with restructuring and downsizing than with morality and character building. In this regard, Rosebush's Thornburg was very different. It is true he wanted order, but he seemed to draw a distinction between order that was merely political and order that was substantively moral. Unlike moral order—which spoke to character and virtue, goodness and excellence, stability and discipline—political order was never certain and could never be trusted: It implied only process and means; it had no ends. It seems the only end of politics, if it had one, was to maximize one's chances to realize one's moral ends. In Machiavellian style, strategy in politics seemed less important than goal. It mattered only, in pursuing a goal, that one be loved, respected, admired, and believed in. So as long as one's followers were pleased, any action would do. Perhaps that is why he failed. Nevertheless, that is how he thought, or so it seems.

In contrast, Gorsich's concern was mainly political, and he never saw his intentions as implicating character and morality. His turn to community emerged from a real, practical need to restore accountability and order. As he was to tell me later, "I had to break the school down into smaller units. . . . That was pretty much right along with the need for . . . order." For him, social order and the desire to serve student needs were connected, with the former being dependent on the latter. "I thought," he also told me, "[that] order comes with meeting the needs of individuals, . . . and you got to change the structure to be able to do this with kids. You can't do this with kids in the structure that we were within." Agreeing with him, school members came to see community in much the same way: as nothing more than a managerial strategy for restoring to teachers authority and power over student learning.

That view has not changed. Community still means what it meant initially. A grouping of teachers and students for purposes of greater control and management is still the most common and consistent response school personnel give to queries concerning its communal arrangement. That the term should mean something more is a suggestion Owen staff find interesting but foreign to the way they think about the notion in the school. Very telling in this regard is the response of a counselor, who has been at the school since the idea was introduced, to the suggestion that the usage of community at Owen did not seem to be "morally loaded." "Yeah," she said, "it doesn't mean the same to me as it means when I say that I want to belong to another group because I want a sense of community. . . . In my own life I [talk about] community and needing a sense of community. But I never thought I want these kids to learn from their experiences in school what it is to have a sense of community." She also doubted that anyone at the school thought any differently or that they shared the view that the reason for dividing Owen into communities was that young adolescents needed to develop a sense of community. As far as she was concerned, the school could have just as easily chosen the terms "pods" or "clusters" instead of community. A colleague agreed: "A lot of people don't even say community. They just say, well, 'I'm in the blue' or 'I'm in the purple.' It's just a word to designate what we mean by group."

Jane Kendrick (1987), the Owen principal who followed Gorsich, often talked about her efforts to take community beyond Gorsich through a "transformational leadership" that "draws leaders and followers to higher levels of commitment and performance, motivation and morality," and "the pursuit of loftier and more intrinsic goals." But indications are that the meaning of community at Owen never moved beyond its initial cast to create a more orderly political environment. Far more interested in the implementation of the concept rather than in clarifying or defining it, Kendrick did more to advance community in its procedural rather than its substantive sense. As it was for Gorsich, so it was for Kendrick: community had more to do with accountability and control than with building a communitarian ethos. Following Basil Bernstein (1975), a way of characterizing Gorsich and Kendrick's application of community is to say that they were far more concerned with the "instrumental" as opposed to the "moral" order of the school.

Principal Watkins, who served as associate principal under Kendrick before succeeding her to the post in February 1992, summarized the consequences of Owen's thin view of community as he discussed with me at length his own perspective on community and the need for change:

> We don't do enough to unite us as Owen, green and gold. We're all into blue, purple, red, and white. . . . The communities don't really do enough or a lot to reinforce the fact that we are a single entity even though we do have different branches. . . . There is no sense of wholeness just like in larger society. We have the Kenwood community; we have the Maywood community; I have the Wallace community; I have the Edison community. And the only time they come together is when we function together at school. But at the end of the school day or at the end of school activities, we go back to our separate *communities* [his stress]. And that is the problem with this community concept. Not that [it] is not working. It does

work well. But what we need to do is get it into a part of our larger society and make these school communities see that they are a part of the larger school and not separate entities unto themselves. . . . I'm looking at it [community] in a much more global sense. I'm talking about taking these different communities that feed into our school, and if we can't get them to interact in a meaningful way that will build relationships beyond their community boundaries, then what we need to do is try to do that in school. But instead . . . we got the kids into the communities and in a sense we reinforced the fact that our communities are our boundaries. And I want to break that notion and say: "Yes, this is the community in which you come to school to work and play, but there is a larger community out there, and that's the Owen Middle School community, and we need to make you a more viable part of the larger Owen school community or have you develop a sense of belonging to the Owen school community." And hopefully that will transfer on when kids get out of here.

We don't know that we still are creating little niches for kids. And that's okay. We have our communities to help kids feel safe and comfortable. But we also need to get them to understand that this community is only part of the whole society, in this case the school society. So one of the things that I hope to do next year . . . is to create those situations. I want to reorganize the school. We're going to have 2 sixth-seventh-grade communities and 1 eighth-grade community; . . . we want to . . . provide some different type of learning experiences for our eighth graders that will take them out into school service, out into community service, and provide them with experiences that just don't occur within school. We're going to give those eighth graders some choice of electives. By putting the sixth and seventh graders together, I feel that chronologically, developmentally, they are more alike than eighth graders and therefore the teachers can work on those academic and social skill-building things that kids need to prepare them for what we want them to do in eighth grade to provide them for success in later life.

Mr. Watkins' candid assessment of Owen's thin view of community bears out in other ways. Absent from Owen's discourse on community, for example, have been important elements typically associated with "thick" applications of the term, such as character, virtue, and civic mindedness (Cochran, 1982), the kind of view Dewey seems to have had in mind. Also, by most accounts, the least developed program areas at Owen are those which require greater cooperation and fraternal relations among faculty: thematic and interdisciplinary teaching, parent and community involvement, and student mentoring. The absence of civic mindedness among school personnel became most evident to me during the 1992 Rodney King–related riots in central Los Angeles. Even though these events captured the nation's attention and became the subject of much discussion and concern across the country, Owen personnel refrained from discussing them with students. In fact, teachers were specifically instructed over the public address system that the events in Los Angeles were not to be discussed and that students violating this directive were to be sent to the office for possible suspension. The fear of losing control overrode any civic obligation to engage the school in the nation's broader conversation concerning race relations.

PROFESSIONALISM AND COMMUNITY

Rosebush and Owen experienced what most other schools during the sixties and seventies experienced as the nation pushed its great society program, and struggled to engineer through public schooling the creation of a more ethnically diverse and multicultural society. The adoption of more egalitarian practices in schools resulted in breakdowns in social structure, moral authority, and civic discipline. Such was the case at schools like Hamilton High, as Gerald Grant (1988) tells us, and Urban, Factory, and Suburban Highs, as Philip Cusick (1983) has also demonstrated. As these and other schools across the nation became more accessible to minority and handicapped students as a consequence of more liberal attendance policies, the more troublesome they became for school members unprepared for the change. The reaction of teachers and administrative personnel in such cases, as the stories of Rosebush and Owen demonstrate, was, and still is, to resort to communitarian principles, which in their more conservative cast tend to conflict with the liberal credo behind public schooling.

What complicated matters at Rosebush at the time Thornburg took over was the fiscal crisis school districts across the nation were beginning to experience. It also did not help matters much that Thornburg fell victim to folly, what some like to simplify as naivete: that he could do it alone by relying solely on the administrative powers of his office. He failed to see the limits of this undemocratic posturing in managing what amounted to a clash of moral visions among members. What if he had taken a more ecumenical style? Liberal-democratic reformers, who represent the majority of today's educational reformers, would argue that the lessons of educational change in public schooling would indeed call for such a style. The story of Owen Middle School, which reinforces that learning, suggests that as well. But my contention here is not really about strategy. It is about the kind of moral visions individuals hold and the ability of public schools to integrate them, independent of strategy. Even if Thornburg had restored order through more ecumenical means, such order, I contend, would have been morally thin. The fact that Owen has had to settle at the end for a thin kind of community speaks to this point: schools are simply unable to integrate just any principle of community. Preventing such integration is the kind of professionalism prevalent in schools today. To illustrate, consider the case of Owen, whose selection is due more to convenience, though the role professionalism played at Rosebush to undermine community could illustrate the point just as well.

Professionalism did not become a central development concern at Owen until Kendrick (1987) took over as principal in 1979. To make community work as Gorsich had intended it, Kendrick felt she needed to move quickly to make school personnel more accountable for their conduct. She was particularly concerned about teacher improprieties during community meetings, which were principally designed for instructional planning and assessment: "people smoking, reading newspapers, working on grades, and writing out personal checks." She also drew attention to "rude behaviors, such as teachers holding private conversations or sitting with their backs turned to the rest of the team during meeting time" (p. 72).

Among the first steps Kendrick took to stop these behaviors and promote a more professional (as opposed to moral) culture among teachers was to mandate and strictly enforce standards and guidelines for the operation of interdisciplinary teams. These accountability measures were subsequently followed with increased staff development efforts in student learning styles, self-assessment, and site-based management. It would take about 8 years for these measures to take effect and for Kendrick to be able to claim with a fair amount of confidence that the level of professionalism within the school had in fact improved. Kendrick (1987) described these accomplishments in terms of increased autonomy and greater leadership and training opportunities for teachers, shared governance and decision making in school affairs, and administrative and peer support in career development.

First of all, teachers at Owen are provided time in the workday to accommodate meetings and training sessions on a regular basis. Second, team leaders receive ongoing training in facilitation and processing skills. Third, opportunities for students and teachers to do what they need to do to learn are created and encouraged. Teacher training and participation in professional conferences, work-related experiences, and partnerships with their schools and agencies are supported. Fourth, leadership is a shared responsibility, as teachers, parents, and students are recognized as partners in governance. Fifth, leaders of the school make keeping up with the educational literature and current trends a priority so that they can serve as guides in the professional learning process. Sixth, teachers are provided an opportunity to share what they have learned. Seventh, teachers are encouraged and supported in their efforts to engage in professional mentoring. (p. 124)

There is a general sentiment among Owen teachers, particularly those who worked under Kendrick, that Kendrick's approach to the development of professionalism in the school may have been too heavy-handed and autocratic. Kendrick (1987) no doubt would agree. That she ran Owen like an autocracy at first is something to which she has readily admitted. "Since I thought I needed to be in charge," she writes, "my behavior was mainly directive. I lectured. I told people how to think, when to think, and what to think. I made up the rules, and I enforced the rules. My actions became: tell, regulate, delegate, evaluate" (p. 115).

However, most Owen teachers, including those openly critical of Kendrick's autocratic style, would agree that Kendrick's professionalization of the school made a substantive difference in how the school is perceived. A school that for many years was considered by district teachers to be among the least desirable places to work now ranks among the most preferred. The school's absenteeism and turnover rates, which now stand among the lowest, illustrates the ranking. Once at Owen, new teachers tend to want to stay, even though they find the school troubling at first. It takes new teachers a while, it seems, to get used to the idea that Owen is in many ways three schools in one. But once they have adjusted to the community arrangement, they begin to see value in their association with a school they come to perceive as a highly innovative and professional setting that seems to care about its members.

Disciplinary professionalism is a reasonable characterization of the kind of professionalism Kendrick had a hand in developing at Owen. The term is Thomas Bender's (1992). Bender distinguishes this form of professionalism, which he associates "with the emergence of industrial and corporate capitalism," from *civic professionalism*, which he traces to the "commercial city and the Florentine tradition of civic humanism" (p. 6). Although in civic professionalism, Bender suggests, practicing professionals are more oriented towards the development of community, in disciplinary professionalism, they are more oriented towards the development of their professional discipline or practice. Bledstein (1976) has captured the differences well in his own assessment of the evolution of professional practice. He writes:

> The new individual professional life had gained both an inward coherence and self-regulating standards that separated and defined it independently of the general community. The inner intensity of the new life oriented toward career stood in contrast to that of the older learned professional life of the eighteenth and early nineteen centuries. In the earlier period such external attributes of gentlemanly behavior as benevolence, duty, virtue, and manners circumscribed the professional experience. Competence, knowledge, and preparation were less important in evaluating the skills of the professional than were dedication to the community, sincerity, trust, permanence, honorable reputation, and righteous behavior. The qualifying credentials of the learned professional were honesty, decency, and civility. Hence, he did not think of a professional life in terms of ascending stages, each preparatory in training for the next, but as a series of good works or public projects, performed within a familiar and deferential society which heaped respectability on its first citizens. (pp. 172–73)

According to Bender (1992), among the reasons for the community orientation of professionals in early America was the way in which professionalism was developed:

> Entry to the professions was usually through local elite sponsorship, and professionals won public trust within this established social context rather than certification. While specialisms were recognized, disciplinary professions did not exist. Medicine, like other professions and learned avocations, represented an emphasis within a shared and relatively accessible public culture that was nurtured by general associations of cognoscenti. (p. 6)

As the most pronounced form of professional practice today, disciplinary professionalism, as Bender and Bledstein describe it, explains why, for Owen personnel, community is not an end but a means and why the end for which it is a means is growth of the individual teacher as an empowered professional. (This is consistent with recent findings on teacher professionalism; see, e.g., Kruse & Seashore Louis, 1993.) The notion captures well the preoccupation on the part of Owen per-

sonnel to establish themselves through training and other development activities as credible experts with a legitimate right to claim in
the school "power in the highest degree," as Derber, Schwartz, and
Magrass (1990) would put it. For Kendrick (1987), strong leadership
and teacher empowerment were key to the attainment of this credibility and legitimacy, and toward the end of her tenure, she characterized Owen as moving in that direction. "We are being transformed at Owen," she wrote, "into a dynamic institution, one in which
a strong leader supports, guides, assesses, and inspires the actions of
an ever-improving, involved, and empowered group of professionals"
(p. 124).

Owen's concern for the development of a professionalism focused
more on the utility of community than on its practice draws its power
from the kind of individualism that undergirds disciplinary professionalism and also saturates the school. One can detect this individualism in such values as moral autonomy, self-regard, and competition that teachers practice and promulgate to students principally
through sermonettes (Jackson, 1988) and other informal ways of
teaching. The workings of this individualism are also reflected in the
social contract that defines professional conduct and binds teachers
and management in the school system. As stated in its preamble, for
example, the Master Contract between the Middle City Teachers'
Federation and the School City of Middle City, as this social contract
is properly called, "embodies the notion that an educational system
based on the involvement of teachers in the decision-making process
will lead to the highest quality of education, enhance the practice of
teaching, and foster human dignity for all at the school site." Furthermore, it goes on to say, "the parties believe that by working together
an atmosphere which promotes professional growth will be established"
(School City of Middle City, 1990, p. 1). Fraternity and shared governance are important under this agreement only to the extent that they
are instrumental to human dignity, a central tenet of individualism
(Lukes, 1973), and to the professionalization of teachers. Development
of community, in other words, is subservient to development of craft
and professional autonomy, especially as these are defined by an agreement forged by two competing interests, one claiming to protect the
individual rights of teachers under the principle of free association, and
the other claiming to protect state rights under the principle of common good. Thus, whenever the values of professional and community
interests compete for loyalty in the school, teachers are more likely to
sacrifice the latter for the former. Such is the case when teachers at

Owen are asked to consider tasks that they perceive as falling outside the bounds of the master contract. The adoption of the Adviser-Advisee (A-A) program offers a good illustration of the problem.

Under the A-A program, teachers were encouraged to serve as mentors to students in an effort "to address the personal development component" of the school curriculum. There were six objectives built into the program:

1. To assist students with their orientation and adjustment to the middle-school setting
2. To help students meet their academic, social, and emotional needs
3. To help students better understand themselves and their relationship with others
4. To help students improve their study, test-taking, time management, and learning skills
5. To help students understand their roles and responsibilities within their family, school, and community
6. To allow students to explore future educational and career opportunities (Robert T. Owen Middle School, n.d., p. 1a)

The strategy for addressing these objectives was to have teachers meet A-A groups during a regularly scheduled 25-minute period Tuesdays and Thursdays. But nothing much happened during these days. Teachers for the most part quietly resisted the program on the grounds that it required the provision of services not covered under the master contract. In the teachers' view, the program's civic dimensions were not sufficiently compelling to warrant an override of what was expected of them under the contract. Of more concern to them was the lack of compensation for the additional demands A-A placed on their roles as teachers in the practice of their discipline. Since they were not being compensated for advising but for teaching, they felt no compulsion or obligation to cooperate. Moreover, for some, the A-A program was management's way of addressing what was fundamentally a structural problem in the school. Instead of expanding the school's two member counseling staff to meet the increasing demands for counseling services that a school the size of Owen engendered, resisting teachers argued, management looked to teachers to flex their roles and take on student advisement as an added chore. Although it may have been in the best interest of the school community for teachers to advise students, language in the master contract precluded any possibility of altering an existing division of labor that worked against it.

CODA

It is clear that the idea of community prevalent at Owen remained relatively thin in conception (Cochran, 1982). What school personnel had in mind when they used the term was an individualistic account in the liberal tradition stressing the utilitarian as opposed to the constitutive side of human association. Thus, terms such as tradition, commitment, character, virtue, or civic responsibility rarely figured in discussions of what community might mean to them. Community in their view was something to be exploited and used in the interest of what may be good for individual teachers or students, not something to be explored and developed in the interest of character development and pursuit of the common good.

I believe that until a more civic-minded professionalism takes hold in schools, the power of communitarianism to provide schools with the moral purpose Dewey envisioned will be somewhat limited. That would be true not only for Owen and Rosebush, but for other schools as well. Disciplinary professionalism tends towards cartel-like behaviors (Rich, 1996) that serve to maintain control through self-serving politics in the interests of members. If it is to avoid such tendencies, professionalism in public schooling must be conceived sufficiently broadly to include civic responsibility and moral development as driving elements. Professional educators are also citizens, with important social responsibilities to the communities they serve. A public education which loses sight of this crucial fact will always fall short of its moral mission.

Communitarianism, of the sort that Mrs. Ennis shared with me, and that my parents went searching for in Catholic education because they could not trust the institution of public schooling to provide it, has much to offer current school reform. That much is clear. But if it is to leave a measurable and lasting impact of the kind Dewey imagined, particularly on our most troubled schools, it cannot shy from challenging the cartel-like and liberal-oriented professionalism internal to American public education.

NOTE

1. Much of what I say about Owen (pseudonym used by the author) here is based on ethnographic material collected at the school over a 2-year period beginning in the fall of 1991. Since I was not present to witness the school's early struggles myself, I had to rely on a reconstruction of them

through interviews with the principal, teachers, and parents who were there. In this regard, I also had the help of Kendrick's (1987) careful and insightful chronicles of reform at the school from 1973 through 1982. By combining both sources of data, I was able to reconstruct the dynamics of Owen's story.

REFERENCES

Baldridge, J. J. (1981). *Class and the state: The origins of populism in Puerto Rico.* Unpublished doctoral dissertation, Yale University, New Haven, CT.

Barth, R. S. (1990). *Improving schools from within: Teachers, parents, and principals can make the difference.* San Francisco: Jossey-Bass.

Beirne, C. J. (1975). *The problem of Americanization in the Catholic schools of Puerto Rico.* San Juan: Editorial Universitaria, Universidad de Puerto Rico.

Bender, T. (1992). *Intellect and public life.* Baltimore: Johns Hopkins University Press.

Bernstein, B. (1975). *Class, codes, and control: Vol. 3. Towards a theory of educational transmissions.* London: Routledge.

Berrios, R. (1993). *Nacionalismo a populismo: Cultura y politica en Puerto Rico.* Rio Piedras, Puerto Rico: Uracan.

Bidwell, C. E. (1965). The school as a formal organization. In J. G. March (Ed.), *Handbook of organizations* (pp. 972–1022). Chicago: Rand McNally.

Bledstein, B. J. (1976). *The culture of professionalism: The middle class and the development of higher education in America.* New York: Norton.

Bryk A. S., & Driscoll, M. E. (1988). *The school as community: Theoretical foundations, contextual influences, and consequences for students and teachers.* Madison, WI: National Center on Effective Schools.

Bryk, A. S., Lee, V. E., & Holland, P. B. (1993). *Catholic schools and the common good.* Cambridge, MA: Harvard University Press.

Carnegie Council on Adolescent Development. (1989). *Turning points: Preparing American youth for the twenty-first century.* New York: Carnegie Corporation of New York.

Cisneros, S. (1991). *The house on Mango Street.* New York: Vintage.

Cochran, C. E. (1982). *Character, community, and politics.* University, AL: University of Alabama Press.

Coleman, J. S., & Hoffer, T. (1987). *Public and private high schools: The impact of communities.* New York: Basic Books.

Colón, J. (1961). *A Puerto Rican in New York and other sketches.* New York: Masses & Mainstream.

Cusick, P. A. (1983). *The egalitarian ideal and the American high school.* New York: Longman.

Derber, C., Schwartz, W., & Magrass, Y. (1990). *Power in the highest degree: Professionals and the rise of the new Mandarin order.* New York: Oxford University Press.

Dewey, J. (1899). *The school and society*. Chicago: Chicago University Press.

Dewey, J. (1902). *The child and the curriculum*. Chicago: Chicago University Press.

Dewey, J. (1916). *Democracy and education*. New York: Macmillan.

Dewey, J. (1934). Character training for youth. *Rotarian, 45*, 6–8, 58–59.

Dreeben, R. (1968). *On what is learned in school*. Reading, MA: Addison-Wesley.

Durkheim, E. (1961). *Moral education*. New York: Free Press.

Grant, G. (1988). *The world we created at Hamilton High*. Cambridge, MA: Harvard University Press.

Henry, J. (1963). *Culture against man*. New York: Random House.

Henry, J. (1972). *Jules Henry on education*. New York: Vintage Books.

Jackson, P. (1988, March). The school as moral instructor: Deliberate efforts and unintended consequences. *The World and I*, pp. 593–606.

Jackson, P. (1990). *Life in classrooms*. New York: Teachers College Press. (Original work published 1968)

Kanter, R. M. (1972). *Community and commitment: Communes and utopias in sociological perspective*. Cambridge, MA: Harvard University Press.

Kendrick, J. (1987). *The emergence of transformational leadership practice in a school improvement effort*. Unpublished doctoral dissertation, University of Illinois, Urbana-Champaign.

Kruse, S. D., & Seashore Louis, K. (1993, April). *An emerging framework for analyzing school-based professional community*. Paper presented at the annual meeting of the American Educational Research Association, Chicago.

Lasch, C. (1991). *The true and only heaven: Progress and its critics*. New York: Norton.

Lightfoot, S. L. (1983). *The good high school: Portraits of character and culture*. New York: Basic Books.

Lukes, S. (1973). *Individualism*. New York: Harper Torchbooks.

McWilliams, W. C. (1973). *The idea of fraternity in America*. Berkeley, CA: University of California Press.

Merz, C., & Furman, G. (1997). *Community and schools: Promise and paradox*. New York: Teachers College Press.

Newman, F. M., & Oliver, D. W. (1972). Education and community. In D. E. Purple & M. Belanger (Eds.), *Curriculum and the cultural revolution* (pp. 205–252). Berkeley, CA: McCutchan.

Oved, Y. (1988). *Two hundred years of American communes*. New Brunswick, NJ: Transaction Books.

Rich, W. C. (1996). *Black mayors and school politics: The failure of reform in Detroit, Gary, and Newark*. New York: Garland.

Robert T. Owen Middle School. (n.d.). *Robert T. Owen Middle School eighth grade advisor advisee curriculum guide*. Middle City, IN: Author.

Rodriguez, R. (1983). *The hunger of memory*. New York: Bantam.

Rosario, J., & Lopes, L. (1983). *Mechanisms of continuity: A study of stability and change in a public school*. Ypsilanti, MI: High/Scope Foundation.

Sarason, S. (1971). *The culture of the school and the problem of change*. Boston: Allyn and Bacon.

School City of Middle City. (1990). *Master contract between School City of Middle City and Middle City Teachers Union*. Middle City, IN: Author.

Sergiovanni, T. J. (1992). *Moral leadership: Getting to the heart of school improvement*. San Francisco: Jossey-Bass.

Sergiovanni, T. J. (1994). *Building community in schools*. San Francisco: Jossey-Bass.

Spindler, G. D. (1982). *Doing the ethnography of schooling: Educational anthropology in action*. New York: Holt, Rinehart, and Winston.

Stein, S. J. (1992). *The Shaker experience in America*. New Haven, CT: Yale University Press.

Strike, K. (1991). The moral role of schooling in a liberal democratic society. In G. Grant (Ed.), *Review of research in education, 17* (pp. 413–483). Washington, DC: American Educational Research Association.

Tyack, D. (1974). *The one best system: The history of American urban education*. Cambridge, MA: Harvard University Press.

Waller, W. (1965). *The sociology of teaching*. New York: Wiley. (Original work published 1932)

PART II

CURRICULUM, DEMOCRACY, AND THE DILEMMA OF SOCIAL CONTROL

Chapter 3

Standards, Markets, and Curriculum

Michael W. Apple

I trust that you will forgive me if I begin my contribution to this book with a personal story. The year is 1970. I have just returned home after working all day, as usual, in Russell Library at Teachers College, Columbia University. I have been putting the finishing touches on the last chapter of my dissertation. The phone rings and it is Herbert Kliebard calling to ask if I am interested in coming to Wisconsin to be interviewed for a position open in the Curriculum Department. Without any hesitation, I say *yes*.

There were a number of reasons for my emphatic *yes*. First, Dwayne Huebner, my adviser at Columbia, received his Ph.D. from Wisconsin, and I know it is among the best places in the country. Second, the intellectual and political awareness and progressive tendencies that dominate both the department there and the university as a whole are well known. Yet, of even greater importance, is the fact that Herbert Kliebard is there. He himself went to Teachers College a generation before me. He returned to give a series of lectures and seminars during the period I was there. His lecture—a detailed and compelling discussion of the historical roots of the curriculum field that pointed to the influences of Taylorism on the formative figures of the field such as Bobbitt and Charters—was one of those rare events when an audience knew that a fundamental transformation was occurring in the ways in which a field was viewed. I came away from that lecture with a considerably deepened understanding of curricular history and an immense respect for Herbert Kliebard.

Being his colleague for nearly three decades has been everything that I had hoped for. His themes and research—the crucial importance of historical understanding, the search for hidden underpinnings in the field, a concern with multiple traditions in deciding what knowl-

55

edge is of most worth, the ways in which metaphors work in creating the horizon against which we interpret our problems—as well as his abiding commitment to the asking of hard questions that tend to be neglected due to the pressures of answering the question "what do I do on Monday morning?"—all of these had a profound influence on me. Herbert Kliebard became that rarity—teacher, mentor, and friend. And I dedicate this chapter to him, knowing full well that we all still have much to learn from him.

RIGHT TURN

In his influential history of curriculum debates, Herbert Kliebard has documented that educational issues have consistently involved major conflicts and compromises among groups with competing visions of "legitimate" knowledge, what counts as "good" teaching and learning, and what a "just" society is (Kliebard, 1986). Although I believe neither that these competing visions have ever had equal holds on the imagination of educators or the general citizenry nor that their advocates have ever had equal power to effect their visions, it is still clear that no analysis of education can be fully serious without placing at its very core a sensitivity to the ongoing struggles that constantly shape the terrain on which the curriculum operates.

Today is no different than the past: A new set of compromises, a new alliance—and a new power bloc has been formed that has increasing influence in education and all things social. This power bloc combines multiple fractions of capital who are committed to neoliberal marketized solutions to educational problems, neoconservative intellectuals who want a "return" to higher standards and a "common culture," authoritarian populist religious fundamentalists who are deeply worried about secularity and the preservation of their own traditions, and particular fractions of the professionally oriented new middle class who are committed to the ideology and techniques of accountability, measurement, and "management." Although there are clear tensions and conflicts within this alliance, in general its overall aims lie in providing the educational conditions believed necessary both for increasing international competitiveness, profit, and discipline and also for returning us to a romanticized past of the "ideal" home, family, and school (Apple, 1993, 1996).

In essence, the new alliance—what I have elsewhere called the "conservative restoration" (Apple, 1996)—has integrated education into a wider set of ideological commitments. The objectives in education are the same as those that guide its economic and social welfare goals. They include the dramatic expansion of that eloquent fiction, the free market; the drastic reduction of government responsibility for social needs; the reinforcement of intensely competitive structures of mobility both inside and outside the school; the lowering of people's expectations for economic security; the disciplining of culture and the body; and the popularization of what is clearly a form of Social Darwinist thinking, as the popularity of *The Bell Curve* (Herrnstein & Murray, 1994) so obviously and distressingly indicates.

The seemingly contradictory discourse of competition, markets, and choice, on the one hand, and, on the other, accountability, performance objectives, standards, national testing, and national curriculum have created such a din that it is hard to hear anything else. As I have shown in *Cultural Politics and Education* (Apple, 1996), these tendencies actually oddly reinforce each other and help cement conservative educational positions into our daily lives.

Though lamentable, the changes that are occurring present an exceptional opportunity for longitudinal research. Here, I am not speaking of merely the accumulation of studies to promote the academic careers of researchers, although the accumulation of serious studies is not unimportant. Rather, I am suggesting that in a time of radical social and educational change it is crucial to document the processes and effects of the various and sometimes contradictory elements of the conservative restoration and of the ways in which they are mediated, compromised with, accepted, used in different ways by different groups for their own purposes, and struggled over in the policies and practices of people's daily educational lives (Ransom, 1995). In this essay I shall want to give a sense of how this might be happening in current "reforms" such as marketization, national curricula, and national testing.

NEW MARKETS, OLD TRADITIONS

Behind a good deal of the New Right's emerging discursive ensemble was a position that emphasized "a culturalist construction of the nation as a (threatened) haven for white (Christian) traditions and values" (Gillborn, 1997a, p. 2). This involved constructing an imagined national past that is at least partly mythologized and then employing it to castigate the present. Gary McCulloch (1997) argues that the nature of the historical images of schooling has changed. Dominant imagery of education as being "safe, domesticated, and progressive" (that is, as leading toward progress and social and personal improvement) has shifted to become "threatening, estranged, and regressive" (p. 80). The past is no longer the source of stability, but a mark of failure, disappointment, and loss. This is seen most vividly in the attacks on the "progressive orthodoxy" that supposedly now reigns supreme in classrooms in many nations.

For example, in England—though much the same is echoed in the United States, Australia, and elsewhere—Michael Jones, the political editor of the *Sunday Times*, recalls the primary school of his day: "Primary school was a happy time for me. About 40 of us sat at fixed wooden desks with ink wells and moved from them only with grudging permission. Teacher sat in a higher desk in front of us and moved only to the blackboard. She smelled of scent and inspired awe" (qtd. in McCulloch, 1997, p. 78). The mix of metaphors invoking discipline, scent, and awe is fascinating. But he goes on, lamenting the past 30 years of "reform" that transformed primary schools. Speaking of his own children's experience, Jones says: "My children spent their primary years in a showplace school where they were allowed to wander around at will, develop their real individuality and dodge the 3Rs. It was all for the best, we were assured. But it was not" (qtd. in McCulloch, 1997, p. 78). For Jones, the "dogmatic orthodoxy" of progressive education "had led directly to educational and social decline." Only the rightist reforms instituted in the 1990s could halt and then reverse this decline (McCulloch, 1997, p. 78). Only then could the imagined past return.

Much the same is being said on this side of the Atlantic. These sentiments are echoed in the public pronouncements of such figures as William Bennett, E. D. Hirsch, Jr., and others, all of whom seem to believe that progressivism is now in the dominant position in educational policy and practice and has destroyed a valued past. All of them believe that only by tightening control over curriculum and teaching (and students, of course), restoring "our" lost traditions, and making education more disciplined and competitive as they are certain it was in the past, only then can they have effective schools. These figures are joined by others who have similar criticisms, but instead turn to a different past for a different future. Their past is less that of scent and awe and authority, but one of market freedom. For them, nothing can be accomplished—not even the restoration of awe and authority—without setting the market loose on schools so as to ensure that only "good" ones survive.

One must understand that these policies are radical transformations. If they had come from the other side of the political spectrum, they would have been ridiculed in many ways, given the ideological tendencies in our nations. Further, not only are these policies based on a romanticized pastoral past, these reforms have not been notable for their grounding in research findings. Indeed, when research has been used, it has often either served as a rhetoric of justification for preconceived beliefs about the supposed efficacy of markets or regimes of tight accountability or such reforms have been based—as in the case of Chubb and Moe's (1990) much publicized work on marketization—on quite flawed research (see, e.g., Whitty, 1997).

Yet, no matter how radical some of these proposed reforms are and no matter how weak the empirical basis of their support, they have now redefined the terrain of debate of all things educational. After years of conservative attacks and mobilizations, it has become clear that "ideas that were once deemed fanciful, unworkable—or just plain extreme" are now increasingly being seen as common sense (Gillborn, 1997b, p. 357).

Tactically, the reconstruction of common sense that has been accomplished has proven to be extremely effective. For example, there are clear discursive strategies being employed here, ones that are characterized by "plain speaking" and speaking in a language that "everyone can understand." (I do not wish to be wholly negative about this. The importance of these things is something many "progressive" educators have yet to understand.) These strategies also involve not only presenting one's own position as common sense, but also usually tacitly implying that there is something of a conspiracy among one's opponents to deny the truth or to say only that which is "fashionable" (Gillborn, 1997b, p. 353). As Gillborn notes,

> This is a powerful technique. First, it assumes that there are no *genuine* arguments against the chosen position; any opposing views are thereby positioned as false, insincere or self-serving. Second, the technique presents the speaker as someone brave or honest enough to speak the (previously) unspeakable. Hence, the moral high ground is assumed and opponents are further denigrated. (p. 353)

It is hard to miss these characteristics in some of the conservative literature such as Herrnstein and Murray's (1994) publicizing of the unthinkable "truth" about genetics and intelligence or E. D. Hirsch's (1996) latest "tough" discussion of the destruction of "serious" schooling by progressive educators.

MARKETS AND PERFORMANCE

I shall take as an example of the ways in which all this operates one element of the conservative restoration—the neoliberal claim that the invisible hand of the market will inexorably lead to better schools. As Roger Dale points out, "the market" acts as a metaphor rather than an explicit guide for action. It is not denotative, but connotative. Thus, it must itself be "marketed" to those who will exist in it and live with its effects (qtd. in Menter, Muschamp, Nicholls, & Ozga, 1997, p. 27). Markets are marketed, are made legitimate, by a depoliticizing strategy. They are said to be natural and neutral, and governed by effort and merit; and those opposed to them are hence, by definition, also opposed to effort and merit. Markets are also supposedly less subject to political interference and the weight of bureaucratic procedures. Plus, they are grounded in the rational choices of individual actors (Menter et al., 1997). Thus, markets and the guarantee of rewards for effort and merit are to be coupled together to produce "neutral," yet positive, results. Mechanisms, hence, must be put into place that give evidence of entrepreneurial efficiency and effectiveness. This coupling of markets and mechanisms for the generation of evidence of performance is exactly what has occurred. Whether it works is open to question.

In what is perhaps the most comprehensive critical review of all of the evidence on marketization, Geoff Whitty (1997) cautions readers not to mistake rhetoric for reality. After examining research from a number of countries, Whitty argues that while advocates of marketized "choice" plans assume that competition will enhance the efficiency and responsiveness of schools, as well as give disadvantaged children opportunities that they currently do not have, this may be a false hope. These hopes are not now being realized and are unlikely to be realized in the future "in the context of broader policies that do nothing to challenge deeper social and cultural inequalities" (p. 58). As he goes on to say, "Atomized decision-making in a highly stratified society may appear to give everyone equal opportunities, but transforming responsibility for decision-making from the public to the private sphere can actually reduce the scope of collective action to improve the quality of education for all" (p. 58). When this is connected, as I shall show shortly, to the fact that in practice neoliberal policies involving market "solutions" may actually serve to reproduce, not subvert, traditional hierarchies of class and race, this should give one reason to pause (Apple, 1996; Whitty, 1997; Whitty, Edwards, & Gewirtz, 1993).

Thus, rather than taking neoliberal claims at face value, one should ask about their hidden effects that are too often invisible in the rhetoric and metaphors of their proponents. Given the limitations of what one can say in an essay of this length, I shall select a few issues that have been given less attention than they deserve, but on which there is now significant research.

The English experience is apposite here, especially since Chubb and Moe (1990) rely so heavily on it. In England, the 1993 Education Act documents the state's commitment to marketization. Governing bodies of local educational authorities (LEAs) were mandated to formally consider "going GM" (that is, opting out of the local school system's control and entering into the competitive market) every year (Power, Halpin, & Fitz, 1994, p. 27). Thus, the weight of the state stood behind the press towards neoliberal reforms there.[1] Yet, rather than leading to curriculum responsiveness and diversification, the competitive market has not created much that is different from the traditional models so firmly entrenched in schools today (Power et al., 1994). Nor has it radically altered the relations of inequality that characterize schooling.

In their own extensive analyses of the effects of marketized reforms "on the ground," Ball and his colleagues point to some of the reasons why one needs to be quite cautious here. As they document, in these situations educational principles and values are often compromised such that commercial issues become more important in curriculum design and resource allocation (Ball, Bowe, & Gewirtz, 1994). For instance, the coupling of markets with the demand for and publication of performance indicators, such as examination league tables in England, has meant that schools are increasingly looking for ways to attract "motivated" parents with "able " children. In this way, schools are able to enhance their relative position in local systems of competition. This represents a subtle, but crucial shift in emphasis—one that is not openly discussed as often as it should be—from student needs to student performance and from what the school does for the student to what the student does for the school. This is also accompanied too uncomfortably often by a shift of resources away from students who are labeled as having special needs or learning difficulties, with some of these needed resources now going to marketing and public relations. Special needs students not only are expensive, but they deflate test scores on those all-important league tables.

Not only does this make it difficult to "manage public impressions," but it also makes it difficult to attract the "best" and most academically talented teachers (Ball et al., 1994, pp. 17–19). The entire enterprise does, however, establish a new metric and a new set of goals based on a constant striving to win the market game. What this means is of considerable import, not only in terms of its effects on daily school life but in the ways it signifies a transformation of what counts as a good society and a responsible citizen. Let me say something about this generally.

Drawing on Kliebard's significant historical work, I noted earlier that behind all educational proposals are visions of a just society and a good student. The neoliberal reforms I have been discussing construct this in a particular way. While the defining characteristic of neoliberalism is largely based on the central tenets of classical liberalism, in particular classic economic liberalism, there are crucial differences between classical liberalism and neoliberalism. These differences are absolutely essential in understanding the politics of education and the transformations education is currently undergoing. Mark Olssen (1996) clearly details these differences in the following passage. It is worth quoting in its entirety.

> Whereas classical liberalism represents a negative conception of state power in that the individual was to be taken as an object to be freed from the interventions of the state, neo-liberalism has come to represent a positive conception of the state's role in creating the appropriate market by providing the conditions, laws and institutions necessary for its operation. In classical liberalism, the individual is characterized as having an autonomous human nature and can practice freedom. In neo-liberalism the state seeks to create an individual who is an enterprising and competitive entrepreneur. In the classical model the theoretical aim of the state was to limit and minimize its role based on postulates which included universal egoism (the self-interested individual); invisible hand theory which dictated that the interests of the individual were also the interests of the society as a whole; and the political maxim of laissez-faire. In the shift from classical liberalism to neo-liberalism, then, there is a further element added, for such a shift involves a change in subject position from "homo economicus," who naturally behaves out of self-interest and is relatively detached from the state, to "manipulatable man," who is created by the state and who is continually encouraged to be "perpetually responsive." It is not that the conception of the self-interested subject is replaced or done away with by the new ideals of "neo-liberalism," but that in an age of universal welfare, the perceived possibilities of slothful indolence create necessities for new forms of vigilance, surveillance, "performance appraisal" and of forms of control generally. In this model the state has taken it upon itself to keep us all up to the mark. The state will see to it that each one makes a "continual enterprise of ourselves" . . . in what seems to be a process of "governing without governing." (p. 340)

The results of Ball and his colleagues' research document how the state does indeed do this, enhancing that odd combination of marketized individualism and control through constant and comparative public assessment. Widely publicized league tables determine one's relative value in the educational marketplace. Only those schools with rising performance indicators are worthy. And only those students who can "make a continual enterprise of themselves" can keep such schools going in the "correct" direction. Yet, though these issues are important, they fail to fully illuminate some of the other mechanisms through which differential effects are produced by neoliberal reforms. Here, class issues come to the fore in ways that Ball et al. (1994) make clear.

Middle-class parents are clearly the most advantaged in this kind of cultural assemblage, and not only, as I pointed out, because the principals of schools seek them out. Middle-class parents have become quite skilled, in general, in exploiting market mechanisms in education and in bringing their social, economic, and cultural capital to bear on them. "Middle class parents are more likely to have the knowledge, skills and contacts to decode and manipulate what are increasingly complex and deregulated systems of choice and recruitment. The more deregulation, the more possibility of informal procedures being employed. The middle class also, on the whole, are more able to move their children around the system" (Ball et al., 1994, p. 19). That class and race intersect and interact in complex ways means that, even though it needs to be clear that marketized systems in education often expressly have their conscious and unconscious raison d'etre in a fear of "the other" and often express a racialization of educational policy—the differential results will "naturally" be decidedly raced as well as classed (McCarthy & Crichlow, 1994; Omi & Winant, 1994).

Economic and social capital can be converted into cultural capital in various ways. In marketized plans, more affluent parents often have more flexible hours and can visit multiple schools. They have cars—often more than one—and can afford driving their children across town to attend a better school. They can as well provide the hidden cultural resources such as camps and after-school programs (dance, music, computer classes, amd so forth) that give their children an "ease," a "style," that seems "natural" and acts as a set of cultural resources. Their previous stock of social capital—who they know, their "comfort" in social encounters with educational officials—is an unseen but powerful storehouse of resources. Thus, more affluent parents are more likely to have the informal knowledge and skill—what Bourdieu (1984) would call the "habitus"—to be able to decode and use marketized forms to their own benefit. This sense of what might be called "confidence"—which is itself the result of past choices that tacitly but no less powerfully depend on the economic resources to actually have had the ability to make economic choices—is the unseen capital that underpins their ability to negotiate marketized forms and "work the system" through sets of informal cultural rules (Ball et al., 1994).

Of course, it needs to be said that working-class, poor, and immigrant parents are not skill-less in this regard, by any means. (After all, it requires an immense amount of skill, courage, and social and cultural resources to survive under exploitative and depressing material conditions. Thus, collective bonds, informal networks and contacts, and an ability to work the system are developed in quite nuanced, intelligent, and often impressive ways here.) However, the match between the historically grounded habitus expected in schools and in its actors and those of more affluent parents, combined with the material resources available to more affluent parents, usually leads to a successful conversion of economic and social capital into cultural capital (see Bourdieu, 1996). And this is exactly what is happening in England.

These empirical findings are made more understandable in terms of Pierre Bourdieu's (1996) analysis of the relative weight given to cultural capital as part of mobility strategies today. The rise in importance of cultural capital infiltrates all institutions in such a way that there is a relative movement away from the direct reproduction of class privilege (where power is transmitted largely within families through economic property) to school-mediated forms of class privilege. Here, "the bequeathal of privilege is simultaneously effectuated and transfigured by the intercession of educational institutions" (Wacquant, 1996, p. xiii). This is *not* a conspiracy; it is not "conscious" in the ways one normally uses that concept. Rather it is the result of a long chain of relatively autonomous connections between differentially accumulated economic, social, and cultural capital operating at the level of daily events as people make their respective ways in the world, including, as I pointed out, in the world of school choice.

Thus, though not taking an unyieldingly determinist position, Bourdieu (1996) argues that a class habitus tends to reproduce the conditions of its own reproduction "unconsciously." It does this by producing a relatively coherent and systematically characteristic set of seemingly natural and unconscious strategies—in essence, ways of understanding and acting on the world that act as forms of cultural capital that can be and are employed to protect and enhance one's status in a social field of power. He aptly compares this similarity of habitus across class actors to handwriting.

Just as the acquired disposition we call "handwriting," that is a particular way of forming letters, always produces the same "writing"—that is, graphic lines that despite differences in size, matter, and color related to writing surface (sheet of paper or blackboard) and implement (pencil, pen, or chalk), that is despite differences in vehicles for the action, have an immediately recognizable affinity of style or a family resemblance—the practices of a single agent, or, more broadly, the practices of all agents endowed with similar habitus, owe the affinity of style that makes each a metaphor for the others to the fact that they are the products of the implementation in different fields of the same schemata of perception, thought, and action. (p. 273)

This very connection of habitus across fields of power—the ease of bringing one's economic, social, and cultural resources to bear on "markets"—enables a comfort between markets and self that characterizes the middle-class actor here. This constantly produces differential effects. These effects are not neutral, no matter what the advocates of neoliberalism suggest. Rather, they are themselves the results of a particular kind of morality. Unlike the conditions of what might best be called "thick morality" where principles of the common good are the ethical basis for adjudicating policies and practices, markets are grounded in aggregative principles. They are constituted out of the sum of individual good and choices. "Founded on individual and property rights that enable citizens to address problems of interdependence via exchange," they offer a prime example of "thin morality" by generating both hierarchy and division based on competitive individualism (Ball et al., 1994, p. 24). And in this competition, the general outline of the winners and losers *has* been identified empirically.

NATIONAL CURRICULUM AND NATIONAL TESTING

I showed in the previous section that there are connections between at least two dynamics operating in neoliberal reforms, free markets and increased surveillance. This can be seen in the fact that in many contexts, marketization has been accompanied by a set of particular policies for "producers," for those professionals working within education. These policies have been strongly regulatory. As in the case of the linkage between national tests and performance indicators published as league tables, they have been organized around a concern for external supervision, regulation, and external judgement of performance (Menter et al., 1997, p. 8). This concern for external supervision and regulation is not only connected with a strong mistrust of producers (e.g., teachers) and to the need for ensuring that people continually make enterprises out of themselves; it is also clearly linked both to the neoconservative sense of a need to return to a lost past of high standards, discipline, awe, and real knowledge and to the professional middle class's own ability to carve out a sphere of authority within the state for its own commitment to management techniques and efficiency.

There has been a shift in the relationship between the state and professionals. In essence, the move toward a small strong state that is increasingly guided by market needs seems inevitably to bring with it reduced professional power and status (Menter et al., 1997). Managerialism takes center stage here.

Managerialism is largely charged with "bringing about the cultural transformation that shifts professional identities in order to make them more responsive to client demand and external judgement" (Menter et al., 1997, p. 9). It aims to justify and to have people internalize fundamental alterations in professional practices. It both harnesses energy and discourages dissent.

There is no necessary contradiction between a general set of marketizing and deregulating interests and processes—such as voucher and choice plans—and a set of enhanced regulatory processes—such as plans for national curricula and national testing. "The regulatory form permits the state to maintain 'steerage' over the aims and processes of education from within the market mechanism" (Menter et al., 1997, p. 24). Such steerage has often been vested in such things as national standards, national curricula, and national testing. Forms of all of these are being pushed in the United States currently and are the subject of considerable controversy, some of which cuts across ideological lines and shows some of the tensions within the different elements contained under the umbrella of the conservative restoration.

I have argued that paradoxically a national curriculum and especially a national testing program are the first and most essential steps toward increased marketization. They actually provide the mechanisms for comparative data that consumers need to make markets work as markets (Apple, 1996). Absent these mechanisms, there is no comparative base of information for choice. Yet, we do not have to argue about these regulatory forms in a vacuum. Like the neoliberal markets I discussed in the previous section, they too have been instituted in England; and, once again, there is important research available that can and must make us duly cautious in going down this path.

One might want to claim that a set of national standards, national curricula, and national tests would provide the conditions for "thick morality." After all, such regulatory reforms are supposedly based on shared values and common sentiments that also create social spaces in which common issues of concern can be debated and made subject to moral interrogation (Ball et al., 1994). Yet, what counts as the "common," and how and by whom it is actually determined, is rather more thin than thick.

It is the case that while the national curriculum now so solidly in place in England and Wales is clearly prescriptive, it has not always proven to be the kind of straitjacket it has often been made out to be. As a number of researchers have documented, it is not only possible that policies and legislative mandates are interpreted and adapted, but it seems inevitable. Thus, the national curriculum is "not so much being 'implemented' in schools as being 'recreated,' not so much 'reproduced,' as 'produced'" (Power et al., 1994, p. 38).

In general, it is nearly a truism that there is no simplistic linear model of policy formation, distribution, and implementation. There are always complex mediations at each level of the process. There is a complex politics that goes on within each group and between these groups and external forces in the formulation of policy, in its being written up as a legislative mandate, in its distribution, and in its reception at the level of practice. Thus, the state may legislate changes in curriculum, evaluation, or policy (which is itself produced through conflict, compromise, and political maneuvering), but policy writers and curriculum writers may be unable to control the meanings and implementations of their texts. All texts are "leaky" documents. They are subject to "recontextualization" at every stage of the process (Ransom, 1995).

However, this general principle may be just a bit too romantic. None of this occurs on a level playing field. As with market plans, there are very real differences in power in one's ability to influence, mediate, transform, or reject a policy or a regulatory process. Granted, it is important to recognize that a state control model—with its assumption of top-down linearity—is much too simplistic and that the possibility of human agency and influence is always there, but this should not imply that such agency and influence will be powerful (Ransom, 1995).

The case of national curriculum and national testing in England and Wales documents the tensions in these two accounts. The national curriculum that was first legislated and then imposed there was indeed struggled over. It was originally too detailed and too specific, and, hence, was subject to major transformations at the national, community, school, and then classroom levels. However, even though the national curriculum was subject to conflict, mediation, and some transformation of its content, organization, and its invasive and immensely time consuming forms of evaluation, its utter power is demonstrated in its radical reconfiguration of the very process of knowledge selection, organization, and assessment. It changed the entire terrain of education radically. Its subject divisions "provide more constraint than scope for discretion." The "standard attainment targets" that have been mandated cement these constraints in place. "The imposition of national testing locks the national curriculum in place as the dominant framework of teachers' work whatever opportunities teachers may take to evade or reshape it" (Richard Hatcher and Barry Troyna quoted in Ransom, 1995, p. 438).

Thus, it is not sufficient to state that the world of education is complex and has multiple influences. The purpose of any serious analysis is to go beyond such overly broad conclusions. Rather, we need to "discriminate degrees of influence in the world," to weigh the relative efficacy of the factors involved. Hence, although it is clear that while the national curriculum and national tests that now exist in England and Wales have come about because of a complex interplay of forces and influences, it is equally clear that "state control has the upper hand" (Ransom, 1995, p. 438).

The national curricula and national tests *did* generate conflict about issues. They did partly lead to the creation of social spaces for moral questions to get asked. (Of course, these moral questions had been asked all along by dispossessed groups.) Thus, it was clear to many people that the creation of mandatory and reductive tests that emphasized memory and decontextualized abstraction pulled the national curriculum in a particular direction—that of encouraging a selective educational market in which elite students and elite schools with a wide range of resources would be well (if narrowly) served. Diverse groups of people argued that such reductive, detailed, and simplistic paper and pencil tests "had the potential to do enormous damage," a situation that was made even worse because the tests were so onerous in terms of time and record keeping (O'Hear, 1994, pp. 55–56). Teachers had a good deal of support when as a group they decided to boycott the administration of the test in a remarkable act of public protest. This also led to serious questioning of the arbitrary, inflexible, and overly prescriptive national curriculum. Although the curriculum is still inherently problematic and the assessment system still contains numerous dangerous and onerous elements within it, organized activity against them did have an impact (O'Hear, 1994).

Yet, unfortunately, the story does not end there. By the mid-1990s, even with the government's partial retreat on such regulatory forms as its program of constant and reductive testing, it had become clearer by the year that the development of testing and the specification of content had been "hijacked" by those who were ideologically committed to traditional pedagogies and to the idea of more rigorous selection. The residual effects are both material and ideological. They include a continuing emphasis on trying to provide the "rigor [that is] missing in the practice of most teachers, . . . judging progress solely by what is testable in tests of this kind" and the development of a "very hostile view of the accountability of teachers" that was seen as "part of a wider thrust of policy to take away professional control of public services and establish so-called consumer control through a market structure" (O'Hear, pp. 65–66).

The authors of an extremely thorough review of recent assessment programs instituted in England and Wales provide a summary of what has happened. Gipps and Murphy (1994) argue that it has become increasingly obvious that the national assessment program attached to the national curriculum is more and more dominated by traditional models of testing and the assumptions about teaching and learning that lie behind them. At the same time, equity issues are becoming much less visible. In the calculus of values now in place in the regulatory state, efficiency, speed, and cost control replace more substantive concerns about social and educational justice. The pressure to get tests in place rapidly has meant that "the speed of test development is so great, and the curriculum and assessment changes so regular, that [there is] little time to carry out detailed analyses and trialing to ensure that the tests are as fair as possible to all groups" (Gipps & Murphy, p. 209). The conditions for "thin morality"—in which the competitive individual of the market dominates and social justice will somehow take care of itself—are reproduced here. The combination of the neoliberal market and the regulatory state, then, does indeed "work." However, it works in ways in which the metaphors of free market, merit, and effort hide the differential reality that is produced.

Basil Bernstein's (1990, 1996) discussion of the general principles by which knowledge and policies ("texts") move from one arena to another is useful in understanding this. As Bernstein reminds us, when talking about educational change, there are three fields with which we must be concerned. Each field has its own rules of access, regulation, privilege, and special interests: (a) the field of "production" where new knowledge is constructed; (b) the field of "reproduction" where pedagogy and curriculum are actually enacted in schools; and, between these two, (c) the "recontextualizing" field where discourses from the field of production are appropriated and then transformed into pedagogic discourse and recommendations. This appropriation and recontextualization of knowledge for educational purposes is itself governed by two sets of principles. The first, *de*-location, implies that there is always a selective appropriation of knowledge and discourse from the field of production. The second, *re*-location, points to the fact that when knowledge and discourse from the field of production is pulled within the recontextualizing field, it is subject to ideological transformations due to the various specialized or political interests, or both, whose conflicts structure the recontextualizing field (Evans & Penney, 1995).

A good example of this, one that confirms Gipps and Murphy's (1994) analysis of the dynamics of national curricula and national testing during their more recent iterations, is found in the process by which the content and organization of the mandated national curriculum in physical education were struggled over and ultimately formed in England. In this instance, a working group of academics both within and outside the field of physical education, headmasters of private and state-supported schools, well-known athletes, and business leaders (but no teachers) was formed.

The original curriculum policies that arose from the groups were relatively mixed educationally and ideologically, taking account of the field of production of knowledge within physical education. That is, they contained both progressive elements and elements of the conservative restoration, as well as academic perspectives within the specialized fields from the university. However, as these made their way from report to recommendations and then from recommendations to action, they steadily came closer to restorational principles. An emphasis on efficiency, basic skills, and performance testing, on the social control of the body, and on competitive norms ultimately won out. Like the middle-class capturing of the market discussed earlier, this too was not a conspiracy. Rather, it was the result of a process of *overdetermination*. That is, it was not due to an imposition of these norms, but to a combination of interests in the recontextualizing field—an economic context in which public spending was under severe scrutiny and cost savings had to be sought everywhere; government officials who were opposed to "frills" and consistently intervened to institute only a selection of the recommendations (conservative ones that did not come from "professional academics," preferably); ideological attacks on critical, progressive, or child-centered approaches to physical education; and a predominant discourse of "being pragmatic." These came together in the recontextualizing field and helped insure in practice that conservative principles would be reinscribed in policies and mandates and that critical forms were seen as too ideological, too costly, or too impractical (Evans & Penney, 1995). Standards were upheld; critical voices were heard, but ultimately to little effect; the norms of competitive performance were made central and employed as regulatory devices. Regulatory devices served to privilege specific groups in much the same way as did markets. Thus goeth democracy in education.

CONCLUSION

In this relatively brief essay, I have been rather ambitious. I have raised serious questions about current educational reform efforts now underway in a number of nations. I have used research on the English experience(s) to document some of the hidden differential effects of two connected strategies—neoliberal inspired market proposals and neoliberal, neoconservative, and middle-class managerial inspired regulatory proposals. Taking a key from Herbert Kliebard's powerful historical analyses, I have described how different interests with different educational and social visions compete for dominion in the social field of power surrounding educational policy and practice. In the process, I have documented some of the complexities and imbalances in this field of power. These complexities and imbalances result in "thin" rather than "thick" morality and in the reproduction of both dominant pedagogical and curricular forms and ideologies and the social privileges that accompany them.

Having said this, however, I want to point to a hidden paradox in what I have done. Even though much of my own and others' research recently has been on the conservative restoration, there are dangers in such a focus of which we should be aware. Research on the history, politics, and practices of rightist social and educational movements and reforms has enabled us to show the contradictions and unequal effects of such policies and practices. It has enabled the rearticulation of claims to social justice on the basis of solid evidence. This is all to the good. However, in the process, one of the latent effects has been the gradual framing of educational issues largely in terms of the conservative agenda. The very categories themselves— markets, choice, national curricula, national testing, standards— bring the debate onto the terrain established by neoliberals and neoconservatives. The analysis of "what is" has led to a neglect of "what might be." Thus, there has been a withering of substantive large-scale discussions of feasible alternatives to neoliberal and neoconservative visions, policies, and practices, ones that would move well beyond them (Seddon, 1997).

Because of this, at least part of the task may be politically and conceptually complex, but it can be said simply. In the long term, scholars need to "develop a political project that is both local yet generalizable, systematic without making Eurocentric, masculinist claims to essential and universal truths about human subjects" (Luke, 1995, pp. vi-vii). Another part of the task, though, must be and is more proximate, more appropriately educational. Defensible, articulate, and fully fleshed-out alternative progressive policies and practices in curriculum, teaching, and evaluation need to be developed and made widely available.

Although in *Democratic Schools* (1995) James Beane and I have brought together a number of such examples for a larger educational audience, so much more needs to be done. Of course, we educators are not starting anew in any of this. As Herbert Kliebard has so forcefully reminded us throughout his long and distinguished career, the history of the field is replete with examples, with resources of hope. Sometimes we can go forward by looking back, by recapturing what the criticisms of past iterations of current rhetorical reforms have been and by rediscovering a valued set of traditions of educational criticism and educational action that have always tried to keep the vast river of democracy flowing. We will not find all of the answers by looking at our past, but we will reconnect with and stand on the shoulders of educators whose lives were spent in struggle against some of the very same ideological forces we face today.

Though crucial, it is then not enough, as I have done in this essay, to deconstruct restorational policies in education. The Right has shown how important changes in common sense are in the struggle for education. It is our task to collectively help rebuild it by reestablishing a sense that "thick" morality, and a "thick" democracy, are truly possible today.

NOTE

1. Whether there actually are significant changes in this regard given the fact that "New Labour" rather than the Conservatives have been governing for the past few years still remains to be seen. Certain aspects of neoliberal and neoconservative policies have already been accepted by Labour, such as the acceptance of stringent cost controls on spending put in place by the previous Conservative government and an aggressive focus on raising standards in association with strict performance indicators.

REFERENCES

Apple, M. W. (1993). *Official knowledge.* New York: Routledge.

Apple, M. W. (1996). *Cultural politics and education.* New York: Teachers College Press.

Apple, M. W., & Beane, J. A. (1995). *Democratic schools.* Washington, DC: Association for Supervision and Curriculum Development.

Ball, S., Bowe, R., & Gewirtz, S. (1994). Market forces and parental choice. In S. Tomlinson (Ed.), *Educational reform and its consequences* (pp. 13–25). London: IPPR/Rivers Oram Press.

Bernstein, B. (1990). *The structuring of pedagogic discourse.* New York: Routledge.

Bernstein, B. (1996). *Pedagogy, symbolic control, and identity.* Bristol, PA: Taylor and Francis.

Bourdieu, P. (1984). *Distinction.* Cambridge, MA: Harvard University Press.

Bourdieu, P. (1996). *The state nobility.* Stanford, CA: Stanford University Press.

Chubb, J., & Moe, T. (1990). *Politics, markets, and America's schools.* Washington, DC: Brookings Institution.

Evans, J., & Penney, D. (1995). The politics of pedagogy. *Journal of Education Policy, 10,* 27–44.

Gillborn, D. (1997a). *Race, nation, and education.* Unpublished manuscript, Institute of Education, University of London.

Gillborn, D. (1997b). Racism and reform. *British Educational Research Journal, 23,* 345–360.

Gipps, C., & Murphy, P. (1994). *A fair test?* Philadelphia: Open University Press.

Herrnstein, R., & Murray, C. (1994). *The bell curve.* New York: Free Press.

Hirsch, E. D., Jr. (1996). *The schools we want and why we don't have them.* New York: Doubleday.

Kliebard, H. (1986). *The struggle for the American curriculum, 1893–1958.* New York: Routledge.

Luke, A. (1995). Series editor's introduction. In J. L. Lemke, *Textual politics* (pp. vi–ix). Bristol, PA: Taylor and Francis.

McCarthy, C., & Crichlow, W. (1994). *Race, identity, and representation in education.* New York: Routledge.

McCulloch, G. (1997). Privatizing the past? *British Journal of Educational Studies, 45,* 69–82.

Menter, I., Muschamp, P., Nicholls, P., & Ozga, J. (with Pollard, A.) (1997). *Work and identity in the primary school.* Philadelphia: Open University Press.

O'Hear, P. (1994). An alternative national curriculum. In S. Tomlinson (Ed.), *Educational reform and its consequences* (pp. 55–72). London: IPPR/Rivers Oram Press.

Olssen, M. (1996). In defence of the welfare state and publicly provided education. *Journal of Education Policy, 11,* 337–362.

Omi, M., & Winant, H. (1994). *Racial formation in the United States.* New York: Routledge.

Power, S., Halpin, D., & Fitz, J. (1994). Underpinning choice and diversity? In S. Tomlinson (Ed.), *Educational reform and its consequences* (pp. 26–40). London: IPPR/Rivers Oram Press.

Ransom, S. (1995). Theorizing educational policy. *Journal of Education Policy, 10,* 427–448.

Seddon, T. (1997). Markets and the English. *British Journal of Sociology of Education, 18,* 165–185.

Wacquant, L. (1996). Foreword. In P. Bourdieu, *The state nobility* (pp. ix–xxii). Stanford, CA: Stanford University Press.

Whitty, G. (1997). Creating quasi-markets in education. In M. W. Apple (Ed.), *Review of research in education, 22* (pp. 3–47). Washington, DC: American Educational Research Association.

Whitty, G., Edwards, T., & Gewirtz, S. (1993). *Specialization and choice in urban education.* New York: Routledge.

Chapter 4

Curriculum as a Problem of Knowledge, Governing, and the Social Administration of the Soul

Thomas S. Popkewitz

I "met" Herb Kliebard during my own doctoral studies when my adviser suggested I write to him about metaphors of curriculum. His historical studies of the curriculum provide the first major, detailed archival examination of the changing formal organization of American school knowledge—its curriculum—during the late nineteenth and first half of the twentieth century. His scholarship brought to the study of schooling questions about the social and historical organization of the curriculum—how the school subjects, teaching, and children are thought about. His research established the importance of relating the internal changes in the school to the intense social and intellectual debates about social and cultural reform. He took an obvious but overlooked fact of schooling—that it is a social practice concerned with the organization of knowledge in the upbringing of children—and made this focus a legitimate scholarly field of inquiry. Through his work with graduate students and his collegial willingness to answer questions about the historical field of curriculum, his influence in recasting the field of curriculum studies was immediately felt by new faculty members such as me. His analytical and historical writings continually serve as a backdrop to my own efforts to understand the practices of schooling. It is what made my coming to Wisconsin after graduate school an intellectual delight.

The importance of Kliebard's work is gauged through students' doctoral studies. Although the department's formal course requirements are almost nonexistent, the cultural mores made Kliebard's courses on curriculum planning and curriculum history a de facto requirement. These courses have helped to provide a historical consciousness in a field that is otherwise historically moribund.

This influence can be shown through a personal story of mine. At the annual meeting of the American Educational Research Association in 1985, I was having breakfast with Ivor Goodson, who edited a series on curriculum history. We talked about my editing a book on the formation of the American school subjects as part of that series. In thinking about such a book, I realized that for it to work, there needed to be people with different disciplinary affiliations who could write historically about their subjects, science or mathematics education, for example. This is not a task for which you just call someone up and say, "Hey, how about a chapter on the history of social studies curriculum or mathematics education?" Most educational researchers assume school subjects rather than ask about them historically. Over the breakfast, I had to make an intuitive assessment about who could write such chapters in order to judge whether such a book was doable. Most of the names that came forward were former graduate students at Wisconsin who were influenced by Kliebard's scholarship in the history of curriculum.

This essay, I hope, maintains that historical questioning of the curriculum that Herb Kliebard made central for thinking about educational phenomena. While I maintain his central theme about knowledge at the center of internal workings of schooling, my point of departure is to pursue questions about the knowledge in curriculum by bringing my past interest in the sociology of knowledge in conversation with postmodern social theories and historical scholarship that I have called a "social epistemology" (Popkewitz, 1991, 1997). My concern with *epistemology* is to focus on the rules and standards of reason that order the principles of action and participation. Concurrently, a social epistemology is to think about how the objects constituted as the knowledge of schooling are produced as social and historical practices. Further, and central to my investigation, the systems of ideas of schooling are produced in an amalgamation of practices and technologies that are the effects of power.

This essay discusses first the particular strategy toward historicizing the curriculum that I am engaging (see Popkewitz, 1997), namely, the study of change through exploring the relation of knowledge, power, and curriculum. I then discuss curriculum historically as a problem of governing and the social administration of the individual, that is, a strategy through which social and political rationalities are brought into organizing the conduct of conduct. In this discussion, I explore how curriculum theory functions as alchemy that transforms the specific disciplinary fields into school subjects. I also explore how curriculum embodies normalizing practices in the sense of producing distinctions and divisions which place the capabilities of children within a continuum of values. The importance of the continuum and divisions, I argue, is to produce principles of normality that function to qualify and disqualify children at the level of dispositions for action and participation. Through this strategy of interrogating the knowledge of schooling is a broadening of the question of the politics of education.

CHANGING THE SUBJECT:
HISTORY AS A QUESTION OF CURRICULUM KNOWLEDGE

I want to pursue a notion of history that is different from social and intellectual history. To make a somewhat sketchy distinction between them, I would say that social history, at least in the United States, focuses on the institutional, cultural, and social flow of practices and ideas, whereas intellectual history is typically that history which follows the development of ideas within a particular grouping of thought (such as pragmatism) or in the tracing of the ideas of a single person (such as John Dewey). Both social and intellectual historical traditions focus on the values and capacities of actors as collective or individual agents who bring about change and activity in the world.

My concern with history is somewhat different. I am interested in how the systems of reason historically construct the objects to which attention is given for action, and from which the actors of change are differentiated and divided. To put this concern for history succinctly, the difference between my interest in historical studies and social and intellectual history is, as Canning (1994) comments, the difference between studying blackness instead of blacks, femininity instead of women, homosexuality instead of homosexuals, childhood instead of children. The central problematic of this approach is to locate historically the changes in the systems of reason (images, narratives, and discourses) through which the objects of schooling are classified and ordered for action and participation. It asks, for example: How is it that people think about and come to reason about change as they do? How is it that they pose problems of school knowledge, children, teaching, and evaluation through reasoning about childhood or particular rationalities associated with science and planning? This discussion of a social epistemology, then, draws on the narratives of historicist traditions, but asks how the rules and standards of knowledge give purpose and intent to action through the organizing and differentiating of the objects of reflection and action in schooling. The concern with a social epistemology is to move the study of curriculum to a study of knowledge as systems of reason.

Knowledge as a Governing Practice

One can think of the ordering and dividing functions of knowledge as a governing practice. My concern is not with the overt rules of school districts about what subjects to teach at what level or with governmental regulations about teaching certification, but rather with the governing that is related to the distinctions, differentiations, and divisions in the school curriculum that construct what is seen, spoken, felt, and thought with respect to the world and the self. For example, although we do not think about the shift from the nineteenth-century discourses about the child as a scholar to the twentieth-century ideas about childhood and learning in terms of governing practices, the shift was one in the system of reason through which school practices are ordered. The new discourses of childhood and learning constructed new principles to govern action in the concrete life of schooling. The change in how one should think, see, and act toward the child was not only in the school but in multiple institutions including health, laws, and the family. The study of curriculum, from this perspective, is the study of the knowledge that constructs, shapes, and fashions action through the ordering principles of pedagogy.

This focus on knowledge inverts a particular trajectory in the studies of schooling. Social and intellectual history in the United States, for example, assumes the identification of the actor in the narrative of historical and sociological studies of schooling. The actor, such social theory assumes, is the agent who makes history. Studies of schooling, for example, view ideas as expressing individual purpose, such as in the work of John Dewey, or as reflecting the intentions of a set of actors, such as the social forces that produce gender differentiation. The strategy of inquiry is to locate the actors who are the prime cause or origin of events. Questions are "who said what" and "how can the events be explained through individual intentions or through an examination of social forces or psychological attributes." Power is to locate who rules and who is ruled, for example, to identify what social forces prevented Progressive Education from being adequately realized in U.S. schools. When the actor is seen as absent in social and historical investigations, it is believed that the research is antihumanistic and the world is deterministic without possibilities of change.

My concern with the governing function of knowledge in schooling entails an absent actor. I admit that; but my interest is to examine critically the modern sense of humanism and its actor that is categorized in intellectual projects as the effects of power. The approach focuses on the rules of reasoning as generating principles that order the participation and actions in schooling, such as the notions of school subjects, childhood, teachers, and so on. The principles of reason make the subject through fabricating identities in the school—the child who has a childhood of stages of development and styles of learning. The identities, however, are not just fictions but govern through placing boundaries on the self who is to act. Within this historical tradition, attention is directed to how reason functions to socially construct action and is a productive intervention in social life rather than merely representative of objects or social interests.

Before proceeding, therefore, I need to talk further about the ideas of humanism and antihumanism as they relate to historical research. Although such distinctions have high value as slogans, they have little substantive value. To speak of antihumanism does not imply something that is against people taking a more active and constructive part in the making of their world. Rather, the word is used to recognize that a particular form of reason that associates intellectual projects with the identification of the actor needs to be historically questioned. As multiple studies have illustrated, the humanist assumption of agents and actors is the effect of power and can obscure the rules that order and discipline the boundaries of fields of action and participation (Dean, 1994; Gutting, 1988; Young, 1990, 1995). The social epistemology is a strategy to challenge the effects of power by moving the agent from the center of the analysis to understand how the construction of agents and the principles that order consciousness have been historically produced (Popkewitz & Brennan, 1997). Making the rules for "telling the truth" contingent, historical, and susceptible to critique is, I believe, a destabilizing strategy to dislodge the ordering principles that intern and enclose action and thus produce the possibility for other actions and possibilities.

I Agree with the Enlightenment, But Can Knowledge Be Dangerous?

My concern with a historical approach to knowledge relates current debates about an Enlightenment commitment to reason and social progress. I realize that to start a section about curriculum history with the heading "Can Knowledge Be Dangerous?" is possibly to strike a nervous cord among intellectuals that seems to go against the grain of modern philosophy and liberal democratic theory. Knowledge, it is believed, is how people have contact with the world, the means by which they assume the security and stability of their place in it, as well as their guarantor in pursuing their commitments toward social betterment. The development of modern institutions is based on commitments to knowledge as stamping out ignorance and promoting a knowledgeable citizen, parent, and worker. The folklore and theories of political and cultural life are that reason (a historically specific attitude that has been directed toward a universalized knowledge about appropriate action) will produce a progressive life. Knowledge is perceived as something that one obtains to gain power. The contemporary landscape is one of linking the faith and virtue of knowledge with the political dictums of empowerment and liberation, popular phrases in today's politics of educational change. "To know" is often seen as the emancipatory project!

While maintaining this general faith, I need to come back to a dual quality of knowledge that was suggested with the concept of governing. While knowledge is viewed as a way to explore social and personal possibilities, it is also a practice that generates principles to order and divide action. The contemporary faith in the commitment of the Enlightenment, for example, is a general attitude toward human involvement in the construction and change of social life, but the system of reason through which this commitment is expressed is not historically stable. The commitment receives its particular expression through a modern sensibility that links reason to the problem-solving rationalities of science and, as I discussed earlier, the actor who is identified as the agent of change. This particular style of constructing knowledge appears forcefully in the nineteenth century and crosses intellectual schools. The focus on the actor inscribes epistemological assumptions that relate social planning, progress, and individuality.

In the nineteenth century, the rationalities of science were transferred into the social realm to interpret and administer social change. One can historically argue that research that makes the actor an agent of change is an overlay of multiple trajectories. It entails, for example, an analytical logic related to Anglo-American linguistic philosophy, a reasoning through probability, populational theories that classified and ordered people for social planning, and the construction of science that told its "truth" through narratives that deployed footnotes, references, and other devices to assert an epistemological authority to the belief that knowledge is cumulative. The overlapping of the different epistemological rules were woven with a social Darwinism that made it possible to think about the logical ordering and control of social change at the microlevel of the community and individuality. The knowledge of science, within this notion of modernity, is to provide direction for social planning, produce social progress, and lead to individual fulfillment. This essay rejects this inscription that relates the actor, progress, and social administration in the epistemologies of research; yet I realize that the essay is bound to its own historicity through accepting the general attitude of the Enlightenment toward reason rather than being "outside" of it.

Modern curriculum theory is a governing practice that carries the duality of knowledge. As Kliebard (1986) has systematically argued, curriculum assumed a particular, though not unified, pattern at the start of the twentieth century. The various forms of modern curriculum thought link science, reason, and progress to the individual through the acquisition of knowledge. The commitments were to a liberal democratic society, although different curriculum theorists thought of these commitments through different routes for salvation. Kliebard's historical explorations about curriculum at the turn of the century point out how schooling joined a number of different strands of thought, technologies, and institutional practices into the micropractices of the family and individual. The administration of school knowledge and the child became intertwined in the quest for social progress. The schools assumed a new function—to borrow from the statement of the President of Harvard, Charles W. Eliot, in the 1890s—that shifted from the external authority of knowledge to a curriculum knowledge that focused on the reason of the individual. Eliot argued that reforming the curriculum would produce the right citizen, one who has "the power of reason, sensitivity to beauty, and high moral character" (Kliebard, 1986, p. 11).

What has interested me over the years is how the governing principles of the curriculum have shifted from the first to the second half of the twentieth century. These shifts are not in the rhetorical forms of the curriculum but in the concrete pedagogical discourses through which teaching and childhood are organized (see, e.g., Popkewitz, 1999; Popkewitz, Tabachnick, & Wehlage, 1982). One can argue that the "New Curriculum" that emerged during the late 1960s reinscribed the conception of knowledge as providing a universalized faith in social and personal progress. There was a continuation of the belief that if educators could just provide more efficient approaches to the curriculum, then society's schools would produce the citizen who acts according to reason (knowledge) in a more progressive and just world. The structure of the discipline debates of the New Curriculum, however, shifted the knowledge of curriculum to a particular professional knowledge. Reforms sought to take the most generalized knowledge of the professions as the content of school subjects in order to give direction for achieving progress. It was asserted that children should learn the broadest and most transferable knowledge in ordering their personal lives.

The seeming reinscription of commitments to change and progress was not merely a continuation of past noble ideas but an amalgamation of institutional and technological ideas that were different from the turn-of-the-century governing principles of the teacher and child. The faith in reason privileged a particular professional knowledge about progress and self-development that was different from moral, political, and religious ideas embodied in earlier expressions of Enlightenment commitments in the school (Popkewitz, 1991). The 1970s focus on how children learn and interpret the content of school subjects received a new authorization through national pedagogical reform efforts of the 1990s that later came to be called *constructivism*.

As with earlier curriculum reforms, the principles of governing make the site of change the pedagogical *soul*—the inner dispositions and capabilities of the problem-solving, collaborative child. The soul targeted in current reforms, however, is not merely a continuation of past concerns. The governing patterns embody a different set of social relations and historical conditions that are homologous to the identities inscribed in other contemporary arenas, such as those of business, culture, and the military (Popkewitz, 1998a, 1999).

My emphasis on curriculum knowledge as a governing practice is a recognition of a particular side of power that is rarely studied in schooling. This relation of knowledge and power in school studies is explored through Michel Foucault's (1979) idea of *governmentality*. Power in social life, he argues, is not found in the public policies of sovereign entities (state bureaucracies, class as entities) or in the unrealized values in the implementation of school reforms. Rather, power is an effect produced through the principles that order thought and reason; that is, the *mentalities* that shape how individuals problematize the world and their action. For example, the tables of ingredients on the back of a package that are used to tell the consumer about the health attributes of food are one such example of how multiple discourses overlap one another to enact principles that bring intent and purpose to action (governmentality). At first glance, the categories seem to be scientific reports of fat content, cholesterol, and calories. However, once one explores the categories and distinctions made through the tables

of ingredients, one is confronted with the realization that the categories that order and give meaning to the experience are formed through
power relations and are the effect of those relations. Joan Scott (1991)
has persuasively argued that what is taken as natural experience is
not natural but is tied to identities that are socially constructed and
to the effects of power. Following her argument, one can understand
that the food content tables that order ingredients overlap with other
discourses. The table of food content is an amalgamation of social,
political, gendered, and scientific discourses, such as those that engender social images of the body (a fat body is undesirable), define
the dispositions and practices through which health is to be understood (through scientific management of the body), and organize by
omission what is not to be considered in questions of health, such as
the use of pesticides, taste and texture, genetic manipulations of foods,
and application of chemicals in agricultural production. It is this se-
lectivity and ordering of principles for action (buying foods that
have the image of being healthy) that function as a system of governmentality, through the systems of reason, that generates principles to
differentiate, distinguish, and divide the world.

I assume that the idea of governing may produce a strong reaction as it hits an American sensitivity—to return to the idea of the
Enlightenment discussed earlier—that places a high value on individual
initiative and human purpose in directing social affairs. My concern
with governing, however, should not be read as disregarding these
Enlightenment sensibilities. Reason and rationality are central to social efforts to improve our human conditions. But we cannot assume
the rules of reason and rationality are unified and universal; rather,
they are historically constructed practices. This interest in knowledge
as governing practices, then, is to make reason and rationality the object
of inquiry. It is to recognize that the seemingly liberatory and redemptive rhetoric of educational discourses to save children may not necessarily be liberatory or redemptive. Particular systems of ideas and rules
of reasoning embedded in the practices of schools are to be made as
problematic. All knowledge is dangerous, to return to the heading of
this section, although not all knowledge is bad.

THE REGISTERS OF SOCIAL ADMINISTRATION AND FREEDOM

At this point, I want to move more directly into the problematic
of governmentality as a way to think about the study of schooling. This raises a question about the traditional casting of school

studies as investigating its realization of principled arguments, such as through the Spencerian question, "What knowledge is of most worth?" It seems to me that the problem of research is not a principled one that asks how some normative idea is being achieved; rather the problem is about the changing rules and standards of knowledge as governing systems. The Spencerian question, for example, assumes an absolute ideal that stands as an unmitigated good; yet the historical practices of schooling include historical ironies and paradoxes as its social practices relate knowledge and power. Let me explore this further.

The governing of the child can be examined through the changing relation of knowledge and politics that appears in the late nineteenth century. The emergence of liberal democratic societies embodied a new relationship between the governing of the state and the governing of the individual, particularly in liberal states where individuals were expected to exhibit self-discipline and self-motivation. The new democratic states entailed the democratization of the individual. People were expected to be seen and to see themselves as individuals who could act on their world with autonomy and responsibility. In one sense, the individual now became a citizen who had certain obligations, responsibilities, and freedoms. The freedoms, however, involved being a citizen who acted responsibly through a new sense of rational self-motivation and self-discipline. The self-discipline of the individual was to be mobilized by the bringing of professionalized knowledge into realms of social administration. Modern pedagogy and the science of education embodied this belief in an individuality that was self-administering.

But this new sense of individuality in liberal democratic states was not one that merely appeared as a complement to political philosophy and state government. New institutions for planning social welfare, health, economy, and education carried the political rationalities of citizenship into the constructions of individuality. The development of institutions of social welfare and economy moved across multiple historical trajectories and multiple overlays of social practices in which the outcomes could be foretold. Thus, while I summarize the outcomes, the interpretations should not be read as one of a conspiracy theory of power and control. The social sciences, whose emergence coincides with the modern state, were not only about interpreting social practices or guiding social policy. The social sciences provided ways to "reason" about the citizen, the child, the family, gender, and the worker. The disciplinary discourses of economy, culture, and education broke the unified systems of theology that preceded them but introduced different, secular systems of administering freedom in modernity (see Heilbron, 1995). The specialized disciplinary discourses included how the worker was to feel, see, think, and act in the new industrial relations, and what dispositions and sensitivities a mother-wife and child were to have in the new social relations of the home.

Although there were ongoing debates and conflicts in this period about organizing society and individuality, there was a pervasive belief that the democratization of the individual was a problem of public administration (see, e.g., Wagner, 1994). At one level, the state was to produce the universalization of policies and routinization of politics that would remove strife and produce harmonious social development. At a different level, this state targeted the "self" as a site of administration. By the nineteenth century, for example, Enlightenment beliefs about the citizen were made into an entity of political reflection and social administration. Nineteenth-century constitutional doctrines of liberty, rights, and law which imposed limits on state activities were predicated on the existence of individuals who were self-governing and took responsibility for their own conduct (Rose, 1989). The state was expected to shape the individual who mastered change through the application of rationality and reason. From Humboldtian to Hegelian and post-Kantian moral and political philosophy, the state functioned to develop people's faculties and the apprehension of the good (see, e.g., Hunter, 1994).

The social administration of freedom is most evident in the construction of pedagogy. Schooling and pedagogy made the soul into an object of scrutiny. Religious motifs of pastoral care and the confessional were brought into the curriculum through the disciplines of psychology and sociology, such as theories of group interaction and community (Greek, 1992). The administration of reflection replaced revelation. Modern salvation and human progress are intricately linked to notions of individual capabilities. The history of citizenship education in the curriculum was a social project to administer the soul (see, e.g., Kliebard & Wegner, 1987; Lybarger, 1987).

But the religious motifs about personal salvation and redemption had new points of reference in the modernizing projects of the nineteenth century in which pedagogical projects were constructed. Categories about attitudes, learning, self-actualization, and self-esteem were words that revisioned religious motifs and placed them in secular discourses of science and rational progress. It became possible to talk about children's inner sense of self in the same way as earlier religious discourses talked about the salvation of soul. Albion Small, for example, at the center of the new social sciences at the University of Chicago, focused on pedagogy as the science that would shape and fashion children's souls in thought and action.

The new pedagogical psychologies gave attention to seemingly secular concerns about personal development, individual dispositions, and fulfillment of the self. Although we do not think of Dewey as related to the psychological construction of pedagogy, he sought to bring a particular pragmatic philosophy into psychology and schooling. Dewey's idea of community, if with different epistemological assumptions than the prevailing psychologies, was to coordinate the emerging individuality of the child with the society through strategies of interaction in a community (Kliebard, 1986). John Dewey, for example, inscribed political and moral assumptions of progress into his conception of personal development within "community." The idea of community embodied a Protestant notion of hard work, a commitment to science as problem-solving in a democracy, and an Emersonian notion of citizen "voluntarism" in social affairs. Dewey's writings further embodied an American "exceptionalism" that transformed Protestant millennial visions about the United States as a New World into a secular belief that the nation had a unique history and a mission to bring about human perfection. (For a general discussion of the inscription of religious and pastoral motifs in U.S. political and social thought, see, e.g., Bercovitch, 1978; Marx, 1964; Ross, 1991; West, 1989.)

The construction of the modern curriculum joined the register of freedom with the register of social administration; this was not a principled project toward some social goal as historical narratives of the development of the modern school imply. The relation of the two registers is illustrated in Fendler's (1998) study of the changing discourses about "the educated subject." She argues that "to be educated has meant to become disciplined according to a regimen of remembering and forgetting, of assuming identities normalized through discursive practices, and of a history of unpredictable diversions" (p. 61). She examines over time the shifting assumptions of "true" and good in the notion of the educated subject, the practical technologies to educate, the systems of recognition and things "examined," and the ways people are "invited" to recognize themselves as "educated." Fendler argues that the systems of reason about the educated subject entail practical technologies that organize the performances and "skills" embodied in a particular type of individuality. These performances and skills appear as "natural" and desirable, but inscribe a normativity through which new forms of supervision and supervision of the self are produced. Fendler's study of the educated subject enables an understanding of how the categories, distinctions, and differentiations embodied in curriculum theory disciplines, shapes, and forms the objects acted on.

The social administration of freedom, thus, should not be construed as a principled argument tied to political philosophy but as a pragmatic one related to multiple historical trajectories that begin prior to and continue into the nineteenth century. The particular joining of the governing of the state with the governing of the individual, assumed, for example, in the curriculum reforms of progressivism in the United States, has a resemblance to the relation of the state and individuality that emerged in the seventeenth- and eighteenth-century European religious wars (Hunter, 1994). While current thought assumes distinct realms of the public and the private (such as distinctions between state and civil society, mind and body, the social and the individual) that are to represent two distinct types of ethical comportment, the distinction between state and civil society historically emerges in a time in which they were to pacify divided communities through the imposition of a politically binding conception of the public good into the construction of the individual self. Freedoms associated with liberal societies—religious toleration and freedom of worship—were produced as part of the administrative state efforts to govern fratricidal communities rather than as the expression of democratic institutions or popular resistance. Nonviolent tolerance and pragmatic spheres of political deliberation were created by forcefully separating the civic comportment of the citizen from the private persona of the man of conscience and by subordinating spiritual absolutes to governmental objectives. Schooling was a mechanism used by the state to conceptualize and organize a massive and ongoing program of pacification, discipline, and training responsible for the political and social capacities of the modern citizen (Hunter, 1995).

If we pursue Hunter's argument, the binaries between state and civil society, the individual and the social, the objective and the subjective, or the cognitive and subjective that are embedded in modern curriculum thought were undermined through the practical linkages between political rationalities and the social administration of the individual that was in place well before liberal democratic theories of the nineteenth century. The governing practice of curriculum goes almost unquestioned in modern educational practices. The problem of curriculum is the administration of the soul with the site of change as the dispositions and sensitivities of the child. The child in the curriculum, no matter from what ideological position, is one who has the correct conduct in acting as a self-governing individual. Thus, when we look at current European Union policy and research in education, an important focus is on producing a European identity among the citizens of its member nations. Current U.S. reforms that embody a constructivist pedagogy in teaching and teacher education reforms, as well, are concerned with the construction of identity through a focus on reconstituting the beliefs and dispositions of the teacher and the child. The strategy of pedagogy is to have a problem-solving, flexible, and collaborative individual. The new psychologies of pedagogy maintain a secularization of the prior confessional systems of church in order to produce a self-disciplined individuality related to modern political projects. The soul is the target but without its explicit mention.

Normalization and the Practices of Curriculum

While I have emphasized the curriculum as the social administration of the soul, the practices of schooling do not occur on a level playing field. The systems of reason are normalizing practices that order and divide the capabilities and dispositions of an individual. The norms that divide, however, are not what we typically talk about as teachers' beliefs and their philosophy of education, bias or stereotypes, or what is publicly spoken about as educational purposes. The normalization is the dividing practice that differentially gives value to the inner qualities of the child and, more recently, the teacher. Modern pedagogy embodies principles that tell the teacher and the child about the average, the normal, and the not-average and not-normal. The normalization practices produce systems of inclusion and exclusion.

To consider curriculum as a practice of normalization and of inclusion and exclusion, I want to focus on a recent ethnographic study concerned with a reform program to train teachers for inner-city, urban and rural schools in multiple sites around the United States (Popkewitz, 1998b). The distinctions of *inner-city, urban* and *rural* are embedded in a particular historically mobilized discourse that at one level introduces the special obligations and needs of American schools (Hennon, in press). At a different level, the discourses of urbanness and ruralness in education deploy a particular normalization that is evident when we place it next to other discourses that also deploy notions of urban or rural. In contexts other than education, *urban* is a word that is associated with high civilization and wealth, such as with the urbane and the cosmopolitan. Further, the particular discourses of urban and rural education are not geographical concepts as certain children who live in the city are not classified as urban and urban schools can exist in suburbia as well as the inner city.

If we focus on the discourses of urban schools, they are embedded in a longer trajectory of school reform dedicated to helping the poor and the needy. It captures a nineteenth century view of schooling as a means to rescue children from their economic, social, and cultural conditions through planned intervention. The rescue of the child combined religious views of salvation with secular notions about the effects of poverty, class, and social and racial discrimination. The groups to be rescued by schools, however, were not merely those who were marginalized, but also the middle classes. But with urban and rural education are historically mobilized discourses about the child who is different from others who are not present but whose norms of behavior and "being" provide the values of comparison. The dividing occurs not only in what is cognitively understood about the child, but in the production of norms that separate and divide children according to their available sensitivities, dispositions, and awarenesses.

The everyday distinctions of teaching had no practical discursive differences between the urbanness and the ruralness of the child or the teacher. The same social, pedagogical, psychological, and management discourses were used in urban and rural schools because the geographical situation did not matter. All children in the schools were classified as having the qualities of urbanness.

The discourses gave teaching and education not only a mission that was social but one that tied religious commitments of saving the soul. The urban and rural schools were sites of pedagogical intervention to rescue the child from the moral conditions of their communities and to make the child into a productive citizen. This missionary quality of redemption was reinscribed and coalesced in pedagogical distinctions to classify school competence-incompetence, and achievement-nonachievement.

One of those operative discourses was the wisdom of teacher's practice. The wisdom of practice was not only for information about teaching. The practices involved norms about the child that organized and evaluated teachers' actions. An inservice program for the training of new teachers, for example, imparted practical information about "what works" in the classroom. The practical information was based on the assumption that future teachers can best learn their craft through the telling of experience. The practical reasoning was a storytelling about teaching.

The storytelling of the wisdom of practice placed boundaries upon what was acceptable and normal, and its opposite—the unacceptable and abnormal—in schooling. The distinctions about inner-city schools, for example, were related to concepts about the streetwise intelligence of the children. The category was intended as a positive expression about the children of the inner-city school. The child in the school was to be viewed as having the potential to be as smart as any other child. But the categories of *streetwise intelligence* and *inner city* are caught in a web of ideas that function to compare and classify the capabilities of children. There were distinctions about children's mastery of school subjects (the children "did not learn" mathematics) and distinctions about psychological capabilities (the children "were not motivated," had "low self-esteem," and had "culturally specific learning styles").

The difference of the urban (sometimes inner-city) child was sanctioned in discourses of psychological development and learning (such as learning styles), conceptions of school subjects (learning as "hands-on"), distinctions about children's intelligence (streetwise intelligence), and technologies of classroom management. The urbanness of the child also joins state welfare policies that target certain populations who are in need of remediation because of what seems to be the psychological and cognitive effects of being inner-city.

The discursive practices constructed the mental capabilities and "being" of children through a reason that normalized what was absent in the children as what was necessary for success. The overlay of psychological, social, pedagogical, and management discourses became a scaffolding that differentiated the children from other children (*these* children required greater attention to hands-on activities and field-dependent learning experiences). But those capabilities could never be obtained because the identities of the children were constructed as being fundamentally outside the bounds of reason and normality.

The urban children, no matter who those children were, were discursively placed as those who can never be average or normal, no matter how hard they try. While most of the children were African American or Latino, the discourses of urbanness racialized also the capabilities of the white child who was classified as urban or rural. The patterns of distinctions *make* the children with the streetwise intelligence of children in inner-city schools appear troubled and somehow different from children who were not present.

The example of *urban*, then, provides a strategy to think about the problem of inclusion-exclusion in curriculum studies. Ideas of inclusion and exclusion are mutually implicated in the other when focusing on discursive practices. What is excluded is no longer the child as the embodiment of populational characteristics—race, gender, class—but the dispositions of the child. The urban child is understood to have personal inner qualities that are not regarded as "reasonable." The normalization that characterizes the child is not mentioned but silently inscribed in the differentiations that compose those that stand outside of thought and reason, and thus become outside of being reasonable. In the study of urbanness that I described above, the normalization related to the "being" of the child that crossed multiple groupings of children—those who were classified as of color but also those who were racialized through their placement in the social space of the *urban*.

ALCHEMIES AND CURRICULUM

One element in the construction of the governing principles of curriculum is its *alchemy:* one can think of curriculum as performing an alchemy on disciplinary knowledge. As the sorcerer of the Middle Ages sought to turn lead into gold, modern curriculum theory produces a magical change as it turns the specific intellectual traditions of historians or physicists, for example, into teaching practices.

To understand the alchemies of curriculum, one can approach science, social science, mathematics, and literary studies as systems of knowledge produced within complex and pragmatic sets of social relations. The knowledge accepted as sociology or anthropology, for example, involves particular institutional relations and systems of reasoning about research, teaching, and professional status. When Thomas Kuhn (1970) spoke about "revolutionary" and "normal" science, in one sense, he was speaking of the competing standards and rules for "telling the truth" and of the different stakes that are authorized (and want to be authorized) as groups compete.

The norms of "truth," however, are not just influenced by the internal dimensions of a discipline. They are produced in intellectual fields that relate ideas to social constellations. Heilbron (1995), in examining the early historical formation of the social sciences in the nineteenth century, focuses on the breakdown of theology and church teaching in organizing the knowledge of society. This decline of church power over knowledge made possible, he argues, the secularization of conceptions and representation and the development of differentiated intellectual fields in which the modern social sciences function. Today, the production of disciplinary knowledge needs to be understood as circulating in different social constellations, such as that of state agencies concerned with welfare questions about the effects of poverty and commercial entities interested in attitude research.

In this sense, the idea of a disciplinary field involves historical configurations between the internal rules and standards of its academic field and those of the social and cultural fields in which it operates.

The relation between these two social spaces in the production of disciplinary knowledge is never straightforward. What counts as knowledge involves struggles among different groups within a discipline about the norms of participation, truth, and recognition.

The alchemy of school curriculum ignores the disciplines as complex sites of struggles about participation, truth, and recognition. School subjects are treated as logical systems of unambiguous content for children to learn. Even the notions of problem-solving in current curriculum reforms focus on the processes of children's thinking while leaving aside the questions about the discursive and rhetorical practices of science (see, e.g., the series, *Rhetoric of the Human Sciences*, edited by John Lyne, Donald McCloskey, & John Nelson, published by the University of Wisconsin Press). Thus, what appears as science, math, composition, or art in schools have little relation to the intellectual fields that bear their names. School subjects are an alchemy in which the pedagogical construction conforms to expectations related to the school timetable, conceptions of childhood, and conventions of teaching that transform knowledge and intellectual inquiry into a strategy for governing the soul. Thus, we can say that there is an alchemy of the discipline of physics into, for example, categories of concept mastery, psychological registers about cooperative small-group learning, and concerns about the motivation and the self-esteem of children.

Perhaps the alchemy of school subjects is necessary because children are not scientists or artists. But that is not my point. My objective is to recognize the significance of this alchemy to the study of schooling as a governing practice in two related ways.

First, curriculum theory revises the complexities and contingencies of disciplinary practices into "things of logic." Concepts and generalizations are taken as logical, nontemporal structures which function as foundations from which learning occurs. Even methods of research are assumed to be logical entities that follow some rules that exist outside of social processes. The alchemy makes it possible to talk about children's learning of social studies as involving conceptions and misconceptions of concepts, as if concepts were stable and fixed entities of knowledge. It also makes possible the teaching of laboratory skills or interview practices as universal procedures of inquiry that enable learning about science or social science. One learns laboratory skills, for example, as a specific instrumental practice that is separate from the discursive patterns through which data are interpreted and practices organized. Yet if we think historically about the laboratory work of psychology, for example, we can see that the idea of an experiment involves a whole range of norms about the relation of the experimenter and the experimentee that emerges slowly in the twentieth century as psychologists redefine the object and epistemologies of research (Danziger, 1990). This alchemy is present when research is classified according to the distinctions in procedures of collecting data, such as the distinction between quantitative and qualitative research.

When research at the cutting edge of science is examined, that knowledge is quite different from that enshrined in the school curriculum. It involves debates and struggles about what is to be studied and how. Further, the conception of knowledge used by research scientists privileges strategies to make the familiar strange, to think about the mysterious and unfamiliar, and to raise questions precisely about that which is taken for granted. The rules of curriculum are quite different as they privilege the stable, fixed, and categorical properties of knowledge, even in recent "constructivist pedagogies" (see Popkewitz, 1991, chap. 7).

The alchemy that makes the world and events seem to be things of logic removes any social mooring from knowledge. The debates and struggles in the production of disciplinary knowledge are glossed over, and a stable system of ideas is presented to children. The disciplines appear in curriculum as natural objects to be learned rather than as approaches that are historically constructed rather than natural.

Kliebard's (1986) discussions of Dewey helps one to understand how the focus on the logic of knowledge distorts the relation of knowledge to human affairs. The difficulty with Dewey's theory, however, is that it is a generalized philosophy of knowledge that is tied to a psychology of the child. Although it gives general references to the social construction of knowledge, its immersion in the logics of psychology is inadequate for curriculum as it lacks a historical specificity to the social production of knowledge.

A second function of the alchemy is related to issues of normalization and exclusion discussed above. The exclusions that I speak about here are related to the distinctions of knowledge and are different from those associated with the children who succeed or fail in a school subject or with those groups that are represented in curriculum. This was evident in the study of urban and rural education discussed earlier. When one approaches the problem of inclusion-exclusion in relation to the alchemy of the curriculum, the stabilizing of the content of school subjects enables a focus on the social administration of the child. The school curriculum functions as a fixed entity through which the strategies of teaching are to change the capabilities and dispositions of the child.

With school subject content stabilized, the pedagogical strategies are directed toward the administration of the soul.

The Politics of Representation and the Politics of Knowledge

The issue of inclusion and exclusion is not only who is represented but the rules and standards of the systems of reason through which school subjects are ordered through pedagogical practices. Let me turn to the example of a multicultural curriculum.

Much of the U.S. research focuses on the inclusion of African Americans and Latinos, among others, in the curriculum. It looks at the ways in which these groups have provided unique contributions to the economic, social, and cultural development of the United States. At the same time, there is discussion about how U.S. curriculum needs to be less Eurocentric. There are efforts to construct historical narratives about marginal groups to be included in textbooks. This notion of inclusion often is phrased as "giving a voice" to those previously excluded from curriculum representation.

This move to give greater representation to various groups that have been excluded from historical and social representation in the curriculum is important. But there is a different question about the politics of inclusion and exclusion when considered through the problematic of knowledge. This question is related to the rules through which these different groups are represented. These rules embody certain normalizing processes about what counts as knowledge, reason, and being. Feminist research, for example, has directed attention to how disciplinary discourses about the body, health, and science maintain images of women that are the effects of power. To give a group representation in the curriculum, if I follow this example, requires attention to the norms generated for action and participation in that representation. Thus, one can examine the new curriculum that increases representation of previously marginalized groups, but also one needs to ask about the normalizations that differentiate and divide the subject.

At a different layer is the hybridity of knowledge, which includes the premise that there is no pure logic or knowledge. This is evident when discussing issues of the Eurocentric focus of the curriculum. The assertion is often that cultural discussions accept European knowledge as valuable and other ways of thinking as not valuable. This discussion is sometimes put into colonial-postcolonial dichotomies to emphasize some non-Western approach to knowledge. But such discussions do not examine how oppositional (postcolonial) images relate with colonial images in a manner that is neither European nor non-European. Within the different social sciences and humanities, for example, there is intense debate about their narratives as hybrids which draw on different European and non-European systems of thought (even the Old Testament is a hybrid, and not of "Western" thought). Gilroy's (1993) discussion of blackness as a "double consciousness" is an example of the construction of self as a hybridity. Gilroy explores various expressions of popular culture and literacy and philosophical ideas of the African communities in North America and Britain as coming out of the African diaspora—in Africa, the Americas, and Europe. The "Black Atlantic," he argues, was a critical transformative site of modernity through these complex engagements. The Nobel laureate, Toni Morrison's (1992) *Playing in the Dark*, also brings in this question of hybridity and race. She discusses how "blackness" is embodied in the literary construction of "whiteness."

This does not mean that certain discursive practices are given greater credibility in social affairs while others are often not heard. But it does mean that the dualism that separates one form of representation (European) from another (a non-European) deflects attention from the effects of power through the epistemological rules applied. Again, there is a need to transpose the Spencerian question of "What knowledge is of most worth" in which knowledge is treated as an object related to other social "facts" to questions of the rules and standards of reason as the effects of power.

EDUCATIONAL KNOWLEDGE AND
THE PROBLEMATIC OF GOVERNING

I have to this point focused on curriculum studies as a historical concern with the governing practices of knowledge. In this last section, I pursue questions about the politics of knowledge that were always present in the previous discussion but not explicitly considered. From the hidden curriculum of the 1970s to current concerns with the cultural politics of education, the question is asked, about whose interests is the organization of schooling, and at a different level, the knowledge of the researcher. In this essay, I have sought to provide a different set of questions related to the principles that order the conduct of conduct in teachers and children. My earlier discussion about the decentering of the subject and a social epistemology was to consider the problematic of knowledge as a productive, material practice that interns and encloses individuality.

I want to return here to a comment of Kliebard's that curriculum is always an imperfect project (Kliebard, 1992). I have sought in this essay to think about this imperfection through examining its systems of knowledge, what I have called a social epistemology. In taking this position, the history and science of education is one that makes skepticism a central attitude. Borrowing for a moment from Stephen Toulmin (1990), a philosopher of science, I argue that in the earlier part of the seventeenth century, science was dominated by uncertainty and skepticism which fell into disuse by the end of the century. By the latter half of the seventeenth century, Newtonian ideas of certainty dominated. This ascension of certainty occurred for a number of historical (rather than solely scientific) reasons. The assumptions still persist. Toulmin suggests at the end of his book that certainty has gotten us to a fixed point, and maybe it is time to give skepticism a chance. I agree! But the skepticism that I have spoken about in this essay is a particular historical question about knowledge as systems of reason and as effects of power.

Curriculum and curriculum studies as an imperfect project entails a continual paradox and irony. It is a problem of social administration of freedom that gives focus to particular historical practices of governing the actions of individuals rather than of freedom as some absolute and universal principle. Perhaps at this historical moment, we educators are bound to the joining of the two registers as the best trajectories available. But acting on curriculum in this manner is not to remove its irony; the irony is in tying the two registers together. It requires that we continually ask questions such as these: "What are the rules and standards by which we reason about the world?" "What are the ways that we 'tell the truth' about teaching, children, historical knowledge, the social sciences in the social studies curriculum?" "How is that knowledge historically an effect of power?"

The irony is embedded in the politics of school subjects and the issues of inclusion-exclusion. The irony is also given expression in the history of science and current sociologies of modernity that have suggested that an important strategy for considering change is through the epistemological constructions of reason.

This last observation is important for considering current reform efforts in pedagogy and teacher education. Asking about the knowledge from which we educators act is difficult because "our" points of communication with experiences are through the discursive systems of categories and differentiations available for that communication. While I do not think that the paradox and irony will be resolved, I do think, as did Toulmin and Kliebard, that we need to give attention to a particular critical skepticism in curriculum work. Although the current pedagogical reforms take for granted that the systems of reason are to socially administer the practices of the teacher and the child, the epistemological rules that order and govern the images and narratives of curriculum cannot be taken as unproblematic.

In this sense, the social epistemology is a history of the present to locate continuities and discontinuities in the knowledge through which the subjects of schooling (in its dual qualities) are constructed. As I suggested earlier, this may seem an "antihumanism" by displacing the acting subject with a concern with the knowledge systems of education. But it is not against people acting to change their world and thus is, like all strategies of intellectual life, one that lives in its own irony. The strategy is to understand the rules of reasoning for "telling the truth" about the actor so as to potentially make the practices of schooling as historically contingent as the effects of power and thus as susceptible to critique and change. The strategy to destabilize the existing doxa of humanism is to dislodge the ordering principles that enclose and intern individuality and thereby to make open the range of possibilities for the subject to act.

To close, I return to where this essay started and the reason for this book. This essay would not have been possible without the historical studies and the disposition toward a historicizing of curriculum in education that Kliebard has provided through his teaching and his scholarship. The collective work of Kliebard provides powerful insights into the profound social, cultural, and philosophical questions that are entailed in the construction of schooling. His scholarship also reminds us educators of the need for continuing deliberation and critical scrutiny of education in a democratic culture. The exploration of the past in the present enables us to consider how the ways of thinking and institutional practices that were formed out of the tensions and compromises of the past are sedimented in current educational reform policy.

REFERENCES

Bercovitch, S. (1978). *The American jeremiad.* Madison: University of Wisconsin Press.

Canning, C. (1994). Feminist history after the linguistic turn: Historicizing discourse and experience. *Signs: Journal of Women in Culture and Society, 19,* 368–404.

Danziger, K. (1990). *Constructing the subject: Historical origins of psychological research.* New York: Cambridge University Press.

Dean, M. (1994). *Critical and effective histories: Foucault's methods and historical sociology*. New York: Routledge.

Fendler, L. (1998). What is it impossible to think? A genealogy of the educated subject. In T. Popkewitz & M. Brennan (Eds.), *Foucault's challenge: Discourse, knowledge, and power in education* (pp. 39–63). New York: Teachers College Press.

Foucault, M. (1979). Governmentality. *Ideology and Consciousness, 6,* 5–22.

Gilroy, P. (1993). *The Black Atlantic: Modernity and double consciousness*. Cambridge, MA: Harvard University.

Greek, C. (1992). *The religious roots of American sociology*. New York: Garland.

Gutting, G. (1988). *Michel Foucault's archaeology of scientific reason*. New York: Cambridge University Press.

Heilbron, J. (1995). *The rise of social theory* (S. Gogol, Trans.). Minneapolis: University of Minnesota Press.

Hennon, L. (in press). The construction of discursive space as patterns of inclusion/exclusion: Governmentality and urbanism in the USA. In T. Popkewitz (Ed.), *Educational knowledge: Changing relationships between the state, civil society, and the educational community*. Albany: The State University of New York Press.

Hunter, I. (1994). *Rethinking the school: Subjectivity, bureaucracy, criticism*. New York: St. Martin's Press.

Hunter, I. (1995). Assembling the school. In A. Barry, T. Osborne, & N. Rose (Eds.), *Foucault and political reason: Liberalism, neo-liberalism, and rationalities of government* (pp. 143–166). Chicago: University of Chicago Press.

Kliebard, H. (1986). *Struggle for the American curriculum, 1893–1958*. London: Routledge & Kegan Paul.

Kliebard, H. (1992). *Forging the American curriculum: Essays in curriculum history and theory*. New York: Routledge.

Kliebard, H., & Wegner, G. (1987). Harold Rugg and the reconstruction of the social studies curriculum: The treatment of the "Great War" in his textbook series. In T. Popkewitz (Ed.), *The formation of school subjects: The struggle for creating an American institution* (pp. 268–288). New York: Falmer Press.

Kuhn, T. (1970). *The structure of scientific revolutions* (2nd ed.). Chicago: University of Chicago Press.

Lybarger, M. (1987). Need as ideology: Social workers, social settlements, and the social studies. In T. Popkewitz (Ed.), *The formation of the school subjects: The struggles for creating an American institution* (pp. 176–189). New York: Falmer Press.

Marx, L. (1964). *The machine in the garden: Technology and the pastoral image in America*. New York: Oxford University Press.

Morrison, T. (1992). *Playing in the dark: Whiteness and the literary imagination*. Cambridge, MA: Harvard University Press.

Popkewitz, T. S. (1991). *A political sociology of educational reform: Power/knowledge in teaching, teacher education, and research*. New York: Teachers College Press.

Popkewitz, T. S. (1997). The production of reason and power: Curriculum history and intellectual traditions. *Journal of Curriculum Studies, 29*(2), 131–164.

Popkewitz, T. S. (1998a). The culture of redemption and the administration of freedom in educational research. *Review of Educational Research, 68*(1), 1–34.

Popkewitz, T. S. (1998b). *Struggling for the soul: The politics of education and the construction of the teacher.* New York: Teachers College Press.

Popkewitz, T. S. (1999). Dewey, Vygotsky, and the social administration of the individual: Constructivist pedagogy as systems of ideas in historical spaces. *American Educational Research Journal, 35*(4), 535–570.

Popkewitz, T. S., & Brennan, M. (1997). Restructuring social and political theory in education: Foucault and a social epistemology of school practices. *Educational Theory, 47*(3), 287–314.

Popkewitz, T. S., Tabachnick, B. R., & Wehlage, G. (1982). *The myth of educational reform: School responses to planned change.* Madison: University of Wisconsin Press.

Rose, N. (1989). *Governing the soul.* New York: Routledge, Chapman & Hall.

Ross, D. (1991). *The origins of American social science.* New York: Cambridge University Press.

Scott, J. (1991). The evidence of experience. *Critical Inquiry, 17,* 773–797.

Toulmin, S. (1990). *Cosmopolis: The hidden agenda of modernity.* New York: Free Press.

Wagner, P. (1994). *The sociology of modernity.* New York: Routledge.

West, C. (1989). *The American evasion of philosophy: A genealogy of pragmatism.* Madison: University of Wisconsin Press.

Young, R. (1990). *White mythologies: Writing, history, and the West.* New York: Routledge.

Young, R. (1995). *Colonial desire: Hybridity in theory, culture, and race.* London: Routledge.

PART III

CURRICULUM DIFFERENTIATION

Chapter 5

The Tracking Show

Reba N. Page

The most intriguing thing about tracking may be the persistence with which we Americans debate it—and continue doing it. The recurrence, over almost a century, might give us pause and prompt perhaps some reconsideration of how we think about, or conceptualize, the curricular practice. That is my purpose in this essay.

First, I pose the ongoing dispute about tracking as cultural rather than technical or straightforwardly political. Hence, if tracking grounds questions about designing effective means of distributing school knowledge among diverse students or about the interest groups that are advantaged and disadvantaged by particular distributions, it also displays a culture's preoccupations (Geertz, 1973b). Its debate offers a "political spectacle" (Edelman, 1988), or show, one that is replete with the look and feel of momentous conflict over what schooling—and "America"—are and ought to be, but without any of the complex contingencies entailed in actual engagement in either politics or curriculum. At a safe remove from troublesome practicalities and conflict, we can reassure ourselves that we care deeply about school and country.

I then illustrate the complexities using a case of tracking-in-practice (Valli, 1990) as well as other scholarship, including case studies of my own (Page, 1987, 1991, 1999). The cases raise three questions that appear frequently in the debate about tracking, but they pose them in a fashion that can generate some reconsideration of how we conceptualize the practice: (a) Does tracking in schools "work"—and, however familiar, is that the right question? (b) How can we generalize about or explain tracking, given a sprawling and often contradictory research literature? (c) Because tracking invariably prompts claims about equal education, what kind of equality do we have in mind when we would hold schools accountable for it?

TRACKING-IN-DEBATE

Argument about the merits of tracking has been standard fare in educational discourse since around the turn of the century, when the practice of differentiating the curriculum offered to different groups of students began to be widely implemented in U.S. secondary schools. Equally persistent, even ritualized, have been the substance, form, and high moral tenor of the argument.[1] Proponents have asserted that tracking is a clearly effective and fair practice because a differentiated curriculum accommodates individuals' distinctive abilities, interests, or aspirations. However, critics have countered with equal certitude, if a diametrically opposed conclusion, that tracking undermines rather than affirms "America"; it is ineffective and inequitable, not least because it provides unworthy knowledge and teaching to students with the fewest social and academic advantages, whereas the most advantaged students receive the best teaching and "high-status knowledge." Because of the acrimony and polarization of the debate, some analysts refer to "the tracking wars" ("Tracking wars . . . ," 1992).

If tracking was the clearly good (or bad) practice that combatants have long maintained and the choice, straightforward, we might expect that we would have settled by now on a victor and a warranted course of action. That is the promise of both a rational politics and technical design. Instead, however, skirmishing continues, its outcomes indecisive (for a recent encounter, see "Exchange," 1994). Equally striking, the inconclusiveness in the war of words goes unremarked. It is mirrored in ambiguous practices that are themselves largely unnoted—in schools, where tracking is widely instituted but with such ambivalence that few educators publicly admit to it; in a research literature that is notable not only for its volume but also for its consistently mixed findings; and in policy initiatives that, paradoxically, exhort educators to further individualize, yet also further equalize, schooling.

The impasse itself might be taken as the phenomenon to be explained. Even though, commonsensically, participants in the tracking wars understand themselves (as do spectators) as rival camps, fighting for the true, if different, visions of schooling and America, the camps are also locked together, dug in in a stalemate, and joined by a no-man's-land between the trenches into which, however, neither side ventures. From that viewpoint, apologists and critics may have more in common than war lets them recognize.

For example, the impasse suggests that tracking's evolution is more pendulum-like than progressive (or regressive), as combatants would have it. Historically, proposals to track have been followed by counterproposals to *de*-track, which in turn have produced moves to *re*-track. The oscillation responds to social conditions, perceptions of which are refracted through an assemblage of resonant yet contrary beliefs about the knowledge schools should teach (Egan, 1997; Kliebard, 1995). For example, in the return to "normalcy" following World War II, life adjustment education promised the harmonious preparation of all citizens for what life had in store by proffering what one might now call a "relevant" curriculum focused on the everyday tasks of life. However, fears engendered by the Cold War and the launching of the Russian sputniks set off demands for academic "rigor" in the service of the national defense, especially honors classes for the "gifted and talented" (Kliebard, 1988). That anxiety notwithstanding, differentiation was again suspect only a short time later when pressures for civil rights and integrated schools took center stage.

The periodic oscillation between a differentiated and common curriculum continues in contemporary schooling. For instance, in 1993 the high schools in a large city in southern California responded to state recommendations to do away with the traditional, tracked science curriculum of a year each of general science, biology, chemistry, and physics. They were advised to replace the "layer-cake" with courses that integrated the natural sciences and also students. Accordingly, the schools developed Integrated Science—at minimum, a 2-year sequence of heterogeneously grouped classes in which all the sciences were to be brought to bear on "practical" themes such as evolution or scale and structure. Within a year, however, the schools *re*-differentiated the undifferentiated course by adding an "embedded honors" component, complete with harder assignments and extra credit for selected students—and, regardless of the reform, the schools never discontinued their honors or special and sheltered courses in science (Crockett, Page, & Samson, 1997; Page, 1999).

The continuing ambivalence over whether curriculum should be specialized or uniform is not acknowledged in technical analyses which pose tracking as a neutral organizational procedure, attainable with sufficiently rational design specifications. Conventional political analyses also neglect the pattern by foregrounding instead the conflict *between* Americans, with groups who value individualism, competition, and freedom pitted against others who value community, cooperation, and equality. A cultural analysis, however, suggests that the source of ambivalence is in a distinctive, if largely implicit, conflict *within* Americans. Americans experience continuing predicaments about membership and differentiation, whether in tracking or other sociocultural institutions, because the culture is oriented around both individualism and the common good, even though the two are contradictory.

Scholars in a variety of disciplines have suggested that American culture is distinguished by ambitious and, therefore, often wavering belief in a Dream in which both union *and* uniqueness hold sway. As historian Michael Kammen (1972) puts it, "the push-pull of both wanting to belong and seeking to be free has been the ambivalent condition of life in America, the nurture of a contrapuntal civilization" (p. 116). Similarly, J. R. Pole (1993), in his classic study of equality, states that American institutions "cannot be understood as the enactment of a single liberal or equalizing principle" because they are also anchored in the contrary idea of status hierarchies—and neither is a "mere aberration" (p. xi). Political scientist Murray Edelman (1977) notes the continuing shifts in direction that mark American social policy and explains that citizens are neither strictly individualistic nor collectivist in their interpretations of enduring social problems but recognize the credibility of both and, hence, sway readily from one to the other.

Anthropologist Hervé Varenne (1977, 1983; see also Bellah, Madsen, Sullivan, Swidler, & Tipton, 1985) clarifies the structured alternation by observing that polarities in America do not present a choice so much as they *engender* each other. A distinctive, ongoing dynamic of fracture *and* coalescence runs through the culture's history, social institutions, and even its everyday discourse. Thus, Americans zealously pursue freedom and individualism but, in achieving them, they begin to worry about a diminished public sphere, a loss of common decency, and neglected traditions; swinging back toward communitarianism, however, they eventually become anxious about threats to creativity, diversity, and local autonomy.

Paradox is certainly not unique to America, but its forms and tensions here have acquired a recognizable texture. As the 13 colonies bent European institutions to fresh purpose in a strange New World, they confronted two radically unfamiliar problems, specifically, questions about the legitimacy of government and an unstable pluralism. They also faced an environment whose very expansiveness promoted divergent experiments to resolve the problems (Bailyn, 1960; Kammen, 1972; Pole, 1993). Both the problems and the expansiveness continue in the contemporary Global Village, as does the penchant to address them by coupling opposites.

Thus, commingled opposites permeate schools, where Americans expect differentiation but without discrimination (Cazden, 1986); they expect that each student's unique qualities will be respected yet, also, that all students will be treated equally. Tracking is one response to the paradoxical imperative for individualized *and* equal education, and schools persist in using the practice because it betokens both the recognition of differences among students and, simultaneously, their reintegration in classes with like-minded peers. The distinctive tension that characterizes American culture arises because distinguishing between aptly differentiated and illegitimately discriminatory coursework is no easy matter. If schools provide the same curriculum for all, they will arouse suspicions of standardization, constraint, and mediocrity even though a common core also promises a form of equality; if they provide specialized curricula for diverse students, they will raise suspicions of prejudice or special privilege, even though relevant content can also support participants' identity, solidarity, and success in learning.

In this complicated context of paradox, the longevity and pattern of the tracking wars suggest that, rather than operating to transform the status quo, they contribute to maintaining it. On the one hand, the wars can be seen as a form of "deep play" (Geertz, 1973b). Like the Balinese cockfight, they provide "the concocted sensation" of fighting for, and watching the fight for, the real America (Geertz, 1973b, p. 443). Even though the wars have not altered substantially the actual conditions and effects of curriculum, any more than the outcomes of cockfights alter more than momentarily the social relations among winners and losers, the wars persist because they are compelling drama. They invest mundane school lessons with deep significance and, precisely because the politics and aggression in the tracking wars are not real, people are safe to fight fervently.

On the other hand, the debate about tracking is not merely symbolic. We *act* with words and create worlds that matter (Burke, 1966; Edelman, 1964/1985; Kliebard, 1990; Metz, 1989). Seen thus, the tracking show functions as a "dummy variable" (Geertz, 1983, p. 79) that diverts attention away from the specific, complex culture that is America. It is a mechanism that promotes and perpetuates Americans' tendency "to ignore their biformities . . . [and remain] unusually perplexed by ambivalence and contradictory pressures" (Kammen, 1972, p. 107).

Hence, the stylized rhetoric of the tracking show maintains American ambivalence about whether education can be both excellent and equal. It keeps citizens uneasy by representing the Dream as hypocritical, in jeopardy, or compromised by pluralistic politicking, yet it simultaneously assuages their uneasiness by projecting resolution as obvious and easy. Put simply, the rhetoric suggests that the polity can simply choose tracking (or detracking). Citizens can ignore viewpoints that differ from their own because tracking is represented as a political conflict *between* Americans; that means diverse views only express some other interest group's different interests, not ideas or evidence with which citizens can better grasp a complex practice or their own position. Further, if tracking is presented as a uniform practice across U.S. schools, citizens can also ignore the remarkable diversity of the American environment (including schools), the indeterminate definition of symbols such as individualism and equality, and the notable fluidity of the symbols and structures that America furnishes. Put simply, the rhetorical formulation of tracking diverts us from the culture's biformities and allows us to couple opposites willy-nilly. Even though in some circumstances cultural paradox can fuel the invention of vibrant hybrids such as a tracked curriculum, described in the next section, that manages to be both differentiated and parallel, it more frequently prompts strange mutants—weapons for peace, legitimate lawlessness, or, in curriculum, amalgamations of relevant and rigorous subject matter that are so muddled that even good students in high-track classes find school knowledge to be of uncertain value (Page, 1999).

In sum, looked at culturally, debate about tracking persists because it displays "America" struggling to be true to its word and, in that display, diverts attention from the complex, ambiguous, and contingent work that curriculum, culture, and democratic politics entail. To grapple efficaciously with the question of whether schools should provide different courses of study to different groups of students will require abandoning the either-or thinking of warfare. Needed instead is attention to the ambitious and multifaceted character of American culture, the ambiguity and diversity of school practice, and a self-consciously provisional rather than peremptory discourse that allows for recognition of differences *and* common ground—and for the practical imagination to put them in felicitous relation.

TRACKING-IN-PRACTICE

If participants in the tracking wars enact a simple yet stirring political scenario, complete with stock characters and a predictable plot, Valli's (1990) careful and intriguing case study takes us backstage, so to speak, to document the obliquity with which the push-pull of individualism and community plays out in actual practice. The case complicates the tracking wars and can be used to reorient our thinking about tracking because, at Central Catholic, an extensive tracking system is key to academic achievement and positive relations among teachers and students, including those placed in lower-track classes. Because most of the students at the medium-sized (1,000 students), all-male, urban high school are working-class or poor and about one-third are African Americans, the school effects are even more remarkable since these are the students who, particularly in qualitative studies (Gamoran & Berends, 1987), are often identified as being especially disadvantaged by tracking.

In accounting for Central Catholic's success, Valli (1990) reframes the question of whether tracking works to portray instead how people work tracking (see, also, Goffman, 1961; Page, 1991, 1998). The shift represents tracking as a social construction, variable in its design and negotiated in its significance. In contrast to the timeless verities represented in the tracking wars, tracking is stigmatizing, fair, alienating, efficient, stratifying, accommodating, or some other quality depending on what people, in particular circumstances, imagine they can use the practice to do.

At Central Catholic, for example, tracking is a publicly acknowledged policy. The course catalog states explicitly that "all courses except Physical Education are tracked" (Valli, 1990, p. 48) and, as Valli reports, "a student's track number is as public as his name" (p. 47).

The school's unusual openness about tracking is matched by a considerable investment in making the practice work, with the goal being to appropriately differentiate courses in accord with students' different skills so that no student is enrolled in a class that he either has no chance of passing or can pass simply by resting on his laurels. Hence, the school designates seven achievement levels: two academic tracks, I and II; a lower, remedial Track IV; and an average, or general, Track III, which is subdivided further into four sections, A, B, C, and D. In addition to establishing the tracks, administrators review student records to determine where students should be placed in the seven levels, and they monitor student progress so that changes can be effected when needed. Teachers make sure that the content and textbooks for the seven levels are suitably different; for example, all students take algebra, but Track I and II students complete the course in a year whereas Track III and IV students take 2 years.

At the same time that Central Catholic acknowledges the importance for teaching and learning of individual differences in academic achievement and skills, the school also works to provide for common, intellectual experiences because it recognizes the discouragement that can accompany permanent lower-track placement and the entitlement that can accompany permanent high-track placement. For example, all students, regardless of their levels, complete an academic course of study, with at least 2 years of a foreign language, 4 of English, and 2 of science and math—a curriculum that many public schools would name "college-prep" and reserve for top students. Central Catholic also phases out tracking when it is no longer needed: By the end of the first year, half of the freshmen in the lowest track will have moved into Track III, and by the junior year, all will have moved out of Track IV.

If we think about Central Catholic in terms of the familiar dichotomies furnished by the tracking wars, its curriculum presents something of a conundrum. For instance, how would teachers mark a survey that asked whether the school tracks, given that Central Catholic makes concerted efforts both to employ and to do away with leveling? Should the school celebrate or be concerned about the fact that lower-track classes take 2 years to complete the algebra course whereas high-track classes finish in a year, given that all students are gaining access to what some call "high-status" mathematics but the gap is widening between the achievement levels and advanced course-taking of students in the high- and low-track classes? Or, as Valli (1990) herself wonders: "Why . . . does Central Catholic go to such lengths to place students into a finely differentiated curriculum while simultaneously going to such lengths to create similarities between the tracks?" (p. 51).

Valli's answer is that Central Catholic uses curriculum as a means to honor both human dignity and community—those bipolar American values that also structure public schools and other Catholic and private schools. Central Catholic is unusual, however, in the viable hybrid it makes of the two. One facet of that viability is the practical thoughtfulness its faculty members invest in curriculum (L. Valli, personal communication, May, 1998). Without setting out to decipher American culture, revolutionize educational politics, or resuscitate individualism or community, they credit the complexity of schooling in America in their conversations with each other and students.

The metaphor, *effort*—a single word—sometimes explicitly but more often tacitly, is a key means by which Central Catholic links, or sets in relation, a differentiated *and* parallel curriculum. Thus, as Valli (1990) delineates, students encounter different rather than the same knowledge in freshman English, with able readers in Track I tackling *Julius Caesar*, for example, whereas less proficient readers in Track IV peruse high-interest/low-ability short stories. However, across the tracks, the school also teaches one "central lesson" (p. 51)—about the value of making an effort. The emphasis on effort puts all students on an equal footing because achieving academically will depend on students' hard work, not on their inborn talents or family advantages (and not on a good-hearted distribution of inflated grades because the school knows the exchange value of a high school diploma in a competitive society). The more academically skilled are not allowed to coast by selecting easy tracks, just as the less academically skilled are not allowed to slide by without having mastered the basics; there is no social promotion, with an "E-for-effort" as consolation prize.

At the same time, effort applies to the school as well as to students and, for this reason, it is not synonymous with "rugged individualism," in which all responsibility for school success is foisted on students who are to pull themselves up by their bootstraps. Adults at Central Catholic are there on students' behalf. As Valli (1990) explains, they use tracking as a means of keeping track of students, not of keeping them in track.

Valli (1990) also notes that the positive meaning of effort in Central Catholic's commingling of individualism and collectivism is not a function of logical definitions or technical design but of the school's culture. Effort signals caring, not bossing, because Central Catholic is a "family" (p. 55). Thus, if the school prizes academic work, its focus is the quality with which people engage together in doing it, not the status that accrues from pursuing high-status knowledge or the notoriety that accompanies high test scores. The "familiness" is pervasive and palpable. It has been built up over decades through Central Catholic's concern for the surrounding neighborhood; it is revivified daily in the give-and-take of school politics and ordinary school lessons. For instance, the public and personal intertwine at Central Catholic in a way that is different from the disengagement or moralizing constructed in many public school classrooms (Page, 1998; Powell, Farrar, & Cohen, 1985). Discussions in the high-track English classes ask students to think about their own aspirations in relation to Julius Caesar's overweening ambition and about the danger of not keeping ambition in proportion. Discussions in lower-track classes are no less serious and engaging, and students who have read in a short story about "street corner society" are asked to think about their ambitions too, including the consequences of having too few or of turning themselves into victims by blaming others for their lack of options. Such pointed lessons attract lower-track students rather than antagonizing them because of the school context within which they are embedded (compare Page, 1998, where, in a different school culture, relevant lessons offer insults).

In short, Valli (1990) portrays what one school makes of tracking as it draws on the paradoxical scholastic and sociocultural resources furnished by America and then refracts those it selects in a fashion that is sensible, or understandable, given the school's particular circumstances. Practically as well as rhetorically, Central Catholic demonstrates that "each student is worth the school's best effort at a suitable and challenging education and each student in turn has an obligation to put forth his best effort to succeed" (p. 51). Although, as Valli notes, tracking is not essential to the school's positive effects, the questions about culture and curriculum to which tracking is one answer would remain if Central Catholic detracked. So would the need for inventive, practical thinking about the questions—thinking which, unlike the slogans deployed in wars, can develop grounded metaphors that move us beyond simplistic dichotomies to the actual concerns, such as ambition, effort, and family, that define us individually and institutionally.

TRACKING-IN-GENERAL

As illustration of tracking's complexity, the case of Central Catholic necessarily evokes questions about how we can generalize about the practice. Valli's is only one study and it considers only a single school; in addition, the case is an outlier in the research literature because practices at Central Catholic run counter to one "commonsense view" (Slavin, 1990, p. 490), that is, that lower-track placement hinders the school success of those students most in need of it. Of what significance is one, apparently aberrant study for a theory or explanation of tracking?

The answer depends not only on how one characterizes America and schooling, as I described in the first section of this essay, but also on whether one undertakes what Bellack (1978) terms a traditional or an interpretive review of research on tracking. This is not to argue about whether interpretive or traditional research is best able to study tracking; both have contributed crucial insights. Rather, my purpose is to raise questions about how we read the empirical record, including both quantitative and qualitative studies and, particularly, how much we weigh the typical case and distinctive ones. Although Passow (1988) warns that "attempts at synthesizing and interpreting research seem more likely to reinforce and harden positions already taken . . . rather than resolving the issues raised by ability grouping" (p. 231), such attempts may nevertheless clarify what those issues are and how, ironically, they fuel the wars and maintain the status quo.

In traditional reviews, a single study of tracking counts for little, particularly case studies of one or a few schools, because the aim is to determine modal, or typical, patterns for a population, such as tracking's effect on academic achievement in U.S. secondary schools. A pattern is often represented by a number—an effect size—which is derived by adding up and averaging the mean scores reported in a sample of studies that are selected according to criteria stipulated a priori.

Reviews by Slavin (1990) and Mosteller, Light, and Sachs (1996) are recent prototypes. Slavin's "best-evidence" is limited to studies which, among other things, compare the effect, in U.S. secondary schools, of heterogeneous and ability grouping on achievement as measured on standardized tests; Mosteller et al. are intent on sound research design and look for studies that are large-scale, controlled, randomized, and quasi-experimental. There is overlap in the studies selected for the two reviews.[2]

In recounting individual studies, both reviews indicate that some heterogeneously grouped classes (but not others) are associated with achievement gains in some studies (but not in others) and that similar variation marks ability-grouped classes. However, the disparities disappear when the results are summed, whether within one study or across several. Thus, both reviews can conclude, as Slavin (1990) puts it, that "the effects of ability grouping on student achievement are essentially zero" (p. 484).

This is a markedly odd result: On the most commonly used measure of school effects—academic achievement, as indicated by test scores—the effects of tracking are zero. Further, the reviews differ in what they make of the result, although both responses reinscribe the tracking wars. Slavin (1990) suggests that the results shift the burden of proof to advocates of tracking because the practice does not produce the achievement benefits it promises and it may have other, unintended negative effects (e.g., stigma, alienation). Mosteller et al. (1996) pin their hopes on better research, arguing that the important questions about tracking cannot be answered because "the appropriate large-scale, multisite research studies . . . have not yet been carried out, even though the issues have been debated as major public concerns within education for most of this century" (p. 814). In contrast to both of these, a cultural perspective views the zero-effect size as suggestive of the degree to which tracking is symbolic rather than instrumental.

Furthermore, despite their authoritative conclusions, both reviews suffer from validity problems. As the authors acknowledge—and as other scholars, too, have long complained about tracking research (e.g.,

Goldberg, Passow, & Justman, 1966; Goodlad, 1984; Metz, 1978; Oakes, 1985; Page, 1991; Passow, 1988)—the studies that meet the criteria stipulated in the reviews only consider grouping itself. That is, none looked inside classrooms to ascertain whether the teaching and knowledge in tracked classes were appropriately differentiated or even whether they were differentiated at all. As a result, the studies count and compare heterogeneously and ability-grouped classes that may differ only in name, or ability-grouped classes that differ more from each other than from heterogeneously grouped classes. Simply put, tracking may not be the operative independent variable.

Traditional theorizing extends to reviews that are less obviously statistical, too. For example, Oakes, Gamoran, and Page (1992) examine not only quantitative but also qualitative studies of tracking (including Valli's) to answer three questions that "have dominated scholarly and policy discussions of curriculum differentiation throughout the century. . . . Does curriculum differentiation 'work'? . . . Is [it] fair? . . . and does [it] affect the quality of schooling and the curriculum?" (p. 593). Here, too, however, individual and interpretive studies count for little. Even though most of the review is given over to describing the variety in tracking's forms, processes, and effects, its conclusions, like those of Slavin and Mosteller et al., revert to modal patterns: "what *most* researchers have concluded are the *most likely* answers to the [three] questions—at least in the *typical* case" (p. 593; emphasis added).

The disjunction in Oakes et al. between the descriptions of tracking's variability and the universal conclusions is particularly unsettling because, unlike Slavin's and Mosteller's et al., this review does not specify the means that were used to reduce the diversity represented in the studies to the central tendencies cited in the conclusion. For instance, did the review tally Valli's portrait with others that show that tracking works or with those that show the opposite—and would either categorization be apt, given that the case describes the mixed effects of tracking? Did the review add the case study of one school to survey data collected in scores or hundreds of schools so that its results were effectively canceled out because of its small sample size? Without information about how the review sorted and counted studies, it is difficult for readers to comprehend the conclusions. For example, how does one understand that "the straight answer [about whether tracking raises achievement] is, sometimes" (p. 594) yet, three pages later, "those who see tracking as unfair do so largely because their assessment of the empirical evidence about tracking's outcomes is that 'it doesn't work' [because it] only rare[ly] . . . remediates educational deficiencies" (p. 597).

By contrast, interpretive reviews of research take the stability *and* variability documented in research on tracking as the pattern to be explained. The aim is to develop a comprehensive but open model that conforms to the complexity of human practices without, however, leaving them a muddle (Egan, 1997). This entails following a metaphorical rather than modal form of theorizing (Dewey, 1902/1956; Kliebard, 1979, 1982)—one which specifies and clarifies the variables that constitute tracking yet does not assume that their significance or the relationships between them are readily predictable. Thus, interpretive reviews posit broad parameters, sometimes a continuum, which can contain the diversity of tracking represented in the research literature: a paradoxical America intent on both individualized and common schooling, as I hypothesized in the first section of this essay; dilemmas that arise as schools alternately seek liberating education and social control (Berlak & Berlak, 1981; Jackson, 1968/1990; Lampert, 1985); or curriculum processes that translate the precepts that define a social order rather than either routinely transmitting them or miraculously transforming them (Page, 1991). Within such frames, tracking's manifestations are not fixed, but neither are they random. For example, we can anticipate that classrooms embody both controlling and educative purposes, but we cannot foretell their combination or which will predominate; that requires examining actual classrooms with attention to the specific contingencies that shape how their alternating values evolve.

Interpretive reviews also proceed recursively rather than in the additive fashion of a traditional review. Employing comparative—metaphorical—thinking, they tack back and forth between a single case and others to which the single case is put in relation. Thus, as Erickson (1986) describes, generalization begins within a single study so as to portray one situation and its elements holistically; it moves then to a second case and considers it equally thoroughly and, finally, it compares the two cases to generalize across them. Because generalizations developed for the first study are tenable only if they also hold for the second, even a single study can reconfigure theory.

An abbreviated example of an interpretive review could begin, as I have here, with a close reading of Valli's portrait of a parallel lower-track curriculum and turn then to a second, complicating case: Southmoor High (Page, 1987). At Southmoor, tracking is similar in many respects to Central Catholic. The large, academically preeminent, middle- and upper-middle-class, public high school makes "effort" a key prescription for student success; lower-track classes command extra resources; the school's ethos is positive, even "heavenly" some participants said, with regular classes engaged in spirited exchanges over a classically academic curriculum. Despite these similarities, however, Southmoor's lower-track classes emerge as caricatures of regular educational encounters, not parallel to them. They couple elements of the creative, intelligent fellowship in regular classes with a distant, moralistic regimen of remedial worksheets so that lower-track lessons are simultaneously energetic and aimless, open but ironic, and inviting yet stigmatizing. In effect, Southmoor's lower-track curriculum is an ambiguous symbiosis of regular and remedial track practices. Neither clearly positive nor unerringly negative, it exacerbates the ambivalence toward schooling of students who must attend but who do not perform very well, yet it also assuages student anxiety by promising that lower-track classes will be easier, but not that different, than regular classes.

On first comparison, the Valli and Page representations might be judged incommensurate: in one, tracking works, in the other, it doesn't. As well, both the high schools differ from one widely cited modal pattern in which lower-class students are disproportionately represented in lower-track classes where they receive lower-status knowledge which ensures their lower-class futures. Instead, at Southmoor, most lower-track students are white, middle-class, and reasonably academically skilled; at neither Southmoor nor Central Catholic are lower-track teaching and knowledge unambiguously "lower-status," and in fact, lower-track classes at the two schools may be more engaging and rigorous than high-track classes in other secondary schools (compare Matthews, 1998; Page & Valli, 1990). How can a theory of tracking accommodate such disparate evidence, short of treating the qualitative data quantitatively to determine the "typical" representation or simply throwing up one's hands and saying each case is unique?

One possibility is to think about tracked classes relationally rather than in terms of categorical distinctions. This entails asking not only the usual questions about the differences between high and low tracks or heterogeneously and ability-grouped classes, but also questions about their similarities and, further, about how the similarities and differences interact in particular situations. Differentiation is thus not considered an absolute or pure condition but the selection of some differences and the ignoring of others. With this orientation, one might review the cases of Central Catholic and Southmoor as follows:

1. The two cases illustrate that lower-track classes can differ significantly from each other. This means they may not be as homoge-

neous as the category, *lower-track*, suggests. They may not be count-able as "apples and apples," as Slavin, Mosteller et al., and Oakes et al. assume, and delineating characteristics that can reliably dis-tinguish lower- and higher-track classes may therefore be impossible. For example, lower-track classes in some suburban schools may more closely resemble the higher- rather than lower-track classes in some rural and urban schools. Further, even though all classes designated "lower-track" would seem to occupy a similarly low position in an implied hierarchy, this assumption too may not be warranted: At some schools, students value rather than avoid lower-track classes because they are seen as a "smart" way to make it through a school system whose purposes students doubt (Page, 1991; Willis, 1977); also, as at Central Catholic, hierarchy may be in tension with or moderated by familial norms.

2. Given differences between the lower-tracks at Central Catholic and Southmoor, lower-track classes can nevertheless be recategorized to-gether if they are conceptualized as versions of the higher-track classes within each high school. Central Catholic's version of lower-track happens to be parallel to its higher-track classes, whereas Southmoor's version is a caricature of its higher track; studies in other contexts document other versions of lower-track (Metz, 1978, 1986; Page, 1991; Page & Valli, 1990), including modal versions (e.g., Oakes, 1985). *Version* is a metaphor that puts lower- and higher-track classes in rela-tion, but without assuming that the nature of the relationship is fore-ordained: it stipulates a bounded, not random, comparison but also acknowledges that many variations on regular-track are possible—not only caricatured or parallel renditions, but parodies, mimicries, puns, inversions, hyperboles, undifferentiated clones, and so forth.

3. The variety across lower-track classes is a function of differences and similarities across schools as well as with higher-track classes. Seen thus, the significance of tracking will depend not only on the dif-ferentiation (and integration) of classes within a school but also on differences (and similarities) between schools (Goodlad, 1984).

4. Differences between schools are not only structural but cultural (Metz, 1978; Page, 1990; Waller, 1932): U.S. high schools vary in size, locale, type, and the sociocultural characteristics of student bodies, and they differ as well in their histories, politics, and social conditions. As a result, such a seemingly standard feature as track-ing will differ in its meaning and form in particular institutions, depending on how people characterize the fact. For example, it is a commonplace that teachers in the United States prefer to teach high-track, socially advantaged students. However, this formula is mislead-

ing, and not only because many socially advantaged students end up in lower-track classes. In some schools, those advantaged students may *not* be seen as "ideal" (Keddie, 1971) but may be characterized as upstarts who challenge authority (Metz, 1978) or demanding "brats" who think they are entitled to favored treatment (Costa, 1997); equally pertinent, teachers may *choose* to teach less academically successful students, some out of political or moral conviction, others because they are intimidated by "the best and the brightest" or by parents who outrank them in social status (Page, 1999).

5. An abbreviated interpretive review concludes, therefore, that tracking's significance is always contextualized, but not in the readily predictable fashion that traditional reviews or participants in the tracking wars suggest. Tracking is neither a neutral technique for tailoring instruction to students' abilities and aspirations nor a foreordained caste system that further disadvantages the already disadvantaged. Rather, it is a social as well as scholastic process in which people negotiate definitions of worthy knowledge and the roles of teacher and student (Keddie, 1971) in particular institutional and sociocultural contexts (Page, 1991). In a paradoxical America, contexts are polysemic rather than determined or determining.

Like other interpretive generalizations, this one about tracking may appear "vacant" without the "thick descriptions" of the cases on which it rests (Geertz, 1973a, p. 25); vacancy may be particularly salient in contrast to the precise "effect size" offered by traditional reviews. However, Geertz (1973a) reminds us that "profundities," or misleading generalizations, such as Equality, American High School, or Lower Track need their "capital letters" taken off (p. 21). Used heedlessly, they divert attention from the complexity of human action and thereby misconstrue the possibility and requisites of social change. If we would credit rather than discount the significance of tracking, including its modal as well as idiosyncratic patterns—not to mention contradictions in what in fact *is* modal (Gamoran & Berends, 1987; Slavin, 1990)—we should not mistake "the typical" for an adequate theory. Interpretive studies in even a single school can point the way.

EQUALITIES-IN-TRACKING

Studies of tracking, like reviews, address most frequently whether tracking works. Usually the question is whether tracking promotes academic achievement as measured on standardized tests. Yet, tracking almost always grounds concern about equal education, too. Indeed, this concern may be responsible for the fervor of the tracking wars.

Equality, however, is largely left as an abstract, apparently self-evident ideal (Pole, 1993). As a result, it operates as a moving target, prompting continuing "demands for larger amounts of the same benefits" (Edelman, 1985, p. 153) and evolving new and usually un-anticipated complications. For example, the 1954 *Brown* decision seemed to guarantee the end of segregated and unequal schooling, but instead, desegregated schools have resegregated, sometimes because of tracking, sometimes because of white flight, and sometimes because of demands from minority groups for separate, ethnically congruent curricula and schools. As a result, it is hard to discern when schools have met expectations for equal education.

Instead of leaving equality a generic if hallowed good, educators and citizens might specify equality of what, for whom, and by whose responsibility. For example, will schools have achieved equal educational opportunity if they use neutral, "color-blind" procedures to determine academic placements, or must they also produce equal educational results? If procedures suffice, will the upshot of equal opportunity necessarily be differentiated outcomes, given that intellectual talents vary across individuals? Or, if equal results are required, must schools guarantee that all students achieve a "threshold level of performance" regardless of their academic abilities (Guiton & Oakes, 1995, p. 331) as well as their race, gender, social class, or interest, and if yes, who will be responsible for determining and enforcing the threshold? Indeed, is either definition of equal opportunity fair? Both operate ascriptively, with the meritocratic definition assigning status according to inborn talents and the egalitarian, according to inborn humanness. As a result, both minimize the extent to which learning is an individual liberty and responsibility.[3]

J. R. Pole's (1993) explication of the history of America's pursuit of equality—what he calls "America's primary moral commitment"—is helpful in thinking more precisely about these issues. He documents that Americans have not pursued equality, but rather equalities, and he identifies three versions: equality before the law, equal opportunity, and equality of esteem. All have been present since the beginning of the Republic, but each has ebbed and flowed in importance depending on changing social conditions, including the evolution of the other kinds of equality, and also, on the ever present, if contrary, American leitmotif of self-advancement, competition, and freedom.

Legal equality is the most elemental in a democratic culture. It provides that all individuals, similarly circumstanced, have equal rights before the law and must be treated alike. As Pole (1993) points out, however, even this seemingly basic principle has not been clear-cut. Until the Second World War, it conflicted with federalism which "stood as a semi-sacred barrier against enforcement of uniform central policies" (p. xiii), even those aimed at securing the equal rights of individuals that are guaranteed by the Constitution. This tension recurs today, when many of the prerogatives assumed by the national government are being returned to the states.

The second equality—of opportunity—surfaced in the early nineteenth century with the awareness of growing disparities in wealth and their impact on competition in a free market economy; it waxed stronger during Reconstruction but then waned until, beginning in the mid-1950s, it resurfaced and underwent dramatic transformation along two dimensions, both of them still salient today: (a) procedural versus substantive equality and (b) individual versus group opportunity. As Pole (1993) documents, in 1964 the focus of the Civil Rights Act was on securing impartial, race-blind procedures for determining individuals' qualifications for jobs, voting, admission to professional schools, and so forth. However, minority groups accustomed to the consequences of a racialized society did not see their experiences individualistically; furthermore, past discrimination limited group members' chances of success on even neutral tests. Consequently, equality of opportunity was increasingly defined in terms of results rather than intent, and the equity of particular results was not measured individualistically but against the proportional representation in society of various social groups. By this reasoning, schooling that results in the disproportionate representation of minorities in lower-track classes can be deemed inequitable, even if placements are made meritocratically, for instance, on the basis of tests of academic skills.

Transfigurations in the concept of equal opportunity continue apace because proportional representation is an unstable basis for policy. For example, a group definition of equal opportunity conflicts with the long-standing ideal that individuals should be treated impartially; it may lead to questions about reverse stigma and whether minority students in high-track classes are "tokens" or about the displacement of students with better skills by those whose groups are underrepresented; these arguments have resurfaced with a vengeance around affirmative action. Similarly, women and minorities once acceded to a "principle of interchangeability" (Pole, 1993, p. xv) when they demanded the same rights to education and jobs as white men by arguing that they were like white men, they were their equals. However, many women and minorities have since come to expect not only equal rights but recognition of their uniquely different identities as women and people of color. Such shifts suggest the continuing allure of both individualism and the common good, as well as the difficulty that inheres in distinguishing differentiation and discrimination.

Pole's third variant of equality is equality of esteem. It is the sense that, regardless of differences in social or idiosyncratic attributes, one is the equal of others, is respected and, as such, has some degree of control over one's environment. Although prominent in the discourse about prejudice during the civil rights era, equality of esteem is less often extolled today, perhaps because it is the most elusive equality and the most difficult to affect by policy.

Equality of esteem may be the kind of equality that schools are best suited to promote, even though more attention has been devoted to equal access to education and equal opportunity, including, most recently, equal results (see Guiton & Oakes, 1995; McDonnell, 1995; Metz, 1986). It may be what distinguishes tracking at Central Catholic. Equality of esteem is basic because schools are among the most diverse and intimate of public institutions. Schoolrooms are crowded places. They are pervaded by a subtle yet telling flow of interchanges in which self-respect and social respect intricately intertwine. They are complicated by "natural inequalities" (Pole, 1993, p. 421), such as variations in talent for scholastic work, and by sociocultural differences regarding whether academic work is deemed an interesting or motivating enterprise. All of these matter for the teaching and learning that go on in classrooms, and they are consequential beyond classrooms, too, because schools serve as evaluative, gatekeeping institutions. However, without equality of esteem, school efforts to persuade youth to engage with knowledge—whose value youth may perceive only dimly, if at all—risk being coercive or insulting—bossing, not caring, as Valli (1990) puts it. Without equality of esteem, school efforts to ensure equal opportunity may be dismissed as mere tokenism or, paradoxically, as a form of discrimination that ignores diversity and choice. (For a different view on commitment to schooling, see Spindler & Spindler, 1994.)

The value and complexity of equality of esteem are demonstrated in the case of Central Catholic (and at Southmoor, by contrast). As with academic excellence, Central Catholic focuses on providing practical educational opportunity rather than abstract equality. For example, the school does not pronounce that all students will study the same curriculum, achieve a minimum standard of competence, or be represented in tracked classes according to group proportions in the community, even though all of these are currently popular policy recommendations for equal education. First, assigning *Julius Caesar* or other purportedly high-status knowledge to all students may look like "equal opportunity to learn," but the same curriculum is not equal if students cannot or will not read the text to begin with; further, little is gained and much lost if all students, including highly motivated or skilled students, are limited to reading the high-interest/low-level stories assigned in a Track IV. Next, for a school to promise that it will produce particular learning outcomes is to confuse the school's and students' responsibilities and prerogatives for learning by overestimating the school's ability to "make" children learn (Page, 1998): teachers cannot "produce" learning, students must do that. Finally, making track placements that are proportional may do nothing to resolve the present differences in academic skills and interests fostered by past allocations which put poor and minority children "at risk" for school failure (Erickson, 1986).

Instead of abstract pronouncements about educational equality, Central Catholic works at establishing the conditions within which it has a chance to flourish. Specifically, it expects students to earn respect, just as it expects them to make an effort to learn. First, the school recognizes that it cannot dictate esteem and social respect but that it can, nevertheless, affect the sentiment of groups and individuals through its own example. Thus, educators at Central Catholic put effort into monitoring tracking policies and practices because they understand that institutional rules and procedures are indispensable if individuals are to recognize the values placed on equitable schooling; such procedures can foster equal intellectual results in classrooms and, consequently, esteem, even though schools cannot guarantee either the same results or esteem, short of engaging in miseducative measures that unduly circumscribe individual responsibility and freedom.

Second, Central Catholic departs from manifest equality when it provides seven levels of classes, but the departure is not arbitrary. The school has an explicit rationale for treating students differently, grounded in propositions about the nature of educative processes and, less explicitly, in community mores that honor both individual differences and human dignity. In contrast to the either-or choices presented in the tracking wars, the school deploys a curriculum that sets powerful aspirations for equal education *in relation with* equally powerful aspirations for self-advancement and the valuing of differences in specific abilities. It eschews choosing between honoring the diverse talents of individuals or securing uniform achievements by all and instead acknowledges the paradoxical values that define America.

Third, Central Catholic's emphasis on practical educational opportunity is also manifest in its focus on the process of education, rather than on foregone inputs or future outputs. The school makes classroom processes its most important product. Mingling educational means and ends, it places foremost the quality of the engagement, right now, of community members in lessons. This is not to say that Central Catholic does not reach important standards—graduation and college-going rates are high, the lowest track can be discontinued—but these results flow from a primary emphasis on the quality of the process of education itself. The important lesson at Central Catholic is that students, regardless of their talents or levels of achievement, see that they are valued members of the school community when they assume responsibility for learning in a school that assumes responsibility for teaching. Thus, rather than trying to guarantee equality of esteem or to assign it, Central Catholic works to persuade and enable its students to develop competence in school tasks so that they can earn esteem.

Central Catholic's tracking program and policies are not directly transposable to other schools and its particular rendition of tracking would change in a different context. However, people elsewhere can think about Central Catholic and use the case to recognize and reconsider their own struggles with the complexities of tracking and a paradoxical America. It may prompt them to consider the limited utility of the tracking wars, whether in terms of accurately representing tracking or as a means of initiating reflection on it. Rather than adhering to war slogans, educators might follow Central Catholic's lead in doing some of the practical, intellectual work on which viable hybrids of individualism and community depend. Then schools may honor difference without discriminating and community without coercing.

NOTES

1. Slavin (1990) asserts that arguments for and against tracking have remained largely the same since the early part of this century, with the exception that current criticism includes discrimination against minority and lower-class students and the low quality of instruction in lower-track classes. However, these criticisms also have a long history. See, for example, Kehliher (1931) or the extensive review in Goldberg, Passow, and Justman (1966).

2. Both reviews also consider studies that compare high- and low-track classes to ascertain whether tracking's impact varies depending on students'

skill levels. Here, too, the reviews find no clear trend indicating that students in high-track classes learn any more or less than high-achieving students in heterogeneous classes or that students in low-track classes learn any more or less than low-achieving students in heterogeneous classes.

3. The similarities between otherwise different meritocratic and egalitarian definitions of equality was a topic discussed by Herbert M. Kliebard in the course, Curriculum Planning, which I took at the University of Wisconsin during the summer, 1980. I retrieve the discussion from my class notes.

REFERENCES

Bailyn, B. (1960). *Education in the forming of American society: Needs and opportunities for study.* New York: Norton.

Bellack, A. (1978). *Competing ideologies in research on teaching.* Uppsala, Sweden: Department of Education, Uppsala University.

Bellah, R., Madsen, R., Sullivan, W., Swidler, A., & Tipton, S. (1985). *Habits of the heart: Individualism and commitment in American life.* New York: Harper & Row.

Berlak, H., & Berlak, A. (1981). *Dilemmas of schooling: Teaching and social control.* New York: Methuen.

Burke, K. (1966). *Language as symbolic action.* Berkeley: University of California Press.

Cazden, C. (1986). Classroom discourse. In M. Wittrock (Ed.), *Handbook of research on teaching* (3rd ed., pp. 432–463). New York: Macmillan.

Costa, V. (1997). Honors chemistry: High-status knowledge or knowledge about high status? *Journal of Curriculum Studies, 29,* 289–313.

Crockett, M., Page, R., & Samson, Y. (1997, April). *Integrated science: Old wine in old bottles.* Paper presented at the annual meeting of the American Educational Research Association, Chicago.

Dewey, J. (1956). *The child and the curriculum.* Chicago: University of Chicago Press. (Original work published 1902)

Edelman, M. (1977). *Political language: Words that succeed and policies that fail.* New York: Academic Press.

Edelman, M. (1985). *The symbolic uses of politics.* Urbana: University of Illinois Press. (Original work published 1964)

Edelman, M. (1988). *Constructing the political spectacle.* Chicago: University of Chicago Press.

Egan, K. (1997). *The educated mind: How cognitive tools shape our understanding.* Chicago: University of Chicago Press.

Erickson, F. (1986). Qualitative methods of research on teaching. In M. Wittrock (Ed.), *The handbook of research on teaching* (3rd ed., pp. 119–161). New York: Macmillan.

Exchange. (1994). *Sociology of Education, 67,* 79–91.

Gamoran, A., & Berends, M. (1987). The effects of stratification in secondary schools: Synthesis of survey and ethnographic research. *Review of Educational Research, 57,* 415–435.

Geertz, C. (1973a). Thick description: Toward an interpretive theory of culture. In *The interpretation of cultures: Selected essays* (pp. 3–30). New York: Basic Books.

Geertz, C. (1973b). Deep play: Notes on the Balinese cockfight. In *The interpretation of cultures: Selected essays* (pp. 412–453). New York: Basic Books.

Geertz, G. (1983). Common sense as a cultural system. In *Local knowledge: Further essays in interpretive anthropology* (pp. 73–93). New York: Basic Books.

Goffman, E. (1961). *Asylums.* Garden City, NY: Doubleday.

Goldberg, M., Passow, A. H., & Justman, J. (1966). *The effects of ability grouping.* New York: Teachers College Press.

Goodlad, J. (1984). *A place called school: Prospects for the future.* New York: McGraw-Hill.

Guiton, G., & Oakes, J. (1995). Opportunity to learn and conceptions of educational equality. *Educational Evaluation and Policy Analysis, 17,* 323–336.

Jackson, P. (1990). *Life in classrooms.* New York: Teachers College Press. (Original work published 1968)

Kammen, M. (1972). *People of paradox.* New York: Knopf.

Keddie, N. (1971). Classroom knowledge. In M. F. D. Young (Ed.), *Knowledge and control: New directions for the sociology of education* (pp. 133–150). London: Collier-Macmillan.

Kehliher, A. (1931). *A critical study of homogeneous grouping.* New York: Teachers College Press.

Kliebard, H. (1979). Curriculum theory: Give me a "for instance." *Curriculum Inquiry, 6,* 257–276.

Kliebard, H. (1982). Curriculum theory as metaphor. *Theory into Practice, 21,* 11–17.

Kliebard, H. (1988). Fads, fashions, and rituals: The instability of curriculum change. In L. Tanner (Ed.), *Critical issues in curriculum.* (The eighty-seventh Yearbook, pt. 1, pp. 16–34). Chicago: National Society for the Study of Education: Distributed by the University of Chicago Press.

Kliebard, H. (1990). Vocational education as symbolic action. *American Educational Research Journal, 27,* 9–28.

Kliebard, H. (1995). *The struggle for the American curriculum, 1893–1958* (2nd ed.). New York: Routledge.

Lampert, M. (1985). How do teachers manage to teach? Perspectives on problems in practice. *Harvard Educational Review, 55,* 178–194.

Matthews, J. (1998). *Class struggle: What's wrong (and right) with America's best public high schools.* New York: Random House.

McDonnell, L. (1995). Opportunity to learn as a research concept and a policy instrument. *Educational Evaluation and Policy Analysis, 17,* 305–322.

Metz, M. (1978). *Classrooms and corridors: The crisis of authority in desegregated secondary schools.* Berkeley: University of California Press.

Metz, M. (1986). *Different by design: The context and character of three magnet schools.* New York: Routledge.

Metz, M. (1989). Real school. In D. Mitchell & M. Goertz (Eds.), *Educational politics for the new century: The twentieth anniversary yearbook of the Politics of Education Association* (pp. 75–91). New York: Falmer Press.

Mosteller, F., Light, R., & Sachs, J. (1996). Sustained inquiry in education: Lessons from skill grouping and class size. *Harvard Educational Review, 66,* 797–842.

Oakes, J. (1985). *Keeping track: How schools structure inequality.* New Haven, CT: Yale University Press.

Oakes, J., Gamoran, A., & Page, R. (1992). Curriculum differentiation: Opportunities, outcomes, and meanings. In P. Jackson (Ed.), *Handbook of research on curriculum* (pp. 570–608). New York: Macmillan.

Page, R. (1987). Lower-track classrooms in a college-preparatory high school: A caricature of educational encounters. In G. Spindler & L. Spindler (Eds.), *Interpretive ethnography of education: At home and abroad* (pp. 445–472). Hillsdale, NJ: Lawrence Erlbaum Associates.

Page, R. (1990). Cultures and curricula: Differences between and within schools. *Educational Foundations, 4,* 49–76.

Page, R. (1991). *Lower-track classrooms: A curricular and cultural perspective.* New York: Teachers College Press.

Page, R. (1998). Moral aspects of curriculum: "Making kids care" about school knowledge. *Journal of Curriculum Studies, 30,* 1–26.

Page, R. (1999). The uncertain value of school knowledge: Biology at Westridge High. *Teachers College Record, 100,* 554–601.

Page, R., & Valli, L. (1990). *Curriculum differentiation in U.S. secondary schools: Interpretive studies.* Albany: State University of New York Press.

Passow, A. H. (1988). Issues of access to knowledge: Grouping and tracking. In L. Tanner (Ed.), *Critical issues in curriculum.* (The eighty-seventh Yearbook, pt. 1, pp. 205–225). Chicago: National Society for the Study of Education: Distributed by the University of Chicago Press.

Pole, J. R. (1993). *The pursuit of equality in American history* (2nd ed.). Berkeley: University of California Press.

Powell, A., Farrar, E., & Cohen, D. (1985). *The shopping mall high school: Winners and losers in the educational marketplace.* Boston: Houghton Mifflin.

Slavin, R. (1990). Achievement effects of ability grouping in secondary schools: A best-evidence synthesis. *Review of Educational Research, 60,* 471–499.

Spindler, G., & Spindler, L. (Eds.). (1994). *Pathways to cultural awareness: Cultural therapy with teachers and students.* Thousand Oaks, CA: Corwin Press.

The tracking wars: Is anyone winning? (1992, May/June). *The Harvard Education Letter, 8,* 1–4.

Valli, L. (1990). A curriculum of effort: Tracking students in a Catholic high school. In R. Page & L. Valli (Eds.), *Curriculum differentiation in U.S. secondary schools* (pp. 45–66). Albany: State University of New York Press.

Varenne, H. (1977). *Americans together: Structured diversity in a Midwestern town.* New York: Teachers College Press.

Varenne, H. (1983). *American school language: Culturally patterned conflict in a suburban high school*. New York: Irvington.

Varenne, H., & McDermott, R. (1998). *Successful failure: The school in the every-day life of America*. Boulder, CO: Westview Press.

Waller, W. (1932). *The sociology of teaching*. New York: John Wiley & Sons.

Willis, P. (1977). *Learning to labor: How working class kids get working class jobs*. Westmead, UK: Saxon House.

Chapter 6

A Historical Perspective on Teaching Low-Achieving Children: A First Account

Barry M. Franklin

Low-achieving children have no doubt been a perennial fixture in American classrooms. Provisions for such children date back to the mid-nineteenth century. In 1838, for example, the Boston School Committee created a number of intermediate schools or "schools for special instruction" to accommodate children who had not acquired the reading skills needed for admission to the city's grammar schools but were too old to attend the primary schools (Osgood, 1997). During the 1870s the Public Schools of Oswego, New York, established the Unclassified School to allow children who had fallen behind their age group to catch up and the Arithmetic School to provide for children whose poor performance in reading, writing, and arithmetic had rendered them over-age for their grade (Zehm, 1973).

Despite these and similar accommodations, teachers of the day did not for the most part recognize achievement as a distinct problem apart from that of conduct. Student failure, to their way of thinking, constituted a moral defect arising from a lack of willpower rather than from an academic problem (Zehm, 1973). As a consequence, they typically treated poor student performance much as they would any of a number of violations of order and discipline. At times, especially as a last resort, they would turn to corporal punishment. As one student in New York City during the 1820s recalled, his teacher employed flogging, as he put it, for both "making a good boy out of what was esteemed a bad one, and a scholar out of a dunce" (Finkelstein, 1989, p. 206). More often, however, they would eschew physical punishment in favor of other forms of coercion, including humiliation and the use of demerits, and such noncoercive techniques as bestowing rewards, emulation, persuasion, and appeals to self-control (Reese, 1995).

During the last half of the nineteenth century, however, teachers began to talk about academic achievement as a distinct issue requiring specific solutions (Zehm, 1973). Beginning around 1880 and continuing through the first three decades of the twentieth century, school administrators, particularly those in urban school systems, established an array of social services to assist children who were experiencing school-related difficulties. Among these programs were medical inspection and other health services, vocational guidance, visiting teacher services, sex and health education, vacation schools, and special schools and classes for the disabled (Reese, 1986; Sedlak & Church, 1982; Sedlak & Schlossman, 1985). During the 1930s, they began to add to this mix of services numerous remedial programs for children with less severe learning problems (Heggerston, 1933). Over the next half century, these services would evolve into the complement of remedial, compensatory, and special education programs that characterize the response of the contemporary American school to the presence of low-achieving children.

We know something of the early effort of teachers to accommodate low achievers as a result of a growing interest since the mid-1970s among educational historians and other scholars in the history of special education (Bennison, 1988; Cuban & Tyack, 1989; Franklin, 1994; Hendrick & MacMillan, 1989; Lazerson, 1975, 1983; Richardson, 1994; Richardson & Parker, 1993; Sarason & Doris, 1979; Tropea, 1987a, 1987b; Wollons, 1993; Zehm, 1973). Yet, we know less about how this educational effort has played itself out among teachers during the last 90 or so years. What we in fact lack is a comprehensive historical account of the work of twentieth-century classroom teachers with low-achieving children. The purpose of this essay will be to begin to construct such a history and to consider how such an account will carry us farther along in our understanding of the problem of low achievement.

I should point out at the start of this essay that I am using the notion of low achievement to refer to a variety of children, including the mildly mentally retarded, slow learners, and the culturally disadvantaged. Such a grouping makes sense when one considers the growing body of research about the efficacy of special education and remedial labels. In brief, this research notes the overlap in the supposed diagnostic characteristics of these conditions, the inability of experts to agree on these defining characteristics, and the failure of assessment instruments to accurately differentiate among individuals bearing these supposedly distinct labels. This research suggests that the single most important criterion that actual schools use to distinguish children with school-related problems from those without such difficulties, notwithstanding the labels that they are given, is poor academic performance, or what I am referring to as low achievement (Franklin, 1987, 1994; Gartner & Lipsky, 1993; Lovitt, 1993; Skrtic, 1991).

The data for this essay come from a series of vignettes of the encounters of classroom teachers with low achievers that have been gleaned from newspapers, school documents of one sort or another, and various archival material. They take various forms, ranging from teacher reminiscences and secondhand accounts of teaching practices to school records and official reports. Taken together, these accounts suggest that there were about five distinct accommodations that schools have made for low-achieving children during this century. They include the establishment of special education programs for disabled students, the introduction of modifications of the regular school curriculum, the creation of remedial programs, the informal efforts of teachers to help such children within their classrooms, and the establishment of compensatory programs for disadvantaged minority youth.

SPECIAL CLASSES FOR LOW-ACHIEVING CHILDREN

Early-twentieth-century urban school administrators promoted the cause of special classes for the disabled as a bureaucratic response to a school population that not only was growing in size but was becoming increasingly diverse in background, interest, inclination, and ability. Special classes offered these school leaders new administrative capacities to accommodate the disruptions that this growth had brought. Of particular concern to these administrators was their belief that these low-achieving children would interfere with the work of classroom teachers and the progress of their students. Special classes provided a way for public schools to make themselves accessible to these children while at the same time removing them from regular classrooms (Tropea, 1987a).

School officials in Atlanta, Georgia, for example, began to contend with this problem as early as 1898. In January of that year, Superintendent William F. Slaton called on the city's Board of Education to adopt a regulation to "prevent children of dull minds and weak intellects from remaining 3 or 4 years in the same grade." As Slaton saw it, their presence in Atlanta's classrooms was leading "to the annoyance of the teacher and the detriment of the grade" (Atlanta Board of Education, January 6, 1898).

Over the course of the next 15 years, the city took a variety of steps to address this problem. In 1908, the Board changed the dismissal time of the city's first-grade classes from 2 p.m. to 1 p.m. to allow teachers in this grade to work with children in the other grades of the city's grammar schools who were behind in their studies. In 1914, the Board of Education authorized the establishment of summer vacation schools to enable students who had failed during the regular year to make up their work. Within 5 years, the city would have seven special classes in its 44 grammar schools for white children and two special classes in its black grammar schools (Atlanta Public Schools, 1920–1930; Strayer & Engelhardt, 1921–1922).

Atlanta was certainly not alone in establishing special classes. Known also as ungraded or opportunity classes, the introduction of these programs was a common response of early-twentieth-century school administrators as they sought to cope with the increasing size and diversity of the school population. A 1931 U.S. Bureau of Education survey of 68 large city school systems reported that 97 percent of these cities had by the end of the 1920s established special classes for their lowest-achieving students, children whom they variously labeled as mentally retarded or backward (U.S. Department of the Interior, 1931).

An important impetus for creating these special classes, no doubt, was the annoyance and disruption that the presence of low-achieving children posed for classroom teachers. The case of two Atlanta teachers is illustrative. At its October 1914 meeting, the Board of Education received a letter from J. E. Ellis, a teacher at Grant Park School, concerning one of her students, who had had, as she put it, an "epileptic fit." According to Ellis, Grant Park's principal, Mrs. W. P. Davis, would not allow the child to return to class "because the presence of the child was liable to cause distraction in the exercise of the school." At the same meeting, the Board also received a letter from Belle Simpson, the teacher of the deaf at Ashby Street School, requesting the removal of one Herbert Manning. In Simpson's words, "he disturbs the class by doing many unusual and unexpected things and continuously distracts the attention of the class and the work of the teacher" (Atlanta Board of Education, October 22, 1914).

Teaching low-achieving children, however, was not easy. In her reminiscences of her career in special education, Ann Covart, who began teaching in 1921 in St. Paul, Minnesota, in a special class for so-called subnormal children, recalled the difficulties:

We had to stay with our children all the time. We took them to the toilets. We ate with them at lunch, presumably to encourage good eating and manners. When school dismissed at 2:30 pm, we were woofed. New students were sent to us anytime all year long. Not only did these children have learning problems, they had become discipline problems, because when you don't comprehend the lesson, you're inclined to do something else. (*A Collection of Memories*, 1960, p. 25)

The responsibilities of special education teachers were, it seems, emotionally taxing. Covart, for example, recalled her encounter with a colleague in the hallway:

She was just coming up from there and was grinning ear to ear. That was unusual and I said to her "What are you laughing at? What is so funny?" She said, "Nothing, but if you don't laugh once in awhile, it'll get you." That remark changed my whole attitude. I had always been a worrier and an extremely sober person, feeling the weight of responsibility, insecurity, and being tense. I decided to try "to laugh it off" and I've been laughing ever since. Ha ha! Really, though, it saved me from a breakdown I'm sure because I had been taking things too seriously and felt as if I might fail. (pp. 24–25)

Assuming responsibility for students who were difficult to teach and often troublesome to manage demanded an extensive commitment on the part of teachers that could, if they were not careful, endanger their mental well-being. Nonetheless, it was a responsibility that teachers like Covart seemed to accept without fanfare as simply part of their job.

MODIFYING THE CURRICULUM
FOR LOW-ACHIEVING CHILDREN

Creating special classes did not, however, free regular classroom teachers from their responsibilities for low-achieving children. There were children with less severe academic deficits who were not candidates for these special programs, as noted in the 1933 report on handicapped children by the White House Conference on Child Health and Protection. These were children who, according to the conference, had specific disabilities in "attention, memory, perception, or language" that were the result of such factors as illness, student-teacher conflict, or inadequate study skills. The conference concluded that these low-achieving children should for the most part be provided assistance on an individualized basis within regular classrooms (White House Conference, 1933).

The suggestions advanced by the White House Conference provided a second strategy whereby urban school systems could provide for low-achieving children. Beginning in the 1930s, the Minneapolis Public Schools, for example, introduced a number of modifications in the regular school program as alternatives to special classes for educating so-called slow-learning children. Writing in March 1932 to the principal of the city's Bryant Junior High School, Assistant Superintendent Prudence Cutright suggested two such schemes (Hardaker, 1932). One involved a series of modified courses that were designed for children with learning problems. Although these courses would bear the same titles as regular junior high school offerings, they would be more practical and related to the day-to-day concerns of young adolescents. Social studies, for example, would be redesigned so that it would include content on community civics, and mathematics would be modified so that it would emphasize basic arithmetic skills.

Another scheme would place slow-learning junior high school students in regular classes for the first semester, during which time counselors would undertake an evaluation of each of these children. Based on the results of this study, an appropriate program would be designed for each of them for the second semester (Hardaker, 1932).

A year later, Barbara Wright, Minneapolis's Supervisor of Counseling, in a letter to a New Orleans school board member identified several experiments that had been introduced to assist junior high school students who were experiencing academic difficulties (Cooley, 1933). At Jordan Junior High School, all seventh- and eighth-grade students were being passed on to the ninth-grade. Those who began exhibiting difficulties in the ninth-grade were placed in a special group that was allowed to remain in this grade for three semesters instead of the usual two. At Lincoln Junior High School, seventh- and eighth-grade students who were experiencing problems were assigned for a half-day to a special teacher who provided instruction in the academic subjects while remaining in their regular classes for homeroom, art, industrial arts, and physical education. And at Phillips Junior High School, the counselor conducted case studies of the entering children. Those identified as being below average were placed in low-ability groups that offered a modified curriculum (Cooley, 1933).

Minneapolis was not the only urban school system that introduced programs for slow-learning children. In 1938, the Detroit Public Schools published a bulletin distributed to all homeroom teachers describing ways in which they could provide for students who were "retarded" in reading. The teachers could, for example, enhance comprehension by providing students with questions for them to answer during their reading assignments. They could drill students on difficult words. Or they could teach students how to read silently. The bulletin recommended that homeroom teachers devote about 2 hours a week during the regular reading period to these remedial activities (Detroit, 1938).

Similarly, New York City had an array of programs for low-achieving students. Within the city's junior high schools a number of remedial and "coaching" classes were established during the 1930s for students who had fallen behind in their work and needed individualized help (New York City, 1935). In December 1934, the administration of Theodore Roosevelt High School opened its Reading School to provide remedial instruction for students with reading difficulties. A number of these children had entered Roosevelt while reading on the third or fourth grade level (New York City, 1937). And with the assistance of the Works Progress Administration (W.P.A.), the city had established remedial reading and arithmetic projects in over two hundred of its elementary schools (New York City, 1939).

In February 1936, the Board of Education joined with Columbia University's Teachers College to establish Public School (P.S.) 500. Housed in the Speyer School Building at Teachers College, the school both provided programs for slow-learning and gifted students and served as a site for developing new curricula for these two groups of children (New York City, 1936). The curriculum for slow learners was a modification of the activity program that was then being introduced in all of the city's elementary schools. Like its counterpart in regular classrooms, the Speyer School activity program shifted the organizing unit of the curriculum from the traditional disciplines of knowledge to daily life activities (New York City, 1935,1936).

One component of this program was a unit entitled Public Services and Public Utilities. Two Speyer teachers, Martha Cook and Cele Brickman, developed the unit because their students seemed to know so little about how these agencies functioned. Cook noted, for example, that although her students were supposed to be in the fifth grade, a good number of them did not know how much it cost to mail a letter, how to dial a telephone number, what a gas meter was, or what the electric company did. The resulting curriculum used guest speakers, films, class discussion, and some reading material to familiarize children with the workings of such agencies as the post office, electric company, bank, and telephone company. During their study of the telephone company, the students viewed a film about the Bell Telephone Laboratories, visited a branch office of New York Telephone, listened to a talk by a telephone company representative, and toured the Museum of Science and Industry at Rockefeller Center. As part of the study, they wrote and illustrated their own book on telephones. Cook believed that the program provided the low-achieving children in her class with a better understanding of the purpose and use of the public utilities they encountered in their daily lives. She reported in this vein that after the unit had been completed, one of her students was playing at a friend's house when his friend's mother had what appeared to be a heart attack. Realizing the seriousness of the situation, Cook's student remained calm, ran to a nearby drugstore, and telephoned for an ambulance. As a result, this woman was taken to the hospital in time to save her life (New York City, 1938).

Students at Speyer School did not, however, simply study public utilities and related topics as ends in themselves. These topics evidently appealed to low-achieving students and kept their interest and attention. They served, then, as ideal vehicles whereby Cook and Brickman could introduce arithmetic, reading, and spelling as well as other traditional subjects to low-achieving children.

The portrait of Martha Cook and Cele Brickman's work at the Speyer School along with the other similar initiatives I cited from New York City, Detroit, and Minneapolis point to the important role that attempts at adjusting the curriculum have played during this century in the teaching of low-achieving children. In each of these instances, it was the introduction of curriculum modifications that enabled teachers in these cities to reduce the demands that they placed on their students, to simplify the tasks that they expected of them, to capture their interest, or to do whatever else was necessary to accommodate their learning difficulties.

SMALLER CLASSES FOR LOW-ACHIEVING CHILDREN

Despite the seeming desire of urban school administrators to keep the least severely impaired of their low-achieving children in regular classrooms, it is not all that certain that the teachers welcomed such students into their midst. It was sometimes necessary for school systems to temporarily provide for these children outside of the regular classroom. In 1928, Detroit's Eastern High School established what was called the Special Grade Room for children who were intellectually normal but who were failing in their academic work. Such students, according to the teacher, Elizabeth Coolidge (1929), either were not interested in school, could not function well in large classrooms, or had experienced any of a number of other situations that had interfered with their academic progress. Enrolling fewer children than other classes at Eastern, the Special Grade Room provided low-achieving students, Coolidge believed, with a less distracting environment and the chance for more individualized attention on the part of the teacher. The program, as Coolidge saw it, was quite successful. She noted that during its first year of operation, about 80 percent of the students assigned to the Special Grade Room were able to return to their regular classes.

One of the most extensive of these programs was Minneapolis's B Curriculum or Small Class Experiment. In 1943, Minneapolis introduced a system of annual promotions to replace its existing practice of promoting students at the conclusion of each semester. As a consequence of this new policy, children in the secondary grades who failed a subject would now have to repeat an entire year's work in that subject, not, as had been the case, a semester. Fearing that this change would increase failures among his less able students, Newton Hegel, principal of the city's Folwell Junior High School, devised a solution the following year that came to be known as the B Curriculum or Small Class Experiment. Selecting those seventh graders who he thought were most likely to receive failing grades, he assigned them to English, social studies, and mathematics classes with enrollments of about 20, which was half the size of the typical class at Folwell (Minneapolis, 1949).

In introducing this program, Hegel at first thought that it would be necessary to modify the existing curriculum to reduce the failure rate among his students. He found, however, that extreme changes were not necessary. The reduced size enabled teachers to provide students with sufficient individual help to improve both their academic performance and their attitude toward school. Some of these students, Hegel pointed out, improved sufficiently to be able to return to their regular classes. In order to allow those students who needed to remain longer in the Small Classes to do so, Hegel expanded the program first to the eighth grade and then to the ninth grade (Goslin, 1945).

In a report on the introduction of the B Curriculum, Eva Bergeland (1945), Folwell's counselor, noted that the experiment necessitated only minimal changes in the school's curriculum. In English, B Curriculum students studied the same content as did students in the regular classes. In comparison to children in regular classes, however, these Small Class students used books written at a lower reading level, devoted more time to reading and spelling, and took more trips to the school library. In mathematics, the teachers spent more time than they did in regular classes on the fundamental operations, used simpler and more practical word problems, and took special pains to make their directions as clear and precise as possible. Despite these changes, Bergeland maintained, the teachers of Small Classes attempted to follow the regular curriculum as much as possible. She argued in fact that the introduction of extensive curricular modifications in the Small Classes would prove harmful to the students:

> Great care must be taken that children in the small classes do not feel inferior. The teachers must be optimistic and wholeheartedly a part of the program. Pupils placed in these classes must understand why they are placed there and also that there is no closed gate for them. They must understand that there is an open road into and out of the regular classes. No child should remain in the class against his will. The success of the B Curriculum program is found in the individual child's achievement, his feeling of satisfaction brought about by being "on his own," thinking independently and taking an active part in the life of the school. (p. 6)

The teachers who were assigned to Small Classes when the program was introduced throughout the city's junior high schools in the fall of 1946 were not, however, as certain as were Hegel and Bergeland about the nature of this program. Some teachers, according to school system curriculum consultant Mary Beauchamp, did not see much difference between the Small Class Experiment and the regular school program and as a consequence supported it. Others, however, believed that the Small Class was "just a glorified special class" for less able students and tended to view the program with skepticism (Gilchrist, 1947).

The reports of junior high school principals about the implementation of the B Curriculum also suggest that teachers were divided in their assessment of this reform. Most teachers, according to these reports, indicated that introducing the B Curriculum was a relatively easy task requiring few, if any, changes in the regular program; some Small Class teachers, however, were making major modifications in their courses and were in effect turning the B Curriculum into a remedial program. According to one of the principals, "no attempt [was] made to cover a definite course of study. Teachers have selected books and materials. [The] method of approach [was] adjusted to the groups." Another principal noted that teachers "have tried to pick and choose materials and topics suited to the abilities and interests of the groups." And finally, a third principal stated that his B Curriculum teachers were using "different books" and assigning the students "easier projects" than were his regular class teachers (Gilchrist, 1946).

The problem was that Minneapolis's teachers had very different and often conflicting ideas of what the Small Class was all about. In March 1947, the B Curriculum Steering Committee met to hear reports from three of its subcommittees that were appointed to look at different aspects of the Small Class Experiment. Composed largely of classroom teachers, these subcommittees seemed hopelessly at odds concerning the purpose of this innovation. The report of the Subcommittee on Learning Materials noted that, with some slight modifications, students in the Small Classes "should have the same curriculum as other students" (Minneapolis, 1947c). The Policies Subcommittee, on the other hand, depicted the Small Class as a special class by describing it as "an adjustment program that will meet the needs of poor achievers such as students having poor work habits, mental and social maladjustments, physical or health handicaps, and language difficulties" (Minneapolis, 1947d). And similarly, the Implications Subcommittee reinforced the difference between the B Curriculum and regular classes when they recommended that Small Class students be evaluated on the basis of their attitudes, not their subject matter achievement" (Minneapolis, 1947e).

In the face of this division, the city's school administration decided that, beginning in the fall of 1947, they would discontinue the practice of placing a Small Class Program in each junior high school. Instead, they offered the principals four choices as to how they could accommodate slow learners. They could continue to offer the Small Class Program, place low-achievers in selected regular classes with reduced enrollments, provide individualized tutorial assistance to slow learners, or leave it up to their teachers as to how to teach such students. Ten principals decided to continue with the Small Class Experiment. The other four, however, chose one of the other options (Minneapolis, 1949).

With a variety of alternative provisions for low-achieving students in place, the school administration decided to evaluate the relative merits of its plans. During the 1947–1948 academic year, all seventh-grade children who were enrolled in each of these four alternative programs were assessed in reading, mathematics, and spelling and given a personality inventory and a behavioral evaluation. Not unexpectedly, the results were inconclusive. While some schools offering Small Classes reported that their students demonstrated academic growth, others reported no gains in achievement (Gilchrist, 1948; Minneapolis, 1947a, 1947b, 1949).

In June 1948, the city's junior high school principals were again asked to choose which of the four plans for teaching low-achieving children they would adopt during the next academic year. This time, 11 of the principals indicated that they would abandon the Small Class Experiment while only 3 decided to maintain the program (Gilchrist, 1948). Within a year the Small Classes would also disappear from these three schools.

Some Minneapolis classroom teachers, it seems, saw the B Curriculum Experiment quite differently than did Newton Hegel. What Hegel envisioned in 1943 as a way to make Minneapolis's junior high schools more accessible to low-achieving children became a separate and segregated class under the tutelage of some of the city's teachers. And what Hegel saw as part of the regular school system, some Minneapolis junior high school teachers saw as a special remedial program.

Based on the B Curriculum Experiment, it appears that the background knowledge and training that teachers bring to their work has an impact on their ability and willingness to teach low-achieving children. Those B Curriculum teachers who knew what Newton Hegel had in mind with his Small Class Experiment and therefore minimized the modifications they introduced ended up as supporters of the program. On the other hand, those who confused the B Curriculum Experiment with a typical remedial or special education program became its opponents.

LOW-ACHIEVING CHILDREN IN THE REGULAR CLASSROOM

Although some Minneapolis teachers were reluctant to embrace the B Curriculum experiment, we should not assume that classroom teachers uniformly rejected low-achieving children. The informal efforts of teachers to help such children within their own classrooms represents a fourth provision that twentieth-century American schools have made for low-achieving children. In 1944, Angelo Patri, principal of P.S. 45, a junior high school in the Bronx, undertook a survey of his teachers' efforts with individual children during the year. He asked his teachers to complete a form in which they offered "a brief account . . . of some interesting developments in the character growth" of a child whom they had taught during the year. Teachers were asked to explain why they selected the particular child that they did and to describe what steps they had taken to obtain "favorable results" (Patri, 1944).

Patri received about one hundred responses to his survey from P.S. 45's faculty. Almost uniformly the teachers who completed the survey indicated that they wanted to help students who were having difficulties in their classes. In some instances, they placed low-achieving children in special programs of one sort or another. Miss Ryan, for example, reported that Howard O'Conner, an eighth-grade student, considered himself a failure. She noted that he came from a good home and was well behaved. Academically, however, he was a "slow-learner." She had him reassigned to a "work-school program" in which he spent a half day in a "slow class" for his academic work and the remainder of the day in a vocational program. As a result of this new assignment, according to Ryan, Howard's academic work improved and his absences decreased. As she put it, "his whole bearing has changed" (Patri, 1944).

In other cases, P.S. 45's teachers simply paid more attention and exhibited more concern for their difficult-to-teach children. Mrs. Keller noted that seventh grader Peter Mastropaolo did not do well academically. "Since he could not shine through his good work," she pointed out, "he tried to get the attention of the class by his clowning and defiance." Her response was to talk to him about his misbehavior as well as to invite him to talk to her when he was bothered. "The fact that I listened to everything concerning him," she reported, "gave him a feeling of such importance that his desire to show off and demand attention disappeared entirely. He then did the best work that he was capable of doing" (Patri, 1944).

Another P.S. 45 teacher, Mr. Law, noted that Dominique Castiello, age 15, was "far below standard scholastically, apathetic, unambitious, [and] unmotivated." Although "firm and unyielding" in his application of classroom rules, Mr. Law made efforts to praise this student for whatever "small success" he attained. As a result, Dominique, according to Law, "commenced to develop an appreciation of, and a belief in his own ability" (Patri, 1944).

Not all of P.S. 45's teachers succeeded in their efforts to improve the academic performance of their low-achieving students. Miss Holding talked about the "great amount of individual attention and time" that she had given to Dominick De Santis in hopes of overcoming his indifference to education. Yet, her report noted her "discouragement" over not being able to really help this child (Patri, 1944). Another teacher reported a similar sense of frustration in his dealings with Joseph Zito. He felt that the child should be able to do "better than average work," but Joseph was failing his class. Encouraging the child to do better seemed to lead to some temporary improvement but did not have "a lasting effect." He was "greatly disappointed" when toward the end of the term Joseph continued to exhibit his "extremely violent temper" (Patri, 1944).

At about the same time that Patri was conducting his survey, Josie Brennan was teaching low-achieving children in an adjustment class at Halsey Junior High School (P.S. 85) in Brooklyn. As she reported in the school's staff newsletter, her students exhibited no initiative when it came to assembling their materials, were unable to ask appropriate questions, and could not complete the tasks that she assigned to them. In some instances, she found that dividing the class into smaller groups and having them work together to complete assignments helped. This seemed to be most effective for tasks that required students to produce written reports. She did not find group work to be effective for teaching the language arts. "Here," she noted, "it was a case of 'blind leading the blind.'" Other strategies that seemed to work for her were field trips, slide presentations, and radio programs. She reported that these approaches worked better in conveying information to her students than did written material. Finally, Brennan pointed out that in managing her pupils, concrete praise and rewards directed to individuals were more effective than offering "general" suggestions to the entire class (Brennan, 1944).

As a reading teacher in Nyack, New York, during the late 1950s, Herbert Kliebard reported that the techniques he learned in graduate school for teaching low-achieving readers were less successful than the strategies he hit upon in working with actual children in the classroom. As a graduate student, he had been discouraged from presenting students with material that was written beyond their reading ability level. Yet, he found that the desire of students in his remedial reading classes to earn their driver's license provided powerful motivation that seemed to overcome their presumed reading difficulties. Although these students read at anywhere from the third to the fifth grade level, they were in fact able to read and understand an array of pamphlets and other material from the New York Department of Motor Vehicles that were written at more advanced levels.

Similarly, Kliebard reported that the approach he was taught in his course on the diagnosis of reading problems, namely, searching for family background factors to explain the reading problems of his students, was useless in actually helping them. What did work, however, for one of his students, Peter, who at 17 could not read, was the textbook that Kliebard created from the verbal comments that this student made to a series of picture advertisements from the local market in which he worked as a stock boy. Kliebard cut out the ads, showed them to Peter, and asked him to name the products, tell where they were located in the store, and to identify their prices. He then took down Peter's comments verbatim and placed them along with the ad in a scrapbook, which became in effect the class text. Once Peter began to associate his own words in the text with the pictures in the ads, Kliebard began to teach him phonics and then introduced other reading material. Coupled with private tutoring lessons, Kliebard's efforts over time were successful: Peter learned to read well enough to qualify for entrance into the army (H. Kliebard, personal communication, May 20, 1998).

Working with low-achieving children was for the teachers at P.S.45, for Josie Brennan, and for Herbert Kliebard something of a hit-and-miss proposition. Some things worked and others did not. There was, it seems, no one definitive way to instruct these children. Teachers who wanted to provide for difficult-to-teach students used their experience and ingenuity to devise a variety of strategies in the hope that one or more of them would work.

Taken together, Angelo Patri's teacher survey and the efforts of Josie Brennan and Herbert Kliebard point to the role that chance has played in the education of low achievers. Among the group of teachers that Angelo Patri surveyed at P.S. 45, some were able to find a way to help the low-achieving student with whom they were working, and others were not. It was not that some of Patri's teachers wanted to provide for such children and others did not. Rather, it seems, some were simply luckier than others in latching on to a strategy that was successful in addressing the learning difficulties of a particular child. Similarly, it was ultimately the serendipitous that accounted for the success of Josie Brennan at Halsey Junior High School and Herbert Kliebard in Nyack, New York.

COMPENSATORY EDUCATION FOR LOW-ACHIEVING CHILDREN

The provisions for low-achieving children that we have examined thus far in this essay were created by urban school administrators to provide for what in their estimation were the particular educational problems of children from poor and immigrant families. Throughout this century, in fact, the problem of educating low-achieving children has been intertwined with the twin issues of ethnicity and class (Bennison, 1988; Cuban & Tyack, 1989; Tyack, 1974). This has been particularly true in the two decades following World War II as the interplay among the forces of racism, deindustrialization, and politics has resulted in a structural transformation of the American city. The key features of this transformation include the racial isolation of an increasing black and Hispanic population as whites have fled to the suburbs, the growing impoverishment of this population as a result of the job losses that have accompanied the relocation of manufacturing to the suburbs and beyond, an eroding tax base that has left cities unable to support their social services and cultural and educational institutions, and a pattern of politics that has propelled these changes forward (Darden, 1976; Darden, Hill, Thomas, & Thomas, 1987; Fine, 1989; Hirsch, 1993; Massey & Denton, 1993; Mollenkopf, 1983; Sugrue, 1993,1996).

Urban schools at the end of the 1950s and the beginning of the 1960s faced the task of educating the children of an increasingly economically distressed minority population with an ever diminishing tax base. Their most pressing problem was a pattern of poor academic performance and low rate of school completion among their largely minority student population that seemed endemic to those living in conditions of economic deprivation and its accompanying social malaise (Kantor & Brenzel, 1993; Mirel, 1993; Rury, 1993). Their response was to establish an array of compensatory programs, which represent a fifth approach that urban schools undertook to provide for low-achieving children.

Illustrative of this strategy are the attempts of Detroit and thirteen other large city school systems during the 1950s to accommodate so-called culturally deprived children. Carl Beyerly, who headed the Detroit effort, described a host of different approaches that were then being introduced at three of the city's junior high schools. Teachers in these schools, according to Beyerly, often appealed to children directly. In his words, they "try to show the child that someone is concerned about him," and they talk to the child about the "advantage of staying in school." Other strategies included adapting reading material to fit the abilities and interests of these children, using remedial or "coaching" teachers to help these children in reading, providing visiting teachers to work with the parents of these children, and establishing at one school a special ungraded class to offer these children individual assistance. Other cities involved in the project introduced their own approaches. In Baltimore, school officials attempted to develop tests to assess the ability of disadvantaged students. And Milwaukee established a number of "orientation centers" throughout the city to place disadvantaged children in the schools that were most appropriate for them ("Schools helping underprivileged,"1959).

In the fall of 1964, New York City established its More Effective Schools (MES) Program, a collaborative effort of the Board of Education, the teacher's union, and the association representing principals and other supervisors. Established initially in 10 of the city's elementary schools, the MES Program included a group of innovative changes in the city's schools designed to enhance the educational success of low-achieving youth, particularly of minority group children (Rogers, 1968; Taft, 1974; "Union backs 10," 1964). Included among the changes were reductions in class size in the elementary schools to 22 children, heterogeneous grouping, lengthening the time during the day that the school was open from 3 p.m. until 6 p.m., the recruitment of enthusiastic and committed teachers, and the provision for cluster teachers to assist regularly assigned teachers ("Joint planning committee," 1964; "Nothing less will work," 1963).

The changes that the MES Program brought were designed to correct an array of inadequacies in the education that New York City was then offering its minority youth. In late November 1966, Rose Shapiro, a member of the Board of Education and a community activist, noted many of those shortcomings in a report she made to the Board about a meeting that she and School Superintendent Bernard Donovan had with about 70 black and Puerto Rican parents earlier that month. According to Shapiro, parents reported numerous problems which they saw as indicative of the inadequate education the city was offering to their children. At P.S. 158 in Brooklyn overcrowding had resulted in half-day sessions for the first through fifth grades. Parents of children enrolled in Manhattan's P.S. 194 complained that their children were rarely given homework, and when they were, teachers never corrected it. At P.S. 123 in Manhattan children were not allowed to take their textbooks home because there was not a sufficient number for the school's population. Children requiring remedial services at Brooklyn's P.S. 76, according to parents at that school, were placed on a waiting list. And one parent reported that a teacher at P.S. 133 in Manhattan stated that one of her students "has no brains" (Shapiro, 1966).

For many of the city's teachers, the MES Program was the vehicle through which they were better able to provide for disadvantaged youth. Barbara Shipley (1968), who taught in the MES Program at Manhattan's P.S. 146, inaugurated a plan to motivate her black and Puerto Rican students by introducing them to well-educated and successful minority group professionals. Exposing her students to such individuals, she reported, was a "very positive approach to teaching racial pride and a positive self-image." During the course of the year, she invited over 20 visitors to her class, including author Claude Brown, the borough presidents of the Bronx and Manhattan, and Olympic athlete Thomas Randolph. For Shipley, these guests were "a living symbol of what the child can be."

Shipley certainly did not believe that her program would cure the problem of low-achievement. Yet, it was an initiative that would offer her children a positive view of the value of schooling:

I will not say that all of my students are going to go to college. However, they now know this is a real live possibility for them, and hopefully, it will make the homework assignments tonight have a slightly higher rating than Batman. (Shipley, 1968)

Shipley's efforts at P.S. 146 point to the role that insightful teaching plays in the education of low-achieving students. At the heart of this teacher's efforts was her understanding of how minority group professionals could serve as role models for her students and her evident flair in devising a teaching strategy that took advantage of the availability of such persons within New York City.

CONCLUSIONS

In this essay I have presented a series of portraits of the teaching of low-achieving children that span the period from the early part of this century until the late 1960s. Taken together, these vignettes provide the beginnings of a historical account of the teaching of low-achieving children that carries us farther along than we were in understanding this enterprise. Specifically, they offer a particularly useful lens, namely, the work of teachers, for exploring some of the key unresolved issues surrounding the problem of low achievement.

The most important of these issues is the relative role that is assigned to in-school factors and out-of-school factors in accounting for low achievement, particularly as it effects urban minority youth. Educational researchers, according to William Boyd (1991), are divided on this subject. On the one side, Boyd argues, are the proponents of so-called effective schools who believe that schools, particularly in respect to their organizational characteristics, do matter in the education of children. Those associated with this viewpoint look to such organizational factors as strong administrative leadership, clear goals, high student expectations, and staff training, to name but a few, as the key attributes in schools that promote academic achievement. On the other side, again according to Boyd, are those researchers who attribute low achievement to such factors as culture, family background, and family economic status.

The portraits presented in this essay suggest that neither explanation in itself is sufficient and call instead for a more nuanced view of low achievement that takes into account both in-school and out-of-school factors. Martha Cook and Cele Brickman's effort to modify the program for slow learners at Speyer School, Minneapolis's B Curriculum Experiment, and a number of remedial programs in Detroit and New York City point to the deliberate initiatives that schools can undertake to address the low educational performance of its students.

Our look at Barbara Shipley's work in the More Effective Schools Program at P.S. 146, however, urges us to be modest in our claims about the effectiveness of schooling in addressing the problem of low achievement. Shipley's practice of inviting minority professionals to speak to her students was clearly an attempt to enhance her instructional effectiveness with children who were difficult to teach. Yet, her comment that the most she could hope for from this approach was that some of her children would take their nightly homework assignment more seriously was telling. She seems to be suggesting that there are real limits to what schools can hope to achieve. In her particular case, the problem of low achievement was tied to the post–World War II social transformation of American cities and their economies. When seen from this vantage point, the problem of low achievement may have had more to do with politics and economics than pedagogy.

A second unsettled issue involves the question of whether low achievers should be provided for in regular classrooms with other students or whether they should be educated in separate settings. This is clearly a longstanding issue that dates back to the turn of the twentieth century with the appearance of special education programs for the disabled. It continues today in the debates among special educators over mainstreaming and inclusion and in the arguments among those concerned with at-risk students over the relative merits of pull-out and in-class programs for educating that population (Lipsky & Gartner, 1996; Natriello, McDill, & Pallas, 1990).

The development of Atlanta's first special classes and the work of Ann Covart in St. Paul's special classes indicate quite clearly why teachers would want to remove low achievers from regular classrooms. These were difficult-to-teach children and providing for them often proved to be physically exhausting and emotionally draining work for teachers. The efforts of the teachers who worked at New York City's P.S. 45 with Angelo Patri, on the other hand, suggest that such children do not have to be removed from regular classrooms. As these teachers seemed to demonstrate, it was often possible to work with low achievers informally in the context of the regular classroom.

The examination of Minneapolis's B Curriculum Experiment suggests that the lack of resolution of this debate may be due to the unwillingness of many classroom teachers to want to work with low achievers. It was this resistance among teachers in Minneapolis that seems to have been the principal reason for the short life of this innovation. It does appear that background knowledge and training can overcome the reluctance of teachers on this score, particularly if it can be shown that the task of teaching low achievers requires, at most, relatively modest departures from the regular school program. At least in Minneapolis, teachers who understood the actual purpose and nature of the B Curriculum Experiment became its supporters. On the other hand, however, the experience of the teachers who worked for Angelo Patri at P.S. 45 and the efforts of Josie Brennan at Halsey and Herbert Kliebard at Nyack point not so much to training but to luck as the key ingredient in the successful teaching of low-achieving children. Teaching low achievers may in fact be an idiosyncratic task whose success relies as much on serendipity as anything else. In that case, the entire question of training becomes problematic. Taken together, the encounters between teachers and low-achieving children presented in this essay indicate that the debate over the separate education of these students may not be easily resolved.

A third and final dilemma on which the portraits shed light is the question of whether or not low-achieving children can master the regular school curriculum. Here again is a perennial educational issue that dates back to attempts to differentiate the curriculum during the early part of this century (Kliebard, 1986). This same conflict is visible today in debates over tracking and ability grouping as well as in the controversy between advocates of remediation and acceleration as the principal approach for educating at-risk youth (Levin, 1991; Oakes, Gamoran, & Page, 1992).

The efforts of Martha Cook and Cele Brickman to modify the curriculum for slow learners at Speyer School suggest why such approaches might be viewed favorably by teachers. Yet, the discussion of Minneapolis's B Curriculum Experiment points to the fact that the changes that were actually required in the regular curriculum to accommodate low achievers may have been few or even nonexistent. As the teachers who worked with Angelo Patri at P.S. 45 during the 1940s and those who taught in New York City's More Effective Schools during the 1960s have shown, astute teachers who care about children seem to be able to provide for such students without altering the regular curriculum.

One of the important contributions that historical inquiry can make to the arena of educational policy is to pull known problems from their all too familiar setting in the present and place them in the less familiar terrain of the past. Viewing these dilemmas in this unknown territory often allows educators to see them in new and more interesting ways and to ask different questions than they normally would. This history of teaching difficult-to-teach children was intended to do just that for the enduring problem of low achievement.

Acknowledgment. The research reported in this essay was assisted in part by a grant from the Spencer Foundation. The data presented, the statements made, and the views expressed are solely my responsibility.

REFERENCES

Atlanta Board of Education. (1898–1915). *Minutes.* Atlanta, GA: Atlanta Public School Archives.

Atlanta Public Schools. (1920–1930). *School directory.* Atlanta, GA: Atlanta Public School Archives.

Bennison, E. A. (1988). *Creating categories of competence: The education of exceptional children in the Milwaukee public schools, 1908–1917.* Unpublished doctoral dissertation, University of Wisconsin, Madison.

Bergeland, E. (1945). Report of the B curriculum department. Minneapolis Board of Education Records, Special Education, Slow-Learning Pupils, B Curriculum Folder, Minnesota State Archives, Minnesota History Society (hereafter MBER).

Boyd, W. L. (1991). What makes ghetto schools succeed or fail? *Teachers College Record, 92,* 331–362.

Brennan, J. (1944). Problems of an adjustment class. *Halsey Clearing House,* 1, 6–7, James Marshall Papers, Box 3, Folder 25, Milbank Memorial Library, Teachers College, Columbia University.

A collection of memories from 1910–1960 as volunteered by St. Paul Educators. (1960). University of Minnesota.

Cooley, E. (1933). Letter from Barbara Wright, May 5, Education, Slow-Learning Pupils, 1929–1964 Folder, Minneapolis Public Schools, Information Service Center (hereafter SLP).

Coolidge, E. (1929). Special grade room of Eastern high school. *Detroit Educational Bulletin, 13*(4), 6, Detroit Public School Archives, Professional Library, School Center Building, Detroit, Michigan.

Cuban, L., & Tyack, D. (1989). *Mismatch: Historical perspectives on schools and students who don't fit.* Unpublished manuscript, Stanford University, Stanford, CA.

Darden, J. T. (1976). The residential segregation of blacks in Detroit, 1960–1970. *International Journal of Comparative Sociology, 17,* 84–91.

Darden, J. T., Hill, R. C., Thomas, J., & Thomas, R. (1987). *Detroit: Race and uneven development.* Philadelphia: Temple University Press.

Detroit Board of Education. (1938). *Causes of retardation in reading and methods of eliminating them.* Detroit: Author.

Fine, S. (1989). *Violence in the model city: The Cavanagh administration, race relations, and the Detroit riot of 1967.* Ann Arbor: University of Michigan Press.

Finkelstein, B. (1989). *Governing the young: Teacher behavior in popular primary schools in nineteenth-century United States.* New York: Falmer Press.

Franklin, B. M. (1987). Introduction: Learning disabilities and the need for dissenting essays. In B. M. Franklin (Ed.), *Learning disability: Dissenting essays* (pp. 1–12). New York: Falmer Press.

Franklin, B. M. (1994). *From "backwardness" to "at-risk": Childhood learning difficulties and the contradictions of school reform.* Albany: State University of New York Press.

Gartner, A., & Lipsky, D. K. (1993). Children at risk: Students in special education. In R. Wollons (Ed.), *Children at risk in America: History, concepts, and public policy* (pp. 157–182). Albany: State University of New York Press.

Gilchrist, R. (1946). Letter from L. E. Leipold, T. O. Everson, and Harold Tallakson, November 5, MBER.

Gilchrist, R. (1947). Letter from Mary Beauchamp, January 11, MBER.

Gilchrist, R. (1948). Letter from Mary Beauchamp, June 24, MBER.

Goslin, W. (1945). Letter from Newton Hegel, May 14, MBER.

Hardaker, E. J. (1932). Letter from Prudence Cutright, March 18, SLP.

Heggerston, A. I. (1933). *Survey of special education in Minneapolis.* Minneapolis Board of Education Publications, Minnesota State Archives, Minnesota Historical Society.

Hendrick, I. G., & MacMillan, D. L. (1989). Selecting children for special education in New York City: William Maxwell, Elizabeth Farrell, and the development of ungraded classes, 1900–1920. *Journal of Special Education, 22,* 395–417.

Hirsch, A. R. (1993). With or without Jim Crow: Black residential segregation in the United States. In A. R. Hirsch & R. A. Mohl (Eds.), *Urban policy in twentieth-century America* (pp. 65–95). New Brunswick, NJ: Rutgers University Press.

Joint planning committee for more effective schools. (1964, June 4). *United Teacher,* United Teacher Records, United Federation of Teachers Collection, Box 2, Wagner Labor Archives, Elmer Holmes Bobst Library, New York University (hereafter UT).

Kantor, H., & Brenzel, B. (1993). Urban education and the "truly disadvantaged": The historical roots of the contemporary crisis, 1945–1990. In M. Katz (Ed.), *The "underclass" debate: Views from history* (pp. 366–402). Princeton, NJ: Princeton University Press.

Kliebard, H. M. (1986). *The struggle for the American curriculum, 1893–1958.* Boston: Routledge and Kegan Paul.

Lazerson, M. (1975). Educational institutions and mental subnormality: Notes on writing a history. In M. J. Begab & S. A. Richardson (Eds.), *The mentally retarded and society: A social science perspective* (pp. 33–52). Baltimore: University Park Press.

Lazerson, M. (1983). The origin of special education. In J. G. Chambers & W. T. Hartman (Eds.), *Special education policies: Their history, implementation, and finance* (pp. 15–33). Philadelphia: Temple University Press.

Levin, H. M. (1991). Educational acceleration for at-risk students. In A. C. Huston (Ed.), *Children in poverty* (pp. 222–240). Cambridge, UK: Cambridge University Press.

Lipsky, D. K., & Gartner, A. (1996). Inclusion, school restructuring, and the remaking of American society. *Harvard Educational Review, 66,* 762–796.

Lovitt, T. C. (1993). Recurring issues in special and general education. In J. I. Goodlad & T. C. Lovitt (Eds.), *Integrating general and special education* (pp. 49–71). New York: Macmillan.

Massey, D. S., & Denton, N. A. (1993). *American apartheid: Segregation and the making of the underclass.* Cambridge, MA: Harvard University Press.

Minneapolis Public Schools. (1947a). Evaluation committee, MBER.

Minneapolis Public Schools. (1947b). Proposed evaluation of small class plans, MBER.

Minneapolis Public Schools. (1947c). Recommendations of the subcommittee on learning materials, MBER.

Minneapolis Public Schools. (1947d). Report of the policies subcommittee of the B curriculum steering committee, MBER.

Minneapolis Public Schools. (1947e). Report of the subcommittee on implications for the curriculum in general, MBER.

Minneapolis Public Schools. (1949). Report of the small class or B curriculum experiment, MBER.

Mirel, J. (1993). *The rise and fall of an urban school system: Detroit, 1907–1981.* Ann Arbor: University of Michigan Press.

Mollenkopf, J. H. (1983). *The contested city.* Princeton, NJ: Princeton University Press.

Natriello, G., McDill, E. L., & Pallas, A. M. (1990). *Schooling disadvantaged children: Racing against catastrophe.* New York: Teachers College Press.

New York City Board of Education. (1935). *All the children: Thirty-seventh annual report of the superintendent of schools.* New York City Board of Education Archives, Milbank Memorial Library, Teachers College, Columbia University (hereafter NYC).

New York City Board of Education. (1936). *All the children: Thirty-eighth annual report of the superintendent of schools.* NYC.

New York City Board of Education. (1937). *All the children: Thirty-ninth annual report of the superintendent of schools.* NYC.

New York City Board of Education. (1938). *Public service and public utilities.* NYC.

New York City Board of Education. (1939). *All the children: Forty-first report of the superintendent of schools.* NYC.

Nothing less will work . . . now is the time. (1963, April). *United Teacher.* Box 1. UT.

Oakes, J., Gamoran, A., & Page, R. N. (1992). Curriculum differentiation: Opportunities, outcomes, and meanings. In P. W. Jackson (Ed.), *Handbook of research on curriculum* (pp. 570–608). New York: MacMillan.

Osgood, R. L. (1997). Undermining the common school ideal: Intermediate schools and ungraded classes in Boston, 1838–1900. *History of Education Quarterly, 37*, 375–398.

Patri, A. (1944). Survey of teachers. Angelo Patri Papers, Box 87. Library of Congress, Manuscript Division, Washington, DC.

Reese, W. J. (1986). *Power and promise of school reform: Grass-roots movements during the progressive era.* Boston: Routledge and Kegan Paul.

Reese, W. J. (1995). *The origins of the American high school.* New Haven, CT: Yale University Press.

Richardson, J. G. (1994). Commons, delinquent, and special: On the formalization of common schooling in the American state. *American Educational Research Journal, 31*, 695–723.

Richardson, J. G., & Parker, T. L. (1993). The institutional genesis of special education: The American case. *American Journal of Education, 101*, 359–392.

Rogers, D. (1968). *110 Livingston Street: Politics and bureaucracy in the New York City school system.* New York: Random House.

Rury, J. L. (1993). The changing social context of urban education: A national perspective. In J. L. Rury & F. A. Cassell (Eds.), *Seeds of crisis: Public schooling in Milwaukee since 1920* (pp. 10–41). Madison: University of Wisconsin Press.

Sarason, S. B., & Doris, J. (1979). *Educational handicap, public policy, and social history: A broadened perspective on mental retardation.* New York: Free Press.

Schools helping underprivileged to adjust to life. (1959, October 10). *Detroit News.* Norman Drachler Papers, Box 57. The Paul and Jean Hanna Archival Collection. Hoover Institution, Stanford University, Stanford, CA.

Sedlak, M. W., & Church, R. L. (1982). *A history of social services directed to youth* (Contract No. 400-79-0017). Washington, DC: National Institute of Education.

Sedlak, M. W., & Schlossman, S. (1985). The public school and social services: Reassessing the progressive legacy. *Educational Theory, 35*, 371–383.

Shapiro, R. (1966). Memorandum from Rose Shapiro, November 28, 1966. Rose Shapiro Papers, Box 7, Folder 7. Milbank Memorial Library, Teachers College, Columbia University.

Shipley, B. (1968, May 29). Development of every child to the uttermost limits. *United Teacher.* Box 3. UT.

Skrtic, T. M. (1991). *Behind special education: A critical analysis of professional culture and school organization.* Denver: Love Publishing.

Strayer, G. D., & Engelhardt, N. L. (1921–1922). *Report of the survey of the public school system of Atlanta, Georgia* (Vol. 1). New York: Teachers College Press.

Sugrue, T. J. (1993). The structures of urban poverty: The reorganization of space and work in three periods of history. In M. B. Katz (Ed.), *The "underclass" debate: Views from history* (pp. 85–117). Princeton, NJ: Princeton University Press.

Sugrue, T. J. (1996). *The origins of the urban crisis: Race and inequality in postwar Detroit*. Princeton, NJ: Princeton University Press.

Taft, P. (1974). *United they teach: The story of the United Federation of Teachers*. Los Angeles: Nash Publishing.

Tropea, J. (1987a). Bureaucratic order and special children: Urban schools, 1890s–1940s. *History of Education Quarterly, 27*, 29–53.

Tropea, J. (1987b). Bureaucratic order and special children: Urban schools, 1950s–1960s. *History of Education Quarterly, 27*, 339–361.

Tyack, D. (1974). *The one best system: A history of American urban education*. Cambridge, MA: Harvard University Press.

Union backs 10 "effective schools." (1964, September 15). *United Teacher*. Box 2. UT.

White House Conference on Child Health and Protection. (1933). *The handicapped child: Report of the committee on physically and mentally handicapped*. New York: Century.

U.S. Department of the Interior. (1931). *Public school education for atypical children*. Washington, DC: U.S. Government Printing Office.

Wollons, R. (Ed.). (1993). *Children at risk in America: History, concepts, and public policy*. Albany: State University of New York Press.

Zehm, J. (1973). *Educational misfits: A study of poor performers in the English class, 1825–1925*. Unpublished doctoral dissertation, Stanford University, Stanford, CA.

PART IV

LIBERAL EDUCATION
AND THE CURRICULUM

Chapter 7

The Philosopher-King of St. Louis

William J. Reese

America's preeminent educational statesperson in the late nineteenth century was William T. Harris. Born in East Killingly, Connecticut, in 1835, Harris first rose to prominence as superintendent of public schools in St. Louis from 1868 to 1880. One of the founding lights of the St. Louis movement in philosophy—a group dedicated to the study of German idealism—Harris founded and edited the *Journal of Speculative Philosophy*, translated Hegel's *Logic* into English, became an early president of the National Education Association and a fixture at its annual meetings, served on its most prestigious committees, edited books, wrote hundreds of addresses and articles, compiled a longer curriculum vitae than most college professors of his day, and served an unprecedented tenure as the U.S. Commissioner of Education (1889–1906). Without question, he was the most famous American educational thinker of his generation. Equally without question, he is now largely forgotten by most students of education or, if remembered, dismissed as a reactionary figure. Merle Curti (1935), the distinguished historian, helped seal his doom by labeling him the "Conservator."

Virtually everything Harris believed in was repudiated within educational circles by the early decades of the twentieth century. Since he was not a university professor, like so many educational theorists at the time, Harris lacked adoring students or disciples to carry on his name or legacy. Unlike John Dewey, G. Stanley Hall, and other academic luminaries, he did not write a major book despite his impressive bibliography. Even his admiring biographers after his death in 1909 were embarrassed by his defense of the common school and an academically oriented curriculum. Harris became an anachronism in his own time, a philosopher-king without many followers or subjects. It makes revisiting him all the more fascinating. What accounts for his dismal place in American educational historiography?

Paying respect to Harris's memory, the editor of the *American School Board Journal* in 1909 recognized the passing of someone distinctive in the nation's educational history. Harris's death, he claimed, "removes the most eminent leader of American educational thought. . . . He was truly an intellectual giant" ("Death of Dr. Harris," 1909, p. 8). Despite the dim view of him held by progressive educators and historians, Harris was probably the most widely recognized American educator in the world in the early 1900s. Yet this renowned Hegelian philosopher-educator reached old age just as new philosophical currents, such as pragmatism, emerged to a position of greater visibility and when the idea of the common school lacked support within dominant educational circles during the progressive era.

A product of the vibrant social changes that transformed America in the nineteenth century, Harris represented the past, not the future. He became famous despite being at odds with a new generation of school reformers who came on the scene after the 1880s: child study advocates, manual training and vocational education enthusiasts, supporters of a differentiated curriculum, Herbartians, followers of Dewey, and other reformers who gathered under the umbrella of the "new education" (Cremin, 1961; Kliebard, 1995). Fellow educationists and later historians might have praised Harris for his sharp wit, analytical skills, and skepticism toward every ascending pedagogical panacea. But he questioned the pieties of progressive education—child study, meeting the interests of the child, disdain for tradition, and so forth—and thus alienated a rising educational establishment that understandably wanted to distance itself from the past. The philosopher did not help himself in yet another fundamental way. As Herbert Kliebard explains, Harris was his era's most vocal and consistent defender of humanistic study in the public schools. Since the turn of the century, progressives have labeled nearly anyone who has endorsed humanism and a core curriculum in the liberal arts as a conservative, outside of polite educational company. While on friendly personal terms with Harris (the "conservator" published some of his early essays), Dewey himself in 1898 described Harris's views of the elementary curriculum as "reactionary." In the 1930s, Curti simply continued the tradition of dismissing those who questioned the assumptions of pragmatism and progressive education. The depth of the disdain for Harris perhaps tells us as much about the critics as about the man and his philosophy of the common school, as this essay hopes to demonstrate.

The path that had led Harris to fame in St. Louis in the 1870s and
to professional infamy later was an unpredictable one. A bookish young
man, educated in district schools, private academies, city schools, and
finally Yale—which he left in good standing in his junior year—Harris
followed Horace Greeley's advice and headed westward in 1857 for the
booming town of St. Louis. The gateway to the West, St. Louis also had
a strategic position on the Mississippi, a commercial link to the north
and south. One of the largest cities in America by the 1870s, St. Louis
offered a challenge to the young and ambitious Connecticut Yankee.
Harris tried his hand at teaching shorthand, selling ink pens, and pursuing other business ventures. He considered purchasing a farm, but
instead became a teacher, then principal, and finally assistant superintendent and superintendent in the St. Louis public schools. Neither
that outcome nor his embrace of idealist philosophy were foreordained.
An avid reader, Harris believed that he had learned all that he could at
Yale. Through his reading out of school, he soon slipped away from
his traditional Congregational moorings, flirted with radical European
thought, and tasted a wide intellectual fare, from phrenology to mes-
merism to spiritualism. This was hardly part of the classical curriculum, which he nonetheless defended in the coming years, adding to
his reputation as a conservative. Before leaving Yale he fell somewhat
under the spell of New England transcendentalism, which helped ease
the intellectual journey to German idealism (Leidecker, 1946).

In his early days in St. Louis, the young Harris still lacked a coherent personal or educational philosophy. Writing to his future wife back
east in 1857, he described himself as follows: he was 5'10", with au-
burn hair, weighed 160 pounds, was mostly a vegetarian, and believed
that most views contained some truth, but not all truth:

> I am somewhat of a spiritualist. Nay, more, I am an entire believer in the
> spiritual nature of man in the communication of man with the spirits
> who have put off the flesh. I totally disapprove of the sensual philoso-
> phy that ignores the intuition of the soul. I love music, poetry and paint-
> ing and sculpture. I love natural science, metaphysics, and above all the-
> ology. I am a phrenologist and moreover I write shorthand at the rate of
> about 100 words per minute. (Leidecker, 1946, pp. 84–85)

He was also "somewhat of an astronomer" and believed he could tell a
fortune-telling faker from a genuine spiritualist. "I am not an atheist
and yet I believe in no God as the popular mind does" (Leidecker, 1946,
pp. 84–85). Not surprisingly, family members and the family minister
worried about the state of his soul. To the end of his life friends said

he was a Christian in an intellectual rather than pietistic sense, and he never lost interest in spiritual communication and mental telepathy (Fitzpatrick, 1910b; Roberts, 1924).

As superintendent in St. Louis, Harris pulled together the many strands of an educational philosophy that would largely cohere for the rest of his life. His annual reports to the St. Louis school board are worth revisiting, even though he refined his positions on specific issues as the intellectual and political climate changed with the rise of the "new education" in later years. Harris's annual reports as superintendent were as famous in his day as Horace Mann's were a generation earlier. Despite tight budgets caused by an economic panic and depression in the 1870s, the city printed 4,000–7,000 copies of them, in both English and German. Their distribution across the nation boosted the reputation of the city and its young superintendent (Troen, 1975). Decades later, an older generation remembered the widespread interest in Harris's annual reports, when educators across the nation had studied how this philosopher-educator organized the schools, conceptualized the course of study, and shaped a growing urban system (Ames, 1909; Brown, 1910; Claxton, 1936; Leidecker, 1946).

In 1906 the editor of the journal *Education* explained in part why these reports were so popular. They were, he argued, "Platonic in their breadth of view, and Aristotelian in attention to details. There are few school documents to-day that better repay careful and critical study" ("Editorial," 1906, p. 50). This was a kind remark, written as Harris, in failing health, stepped down as U.S. Commissioner of Education. In truth, few up-and-coming administrators or educational thinkers cared much about what Harris said by this time. Many ideas which he regarded as fads (like child study) or harmful (such as vocational education) were now common coin in educational circles, and his idealist philosophy, "reactionary" defense of the traditional common curriculum, and support for humanistic study were out of step with pragmatism and the latest progressive views. In its essence, his philosophy of education had not changed fundamentally since his St. Louis years. Harris was respected for his erudition and stature as a thinker and educational leader in a professional world that cared little for his ideas.

PHILOSOPHER AND ADMINISTRATOR

Even before his reputation sagged, many people regarded the Connecticut Yankee as a very odd combination: the philosopher and administrator. Upon his death, one educator wrote that even "his intimate friends wondered at the practical acumen of the philosopher" (Brown, 1910, p. 223). In his St. Louis days, businessmen on the school board, newspaper reporters, and others also saw something they thought was remarkable: a philosopher who could run a rapidly expanding school system, a scholar who by day could work with teachers to improve science instruction and by night discuss Hegel, Fichte, and Kant with other highbrow intellectuals. The stereotype of the monkish intellectual who counts angels on the heads of pins but who gets lost traveling home at night is common in a society that has long distinguished the practical from the cerebral. And so, when reporters, key figures in the popularization of information, wrote about Harris, they all noted his capacity for theorizing as well as for practical action. The *St. Louis Globe-Democrat* typically wrote that:

> Mr. Harris is a transcendental philosopher, and when he gets hold of the Philosophy of the Conditioned he can puzzle a spelling class; but when he takes hold of a plain question of fact, or explains the management of the public schools, he can satisfy the dullest intellect that his dealings with the abstruse mysteries of Kant and Hegel have not unfitted him for his practical work as a Superintendent. (Leidecker, 1946, p. 262)

As early as 1858 he wrote a paper entitled "Practical Idealism." Man, he wrote, was a transcendent being, moving through "time and space," drawn to eternal values such as Truth, Beauty, and Holiness. At the same time, he realized that most parents wanted their children to learn to read and write, mundane but vital accomplishments to allow youth to share in the inherited wisdom of civilization. The sublime and ordinary lived in creative tension. Like so many Western intellectuals after the Enlightenment and before World War I, Harris believed in progress, a view reinforced by his attraction to Hegelian dialectics in the coming years. Darwin's controversial views, he assumed, would ultimately be absorbed into Christian cosmology, and change and improvement were ever present and irresistible. "All things in nature are in a perpetual flux and reflux. No sooner does a thing become what it is than it begins to become something else. A seed becomes a plant[;] the plant decays" (Harris Papers, "Practical Idealism," December 10, 1858, Box 14). In the next decade, as his grasp and embrace of idealist philosophy became more sure, he was confident that through the familiar process of thesis-antithesis-synthesis, progress was inevitable.

By the time he became superintendent of the St. Louis schools in 1868, Harris was already routinely juxtaposing dualisms such as reflection and action in his prose as examples of the dialectic. While commentators would continue to note the apparent contradiction of the philosopher who could act as well as think, the superintendent pursued his double life, searching for a new educational synthesis in a world of constant change. Like life itself, America was dynamic, on the move: from countryside to city, from farm to factory, from east to west. These tensions would ultimately be resolved into a higher, different reality, he confidently predicted. In educational circles as elsewhere, ideas clashed as rival notions struggled for dominance on such issues as foreign language instruction, free high schools, early childhood education, moral training, a common curriculum, and teaching practices. While cities, factories, and immigrants remade the face of America, educational reformers criticized schools from a variety of positions. Harris believed that nearly every critic possessed a worthy insight and caught at least a partial truth, though he consistently believed that reformers were also prone to exaggeration and often believed in panaceas and slogans. Harris outraged a younger generation after the 1880s by suggesting that the premises of their "progressive" ideas were often ill-founded, undemocratic, and harmful to the child. Indeed, before he left St. Louis in 1880, he had worked out a philosophy that made him an easy political target for a variety of progressive educators.

SUPPORTER OF THE COMMON SCHOOL

Like most educators at midcentury, Harris was heir to the ideals of the common school and the belief that free, tax-supported public education was a grand republican achievement. As Harris worked his way up the administrative ladder, from teacher to principal to superintendent, he participated in what many contemporaries saw as a great social experiment. While late-twentieth-century Americans often bemoan the ills of cities, large-scale organizations, and institutions, Harris and most contemporary educational theorists knew that despite their many problems, cities were the site of culture, civilization, and remarkable pedagogical experiments. Like other urban areas, St. Louis initially offered free education only for the poor in charity schools, taught by Lancasterian methods. Middle- and upper-class children attended private, often religiously oriented schools that charged tuition. By the time Harris arrived in St. Louis, however, America's urban public schools were free, growing in popularity, and becoming more central in the lives of more children (Barnard, 1880; Troen, 1975). Cities built the first graded classrooms, hired women as elementary teachers, assigned uniform textbooks, improved school design (including heating, lighting, and ventilation), and often constructed architecturally magnificent high schools to crown the system (Kaestle, 1983). St. Louis followed suit. And despite his reputation later as a reactionary and opponent of Rousseauean romanticism, Harris would also become famous for establishing the first public kindergartens in any large system.

Imagine the enthusiasm that this young Hegelian experienced in the city! The workaday world of the educator and the cerebral world of the philosopher were mutually reinforcing. Harris could see at first hand the Hegelian idea that the individual in the modern world would work, live, and gain identity and greater freedom through interaction with institutions. To Harris, history was the unfolding of ever greater movements for freedom and enlightenment. The separation of church and state generally and the Protestant Reformation specifically had liberated the individual from arbitrary authority, and the free public school became one of the many new institutional expressions of a changing world (Harris Papers, "Do the Signs of the Times Indicate a Degeneration of American Character?" n.d., Box 14, and *Commonplace Book*, Essay XVII, 1864, pp. 1–3). As competing ideas struggled for dominance, the public school was wracked with dissent over how best to educate, socialize, and prepare the young for their role in a dynamic nation undergoing constant transformation. Searching for a synthesis of divergent educational perspectives was difficult but essential.

The common school, as Harris never tired of saying, was only one of many modern institutions that had its special role to play in building a better society. Families, churches, neighborhoods, and the workplace all had their own, somewhat overlapping part in the great human drama. Too often people expected schools to solve every imaginable social ill, though as he regularly pointed out, most children in St. Louis in the 1870s attended school for only 5 years. Those 5 years were crucial, but Harris warned that only so much could be done in so short a period. Everyone who attended, therefore, should share in the same curricular bounty (St. Louis, 1874).

In words that Dewey and other progressives would echo a generation later, Harris wrote in 1872 that the public school was a "miniature community" (St. Louis, 1872, p. 35). His dream, shared by public school reformers since the 1830s, was that the schools would enroll children of all social backgrounds into a common system, where they would study with the same teachers and to the degree possible have equal access to learning. This helps explain Harris's well-publicized endorsement of coeducation in the 1870s, at a time when conservative critics attacked it on the national level for a host of supposed abuses. While coeducation had fairly solid support within the public schools of St. Louis, more politically dangerous was the issue of foreign language training (St. Louis, 1871, 1874; Roberts, 1924). While Harris noted that at least 10 different languages were spoken in the city, for a variety of reasons German was the center of political debate. As in his endorsement of the coeducation of the sexes, the Superintendent offered numerous reasons why the city should fund high quality foreign language programs in German.

Germans constituted the largest immigrant group in St. Louis, and the establishment of foreign language courses was a major sticking point in local politics. By the 1870s, Germans, usually Republicans, were powerful on the city school board, where they often firmly supported foreign language teaching as well as German-inspired innovations like the kindergarten. In some districts of St. Louis, nearly 80 percent of the children in the schools had German ancestry. Irish politicians, usually Democrats, often introduced resolutions to the school board to establish Gaelic language courses, less because they wanted such programs than to stir animosity against their political rivals. A great admirer of German culture and philosophy, Harris repeatedly went on record in support of German language instruction, a political necessity as well as an intellectual imperative (St. Louis, 1874; Troen, 1975). But Harris's position on this issue essentially reflected his wider faith in the assimilative powers of the common school, but from a unique perspective.

In his many writings on educational thought and practice, the superintendent assailed private schools for dividing the community and for weakening support for the public sphere. By meeting on a "common ground" in the common school, a distinctive American nationality would emerge as the various traits of diverse groups competed for favor. Like other educators of his time, he endorsed the idea that schools should assimilate all children into a common culture, one however that was in the making, not already formed. The practical problem was that St. Louis had many private schools in which German was the language of instruction, so Harris and his allies on the school board pressed for their elimination through the addition of German language programs in the public system. Without question, the strategy worked: German Americans abandoned the private sector in large numbers during Harris's tenure (St. Louis, 1870; Troen, 1975).

First added as an elective in the schools in 1864, German was therefore an important way to draw more immigrants into the school, without whom the common system would exist only in name. Harris recognized the power of German voters and politicians and admired their intellectual contributions to America, and he insisted that the addition of foreign language programs was not an outrageous concession to an immigrant group. It was natural, he said, for the adults in any immigrant group to want their children to have some memory of their family's ethnic and cultural past. As immigrant children mingled with English speakers—whether native born or from England or Ireland—the process of assimilation of old and new was inevitable; a new synthesis would emerge (St. Louis, 1871, 1876, 1878). Attending school together would ultimately help break down the clannishness of all groups. In this context, just as free schools enabled rich and poor to meet (supposedly) on a common plane of competition, making German available both to immigrants and native born alike ensured that the school was in fact a miniature community. That schools should preserve the distinctiveness of groups was not a central theme within nineteenth century educational thought, so Harris's paean to assimilation was neither novel nor politically reactionary in this historical context. "With differences of languages there go, also, differences of manners and customs—of feelings, convictions and ideas," he asserted in 1874. "And yet the process of forming one community, one nationality of these heterogeneous elements, must necessarily go on. We are all to live in one community, and the relations of family, commerce, social intercourse, and fellow citizenship shall bind us together" (St. Louis, p. 136). Through a dialectical interaction between differences emerged a new American synthesis, assuring social harmony until new contradictory forces challenged the status quo. How to find this "common ground" was something educators like other citizens inevitably struggled over.

"The public school is the instrumentality designed for the conservation of true democratic principles," he wrote in 1876. "It protects one class against another by giving an opportunity to the children of all classes for free competition in the struggle to become intelligent and virtuous. An aristocracy built on the accident of birth, wealth, or position can not resist the counter-influence of a system of free schools wherein all are given the same chances" (St. Louis, p. 111). Two early theorists of mass education, Thomas Jefferson and Horace Mann, had popularized these notions. Indeed, most public school leaders shared this faith that schools prevented the hardening of inherited social distinctions while rewarding the most meritorious individuals. The superintendent added that vast social changes during recent decades only reinforced the special mission of the public school, whose influence, he predicted, would continue to expand in the modern world.

FAITH IN THE POWER OF EDUCATION

In the modern world, the division of labor in the political economy found its expression in the educational world. Hence the division of classes into grades, the distinctions between district schools and high schools, and a curriculum constructed upon a gradient of difficulty. As Harris confided in his *Commonplace Book* in 1864, man alone was an improving being, and as the adage had it, knowledge is power. But now knowledge grew in quantity and complexity. Universal education thus remained an absolute necessity in a free society: "Free thought is the privilege of the educated." Patriarchal, monarchical forms of government had been repudiated during the American Revolution, and the "greatest institutions" of the modern world "will be the arrangements for education. Schools of all grades for the beginners and advanced and universities to finish the development. Education develops the inventive powers" (Harris Papers, *Commonplace Book*, "Necessity of Universal Education in a Democracy," 1864, pp. 1–3). Machines and labor saving devices would help eliminate drudgery and allow more time for men, women, and children to cultivate their minds.

This faith in the power of education to enhance individual and national productivity was a constant theme in Harris's writings. The notion was an old one, made famous by Horace Mann, who in the 1840s had polled manufacturers and business people to prove that educated workers were more dependable, moral, and productive. By the 1870s, national exhibitions in Europe and America emphasized the role of education in shaping an industrial workforce, scientific invention, and even the strong Prussian military. Harris was hardly unusual in believing that education promoted economic productivity and thus national greatness. With each added year of schooling, children learned the values, sensibilities, and skills that would serve them well in the workplace. In particular, in a world of factories and machine production, a new set of values unnecessary in a rural, agrarian society now had to be learned for sheer survival. While Harris adamantly opposed trade training and vocational education in the public schools, he saw clear connections between what was learned in school and an individual's economic success. His failure to join the bandwagon of enthusiasts for manual training, industrial education, or vocational education contributed to his reputation as a conservative. Attending school made one more moral, more intelligent, and more productive. But it was not the job of the school, he believed, to train youth for specific jobs.

In one of his stock phrases, Harris assumed that attending school enhanced one's "directive power," or capacity to gain more control over nature (St. Louis, 1870, 1871). He was confident that schools helped ensure that America would be a nation that promoted talent, spelling doom for any aristocracy based on inherited wealth and family background. Schools were severely criticized in the 1870s, a time of economic panic and depression, when pressures to cut costs and school programs accelerated. With the firm support of the school board, Harris championed the high school throughout these hard times, answering those who attacked it for its academic pretensions and high costs. And he refused to budge in his defense of a common academic curriculum. From the elementary grades through the high school, only academic subjects belonged in the course of study, otherwise the breadth of learning to which all children were heir would be denied. Relatively few children would stay in school long enough to attend, never mind graduate from high school, but Harris insisted that whoever attended for however many years should receive an academic education.

Throughout his tenure in St. Louis, he wrote in 1880, "there has been . . . a popular clamor in favor of the introduction of the arts and trades into public schools. It has been supposed by self-styled 'practical' writers upon education that the school should fit the youth for the practice of some vocation or calling." Harris feared that these reformers would substitute trade training "and not much else" for the common academic curriculum. A more general education was better for everyone, he argued. Moreover, "Who can tell, on seeing the child, what special vocation he will best follow when he grows up?" (St. Louis, 1880, pp. 126–127). This was a voice of the nineteenth century. For the typical child attending school for a few years, exposure to common moral values, habits, and subjects seemed sufficient preparation for adult responsibilities. Children generally left school by the age of 12, so what the schools chose to emphasize was crucial. Narrow trade training in a world where old jobs disappeared and new industries appeared overnight might doom the child to the static here and now and not teach the flexibility needed in the ever changing present.

ADVOCATE OF MORAL TRAINING IN PUBLIC SCHOOLS

What did children need to learn at school? Harris hardly thought that preparing for work was the only reason why society had created public schools, as some reformers seemed to think. Moral training above all helped prepare children for adulthood. Given the specialization of function of institutions in the modern world, however, the work of the key religious institution—the church—must not interfere with the sort of moral training offered in the secular school. Because of Harris's deep spiritualism (if not conventional Christianity), some critics were puzzled that the St. Louis system forbade Bible or prayer reading, familiar school practices in many places. Curious about the bans, which he avidly endorsed, Harris scoured the local archival record, learning that this was a policy of very long standing. Periodically, orthodox Protestants, many Catholics, and various sectarians attacked the secular system as immoral, and Harris was still being criticized for favoring "Godless" schools at the turn of the century. Certain that schools in fact taught important moral lessons and virtues, he firmly supported the continued separation of church and state and opposed diverting public funds to private schools. Religion at school was divisive, which would drive a wedge between groups who needed to embrace the secular values of the common school (Barnard, 1880; McCluskey, 1958; St. Louis, 1873).

"Moral virtues": schools taught many of them, including the importance of punctuality, obedience to authority, kindness, fortitude, honesty, and delayed gratification. As early as 1869, Harris told the board of education that churches had their proper division of labor, and so did the schools. "On this groundwork of Punctuality, the public school teachers proceed to build up the moral superstructure, by cultivating habits of SELF-RELIANCE and INDUSTRY; OBEDIENCE and RESPECT to superiors, COURTESY toward equals, and KINDNESS toward inferiors. These are the fundamental characteristics of a civilized demeanor" (St. Louis, 1870, p. 18). Showing up at school on time, like obeying all the other rules, taught a "moral lesson," but not a sectarian lesson per se; yet what was learned at school supplemented religious training and was invaluable in an interdependent world. He wrote in 1875 that, in an earlier period of history, learning the three Rs at the most basic level enabled most people to function reasonably well in society. The coming of the railroad, telegraph, industry, and urban life had transformed traditional society, demanding a new type of human personality, one which had a "disciplined will and habits of regularity, punctuality, and attention" (St. Louis, 1875, p. 79).

How did a child learn these moral virtues? Instead of believing that educational institutions oppressed the child, Harris consistently argued that attendance there trained the will along certain lines and this was more valuable than courses in woodworking or sheet metal. Participation in the institution allowed the child to gain greater freedom through exposure to the wider world by mastering the academic curriculum and by absorbing the moral values taught throughout the school day. To function productively, harmoniously, and morally in an interdependent society, the untutored and self-centered child had to lose his or her individuality at first, while gaining greater freedom and success later. "No one will question the great importance of habits of punctuality," he wrote. "In a civilization that is every year becoming more complex and more dependent upon the combination of each individual with the whole of society, punctuality becomes a moral virtue" (St. Louis, 1876, pp. 20–21; see also 1870, 1871, 1872, 1880).

On this point Harris was not a hypocrite. He himself danced to the familiar meter of the Yankee work ethic to show how self-discipline, hard work, and application in an institutional setting made one freer by leading to higher achievement and productivity than if one lived and worked alone. Harris monitored himself: he was late for work a total of 13 minutes in one 7 year period, and absent 3 ½ days, which included time for a friend's funeral (Leidecker, 1946). As in other cities that labored to address the need for more industrial time discipline in the shaping of school culture, his annual reports bulged with statistics on punctuality, tardiness, and deportment, among the many presumed indicators of institutional, and thus social, advance. A critic of corporal punishment, which he thought more common in rural than city schools, he shared the faith of many school men that teaching self-control, self-discipline, and the internalization of the moral values of the classroom was a benevolent feature of the secular system (St. Louis, 1870, 1871, 1873, 1875; Leidecker, 1946).

CHAMPION OF AN ACADEMIC CURRICULUM

While the values of Poor Richard still proved functional in this more complex social system, Harris's confidence in the causal connection between education and productivity never caused him to champion the cause of manual training or industrial education in the schools. These reforms had gained a following before the Civil War, but with nothing like the accelerated passion of the 1870s. Harris did not doubt that training the "hand and eye" was a worthy educational goal; he endorsed kindergartens in part to promote dexterity, physical coordination, and similar traits in little children. But he doubted that manual training or industrial education was quite the panacea its champions assumed, that it would cure labor unrest, solve unemployment, and undermine socialism. Moreover, in 1874 he warned that public schools should never be "caste schools," where workers' children were only trained to become future workers. Everyone in the same grade should study the same subjects, whether they went to high school or stopped at fourth grade, "whether they are preparing for a liberal education [at college] or intend to enter the sphere of productive industry at an early age" (St. Louis, 1874, pp. 56, 105). Near his final year as superintendent, he again said that every individual should have access to the same knowledge and criticized those who wanted "to convert common schools into apprentice-shops wherein the trades of art and life are taught" (St. Louis, 1879, p. 203).

In the simplicity of the common school curriculum lay the best guarantee of the intellectual and cultural development of the child. To go to school opened the possibility of freeing the child from the specific influences of family, social background, and sectarian religion, and of expanding his or her mental universe beyond a necessarily parochial past. An ideal school drew upon children from all sorts of families, all kinds of nations, all variety of situations. There they acquired the intellectual tools to become what later generations would call "lifelong learners." Even in a few short years, by learning a handful of basic subjects, the child gained access to the "common stock of ideas" worth knowing (St. Louis, 1870, p. 110). As they matured, individuals would make their own intellectual discoveries, possibly adding to the canon of the world's wisdom. But the major obligation of the school was to provide everyone with the same knowledge . Everyone was expected to be punctual and well-behaved and to exhibit other important moral virtues; so too each child in a democratic republic needed access to a common curriculum, best represented by a few key subjects. These areas of study were veritable "windows of the soul" (Kliebard, 1995).

These windows of the soul (occasionally called the windows of the mind) included five areas within the common school: arithmetic and mathematics, geography, history, grammar, and art and literature. Although there were a host of fascinating, worthy subjects worth knowing, everyone needed to master these subjects in the elementary grades. The curriculum was the heart of the classroom and, for many children, the foundation for their learning for the rest of their lives. This was worth defending, since in the poorest industrial districts the most disadvantaged children only attended school for 3 years. Schools taught them habits to counter the hard lives they faced on the streets, said almost every urban educator at the time, including Harris. But Harris also emphasized offering every student a chance at intellectual development, impossible without an academic course of study.

Arithmetic and mathematics served as a window into a world of abstract relationships, beyond the usual ways an unlettered child perceived life. While practical—teaching you how to make change, to count, and so forth—they had more profound potential, to allow everyone to gain "theoretical dominion over time and space, and by it [a student] can formulate the entire inorganic world" (St. Louis, 1870, p. 76; see also 1874, 1879). A few years of arithmetic could not do this, but it offered what a beginner needed to advance still higher, whether one progressed to the high school or later studied on one's own. Geography, like all the other subjects, also removed children from their immediate environment; it allowed them to see the larger world around them, how food was produced, how humankind struggled to tame nature, and so forth. "Shut up the geographical window of the soul and what darkness ensues!" (St. Louis, 1870, p. 112; see also 1871, 1872, 1874). Mastery of geography opened up the study of the heavens, other nations, and nature in every form, helping the school to expand the mental horizons of even the poorest student.

Without grammar, and all the related subjects in the language arts, students were imprisoned in their own thoughts. Central to all oral and written communication, grammar helped everyone share ideas, correct misperceptions, and expand appreciation for the immense intellectual universe found outside family, neighborhood, and church. All basic subjects, such as reading and writing, had "universal significance" or did not belong in the common school curriculum. Reading and writing allowed the child to transcend "the circumscribed life of the senses, in which he is confined to the narrow circle of individuals constituting his acquaintances; he issues forth from this immediate inclosure, and finds himself in the community of the world at large" (St. Louis, 1870, p. 111). To learn to read and write was something that nineteenth-century Americans still marveled over; only around 1800, had the most privileged citizens—white men and women—achieved basic universal literacy. Language enabled the young to share in this bounty: "The printed page, conversation, and everything else now opened up to [the child]" (St. Louis, 1874, p. 77).

History, difficult to understand apart from geography, similarly gave students an opportunity to imagine a world of experience beyond their own, by learning something of what came before. With a keen awareness of change and development, Harris frequently made historical allusions in his philosophical writings, so it is not surprising that the historical window was an important one in his curriculum theory. History recorded all that people were capable of, from the highest forms of justice to the worst forms of avarice and incivility. Again, it provided avenues of learning and of understanding how things came to be, placing the individual in a long train of time and human achievement, as the world progressed toward a realization of greater human freedom. History was "the revelation of what is potentially" within each person (St. Louis, 1871, p. 169; see also 1872, 1874). And, lastly, art and literature—including music—offered children access to aesthetic realms, novel and creative forms of self-expression, ideas about high culture, taste, and refinement (St. Louis, 1870, 1874). All five windows provided an entree into an expansive intellectual world impossible within the narrower confines of family, church, or neighborhood. A course in woodworking was not a waste of time but seemed to pale in significance compared with the liberal core of the school curriculum.

The St. Louis Hegelian was fully aware of the great clash of ideas that struggled for dominance in the public school curriculum. "The Course of Study," he wrote in 1879, "is dependent upon the great currents that flow in society and in the nation." A man who enjoyed debate and constantly remarked about emerging contradictions in school and society watched the sides line up:

> In the days of financial inflation when the nation is sending its bonds abroad and is realizing material productions for its obligations, there is a giddy inflation of its educational theories. When the nation comes to economize and take up its obligations, it becomes unreasonably conservative and reactionary. Thus the Bulls and Bears in Education hold alternate sway. The work of teachers and school boards must be to prevent too great reactions in either direction. (St. Louis, 1879, pp. 203–204)

VIEWS ON THE "NEW" EDUCATION

Ironically, given his reputation as a reactionary late in life, Harris never really believed in a fixed curriculum or a world without change. When Dewey and other progressives at the turn of the century described the "old" education, as opposed to the "new" or progressive alternative, they usually offered a stereotyped view of the past: that before the 1890s educators opposed all change, that they allowed children to suffer under the tyranny of a teacher-dominated class, and that pedagogy was medieval in its emphasis on order and silence. All this had been said about schools by the 1870s. Harris, in fact, said then and later that there were some truths in the criticisms, but that the critics were talking about the worst schools and were unwilling to recognize any philosophical shortcomings within the "new" education.

Harris never shied from intellectual combat, understanding that antagonisms were inevitable and their resolution part of the natural path to progress. Despite his subsequent negative press, Harris in the 1870s was not especially regarded as some out-and-out opponent of the new education. Consider his views on pedagogy, early childhood education, and other changes proposed in the curriculum. He supported manual training, industrial education, and vocational education—but regarded them as inappropriate for the common schools or even the high school. Harris did not deny that critics of bad teachers were on the mark and did not doubt the great insights made by Johann Pestalozzi, Friedrich Froebel, and at times even J. J. Rousseau (his least favorite, often his nemesis). He hardly thought that the school subjects would not adapt or change. He argued that change was the only constant in the modern world, even though his defense of the common school in the face of untested but newly popularized reforms ultimately made him appear to later educators and historians as hopelessly irredeemable.

Throughout the 1870s, Harris, in fact, joined those who complained that schools were too formal and resistant to change. He inaugurated a plan of periodic student promotions, rather than the usual annual ones found in most city systems, in order to make the system more flexible (Barnard, 1880; Leidecker, 1946). While the five major subject areas remained the core of the curriculum, he added natural science to the course of study and insisted that it be taught not from textbooks but through object teaching, or oral methods. In progressive circles, object teaching was the rage, inspired directly by Pestalozzi, who believed that young children learned more from concrete objects than from books. Characteristically, Harris believed that Pestalozzi had made a significant contribution to pedagogy but that his followers zealously exaggerated its importance. As early as 1866, Harris filled a notebook with some thoughts on "Educational Methods," where he noted the growing popularity of object lessons. He concluded that their use was really more limited than Pestalozzi's disciples believed; children at certain ages studying particular aspects of a subject might indeed benefit from the method. "But how is it with objects that possess universal necessity? Can we present to sensuous perception, God, Mind, Reason, or Truth? If not then the Science of Government, of Religion, & of Mind cannot be much helped by object lessons. On the contrary these require the profound reflection of the soul into itself" (Harris Papers, "Educational Methods," October 2, 1866, Box 1; see also St. Louis, 1872, 1873, 1878). Object lessons seemed especially promising in teaching natural science, though hardly to the exclusion of books (St. Louis, 1873). But even a promising method had limitations, and no single method was a panacea for every classroom difficulty.

Education, however, seemed to attract all sorts of visionaries and theorists, most of whom had some worthy insights but also often confused "idiosyncrasy for originality" (St. Louis, 1877, p. 186). Without question, too many teachers crammed their students' minds with mountains of facts, but the attack on textbooks that became a staple of progressive pedagogy seemed excessive to Harris. Would individual teachers who dispensed with or minimized the importance of books forget that schools should teach the inherited wisdom of the past? This was not something easily taught through object lessons alone, however well conceived.

> Since it has become common in this country to blame the text-book method, and to lay stress on oral instruction, most schools seem to prefer to let some form of object-lessons pass as the type of their instruction method; and a teacher is prouder of his collection of bugs of "native woods" or specimens of rocks and fossils than he is of a method of teaching how to read and write. It is fashionable to speak of the "objective method" as applicable to all branches, even those of grammar and arithmetic. (St. Louis, 1877, p. 188)

The disciples of Pestalozzi seemed bedazzled by their discovery that children learned from more than books, but they had ignored the great value of the printed word and were blind to their own pedagogical fetishes.

Friedrich Froebel, another European romantic, had also made a notable contribution to the history of pedagogy and early childhood education. By midcentury his followers had brought the idea of kindergartens to America. Harris hardly dismissed all that the major romantics said about the nature of the child, the importance of play, or in particular the desirability of kindergartens. In fact, St. Louis almost stood alone in the 1870s by establishing free public kindergartens, for children of all social classes, and including black children; most kindergartens in America were private, in tuition schools for the rich or in charity schools for the poor. This violated Harris's belief that all children should attend school together. Working with some prominent women reformers and with Germans on the school board, Harris pushed for the creation and expansion of public kindergartens. Like nearly everyone else advocating the reform, Harris believed that the kindergarten taught children moral values and also provided hand and eye training, improved motor skills, and some intellectual preparation for the first grade (Troen, 1975).

Himself an exceptional athlete and advocate of physical fitness, Harris did not have to be persuaded about the value and importance of play (Fitzpatrick, 1910a). He defended recess from conservative critics, pressed for the continual expansion of the kindergarten budget, and yet very much doubted that play should be elevated to an unreasonable height in the few short years most children attended school. Much valuable knowledge was gained by sometimes very unpleasant means, namely through hard work, self-discipline, and the mastery of sometimes difficult and demanding textbooks. Play had real educational value, but reformers could easily ride a hobby horse and exaggerate its centrality in the life of the child at school.

How to treat children in a more kindly way was an important question in reform circles throughout the nineteenth century. Like many educators, Harris believed that the romantics had left some desirable marks on school practice and that the hiring of women teachers helped to reduce the frequency of corporal punishment. Harris criticized physical punishment and lamented its use and popular support, in St. Louis as elsewhere. Self-discipline was preferable and consistently advocated (St. Louis, 1871, 1873, 1875; Leidecker, 1946). Similarly, he agreed that too many teachers were martinets who forced children to memorize unconnected bits of information rather than employing class recitations in a more humane, interesting way. Who could approve of any classroom method through which "the child gets his individuality crushed out of him and he becomes a wheel in the clockwork of society?" (St. Louis, 1879, p. 201)

The superintendent doubted, however, that oral instruction, if pursued by the legions of untalented teachers found in most school systems, would solve the age-old dilemma of bored students and dull instruction. Again, an understandable reaction against the worst classrooms too often led people to seek a panacea, in this instance, the elimination or lessened use of textbooks or homework. All good teachers recognized an inherent tension between discipline and spontaneity, between order and freedom. This dialectical struggle was a natural process, the way change and improvement occurred in the world. But advocates of the new education who thought that play, manual training, and the elimination of textbooks would not create problems of their own needed to stop and reconsider their philosophical premises. The damage that could be inflicted on children, Harris thought, might be serious, worse than the effects of unenlightened teachers who crammed undigested nonsense into their scholars' brains.

Many reformers late in the century claimed that the "old" education of Harris's generation was overly dependent upon textbooks and the written word. The "conservator" agreed that many poorly trained, uninspiring teachers misused textbooks. He found little to commend in a geography teacher who took a fascinating subject and reduced it to lists of mountain ranges, rivers, and national boundaries that children had to memorize. Yet Harris quite unromantically thought that there would always be a short supply of really talented teachers. The growth of Normal schools, which taught the latest progressive methods, would help somewhat, but the shortage of first-rate, creative teachers would always plague the system. Moreover, even if the printed word could be deadly, hard work, and not much fun, knowing the names of important mountain chains, rivers, and so forth was not an inappropriate thing to learn in geography class. Talented teachers could make otherwise dull books come alive; talentless teachers did not become geniuses and inspiring Pestalozzis upon discovering object lessons. Books allowed every child to read and think on their own, no matter the quality of his or her teacher, and this brought something new and potentially desirable into a child's life (Leidecker, 1946; Roberts, 1924).

By the time he became superintendent, the bookish philosopher was convinced that reading, including the mastery of textbooks, was a democratic force in pedagogy. "The printed page is the mighty Aladdin's lamp, which gives to the meanest citizen the power to lay a spell on time and space. It is the book alone that is reliable for exhaustive authority" (St. Louis, 1870, pp. 27–28). Moreover, the aim of instruction was to teach all pupils how to learn on their own, after school days ended, through "perpetual self-education." The public library, a central means of popular education, would help promote this democratic end. "Every step toward the ability to master the printed page," he wrote in 1870, "is a step toward freedom from, and independence of, living teachers" (St. Louis, 1870, p. 28). This was another way in which socialization to the norms of the school led to wider intellectual horizons and thus ultimately greater individual freedom.

As a former teacher, Harris had great respect for the profession, even though he believed that like all occupations it attracted many dull, conservative people. Only clergymen, he thought, were more conservative than teachers. By all reports Harris overall enjoyed very good relations with the St. Louis teaching staff. Upon his retirement, the local teachers presented him with a beautifully bound volume, with an inscription to warm any superintendent's heart. It said that Harris had not only brought the city schools fame but that they "reflect to an eminent degree the personality of the man through whose comprehensive grasp that system has taken shape" (Harris Papers, Volume entitled "Teachers of St. Louis Public Schools to Prof. Wm. T. Harris, L.L.D.," May 12, 1880). The textbook had remained an essential part of the system that, according to the superintendent, allowed students to have authoritative knowledge at their disposal no matter how poor their instructor and helped them cultivate a life-long love of reading and learning. Reading books was hard work and not always as pleasurable as kindergarten, manual training, or recess. Without them, however, students were at the mercy of teachers who were not always well informed or a master of every intellectual domain.

CONCLUSION

As his tenure in St. Louis ended, Harris had established an impressive record, one complex enough to merit different sorts of historical appraisals. At the time, the young Hegelian had done some things that might have earned him credits among a rising cadre of progressive educators. He had actively pressed for a comprehensive system of public kindergartens, defended coeducation despite noisy calls for the establishment of single sex schools, loudly championed the cause of free high schools, expanded an extensive foreign language program for Germans, and had often eloquently stated the democratic purposes of modern education and the common school. But he had also exposed the excesses of the romantic critique of education, warned against panaceas such as manual training and industrial education, and defended textbooks and a formal curriculum despite the chanting on behalf of object teaching and pedagogical experimentation. Anything "progressive" he might have said was forgotten or downplayed in the years to come. Harris soon appeared out of step, as he criticized each wave of reformers, from the Herbartians and their focus on the interest of the child in learning in the 1890s, to the various advocates of a differentiated secondary curriculum, tracking, and other reforms that buried forever the idea of a common school (Claxton, 1936).

The five windows of the soul now seems like a quaint way of talking about what academic knowledge is worthy of study. To Harris, studying the common subjects in a common curriculum was the only way to receive the rudiments of an academic education; only then could democracy thrive. In his lifetime, the proponents of the new education would stereotype an older generation, saying they cared more about textbooks and rows of orderly desks than the welfare of the child, more about academics than vocational preparation. Merle Curti (1935) summed up the views of other progressives by calling Harris a conservative, and other biographers, though more admiring, remained embarrassed by the philosopher-king's faith in the power of tradition and common access to knowledge in a democratic society. Harris's defense of humanistic study for everyone in the nation's schools sounded reasonable to some educators in Victorian America but gradually faded in popularity in the education profession. I.Q. tests, a differentiated curricula, and shop class had become the new windows into the modern educational soul.

Acknowledgments. I would like to thank Barry Franklin, Herb Kliebard, Ed McClellan, Jeff Mirel, and Fran Schrag for their constructive criticisms of an early draft of this essay.

REFERENCES

Ames, C. H. (1909, December 23). William Torrey Harris. *The Journal of Philosophy, Psychology, and Scientific Method, 6,* 701–709.

Barnard, H. F. (1880, September). William Torrey Harris and the St. Louis public schools. *American Journal of Education, 30,* 625–640.

Brown, G. P. (1910, March). William T. Harris. *School and Home Education, 29,* 220–224.

Claxton, P. (1936). William Torrey Harris. In W. C. John (Ed.), *William Torrey Harris: The commemoration of the one hundredth anniversary of his birth, 1835–1935* (pp. 19–31). Washington, DC: U.S. Department of the Interior, Office of Education.

Cremin, L. A. (1961). *The transformation of the school: Progressivism in American education, 1876–1957.* New York: Knopf.

Curti, M. (1935). *The social ideas of American educators.* Totowa, NJ: Littlefield, Adams.

The death of Dr. Harris [Editorial]. (1909). *The American School Board Journal, 34,* 8.

Dewey, J. (1898, December). Harris's psychologic foundations of education. *Educational Review, 16,* 1–14.

Editorial. (1906). *Education, 27,* 49–50.

Fitzpatrick, F. A. (1910a, March 10). William Torrey Harris: An appreciation. *Journal of Education, 34,* 257–259.

Fitzpatrick, F. A. (1910b, March 31). William Torrey Harris. *Journal of Education, 34,* 340–341.

Harris, William Torrey. Papers. Missouri Historical Society, St. Louis.

Kaestle, C. F. (1983). *Pillars of the republic: Common schools and American society, 1780–1860.* New York: Hill & Wang.

Kliebard, H. M. (1995). *The struggle for the American curriculum, 1893–1958.* (2nd ed.). New York: Routledge.

Leidecker, K. F. (1946). *Yankee teacher: The life of William Torrey Harris.* New York: Philosophical Library.

McCluskey, N. J. (1958). *Public schools and moral education: The influence of Horace Mann, William Torrey Harris, and John Dewey*. New York: Columbia University Press.

Roberts, J. S. (1924). *William T. Harris: A critical study of his educational and related philosophical views*. Washington, DC: National Education Association of the United States.

St. Louis Public Schools. (1869–1881). *Annual Report of the Board of Directors*. St. Louis.

Troen, S. W. (1975). *The public and the schools: Shaping the St. Louis system, 1838–1920*. Columbia: University of Missouri Press.

Chapter 8

Integrated Curriculum and the Academic Disciplines: The NCTE Correlated Curriculum of 1936

Kathleen Cruikshank

The structuring of the secondary school curriculum through subject area divisions roughly reproducing the college and university academic disciplines has, despite its tenacity (Kliebard, 1995), been repeatedly challenged ever since it became obvious in the late nineteenth century that secondary schools would be called upon to serve more students than merely those preparing for college. The explosion of secondary school students who had no aspirations to college attendance in the first two decades of the twentieth century led to increasing interest in finding principles for curriculum organization based on perceived student needs rather than on the logical organization of the academic disciplines. When, after 3 years of work along subject area lines, the Committee on the Articulation of High Schools and Colleges of the National Education Association's Secondary Department recommended the establishment of an independent commission to consider serious reorganization of the subject areas for the high school curriculum, the stage was set for a final break with the traditional disciplinary organization of knowledge. That break came with the 1918 report, *Cardinal Principles of Secondary Education* (U.S. Bureau of Education, 1918), which recommended a high school curriculum built around the seven themes of health, command of fundamental processes, worthy home membership, vocation, civic education, worthy use of leisure time, and ethical character, to which end the traditional subjects were to serve merely as means. Thus the academic disciplines were not to be studied for their own sake but strictly as tools for meeting a wide range of student needs not unlike those which challenge schools today.

Among the forms through which this was to be accomplished over the next two decades were the correlated curriculum, integrated curriculum, fused curriculum, project curriculum, and activity curriculum, all of which claimed to be improved approaches to a more relevant preparation of young adults for the realities of life. "Life" was increasingly defined in terms of the concrete and mundane, as secondary teaching attempted to reach more and more students to whom schooling seemed a barely desirable alternative in any event. In this context, the potential for a progressive but academically grounded curriculum implied by John Dewey's contention that the organized adult knowledge contained in the academic disciplines represents "the possibilities of development inherent in the child's immediate crude experience" (Dewey, 1902/1990, p. 190) was lost in attempts to define ever more specifically the experiences and activities that would characterize students' daily lives as adults and to train them directly for those.

Yet despite these dominant tendencies, it was still possible to advocate a rigorous, academically based curriculum and, indeed, one within the context of a definition of schooling as preparation for life. Ruth Mary Weeks, as president of the National Council of Teachers of English, not only placed herself in the mainstream of curriculum thinking by her support of interdisciplinary curriculum and the creation of the commission that produced an exemplary all-grades curriculum based on and geared to the ordinary experiences of life, but she was also responsible for a comprehensive study of academically oriented interdisciplinary curricula and an attempt to link precollegiate curriculum to the most profound insights offered by leading thinkers in the disciplines. In her latter role, she represents a link between the thinking of Dewey and contemporary work that strives to identify the "enduring understandings" offered by the academic disciplines and to transform those into "essential questions" or overarching goals that will drive the curriculum (Blythe et al., 1998; Wiggins & McTighe, 1998; Wiske, 1998). That she was able to make her voice heard in an era dominated by a very different and in many ways contradictory perspective not only offers insight into her era but is suggestive as well for how contemporary change might be pursued.

RUTH MARY WEEKS AND THE CURRICULUM
COMMISSION OF THE NCTE

The National Council of Teachers of English (NCTE) was born in 1911 in response to a perceived need for redefinition of English as a secondary school subject, and its membership was largely secondary school English teachers who defined themselves over against the professors in those colleges and universities from whose requirements they were seeking to free their work. So strong was their opposition to collegiate disciplinary domination that in the first decades of the organization's existence they apparently never considered involving college professors in either the organization itself or its discussions (Fay, 1979). Between 1911 and 1936, they produced three major studies which reflected a steady progression away from the intellectual content of literary study toward the activities and skills of daily life (Clapp, 1926; Hatfield, 1935; Hosic, 1917). The last of these, *An Experience Curriculum in English* (Hatfield, 1935) sold over 25,000 copies in the first few years after publication and remained in print into the 1960s (Hook, 1979), testimony to the extent to which it captured the spirit of curriculum change in the mid-twentieth century. That spirit held the intellectual disciplines in a state of constant siege.

Yet even as that report was being developed, a study with equally potent but quite different implications was being compiled, launched by the same person and under the auspices of the same Curriculum Commission of the NCTE. That study, *A Correlated Curriculum* (Weeks, 1936), has remained virtually invisible historically, yet it represents one of the few serious attempts in U.S. curriculum history to articulate the optimum relationship between the curriculum of secondary education and traditional disciplines as manifested in college and university curricula. Further, it offers a vision of secondary school education that joins the rhetoric of democratic education for "life" with a vision of a life that incorporates the deeply held convictions of those who see the intellectual pursuit of a higher understanding as part of the shared democratic enterprise. That it does so in conjunction with an exploration of the many possibilities of a correlated curriculum gives it particular relevance in the context of contemporary discussions and experiments in interdisciplinary and integrated curriculum at the secondary level (Beane, 1995, 1997; Brady, 1989; Clarke & Agne, 1997).

Both *An Experience Curriculum in English* and *A Correlated Curriculum* were products of the NCTE's Curriculum Commission, which Ruth Mary Weeks established during her presidency in 1929–1930 with the announced goal of building "a course of study in English from the kindergarten through the university" (Hatfield, 1932, p. 407). Weeks was a relatively young woman of 43, somewhat flamboyant perhaps, certainly self-assured (Hook, 1979), when she assumed the presidency of the NCTE in 1929. Her parents were prominent Kansas City reformers in humanitarian and educational causes, whose commitment to the full development of their only child nurtured in her a highly educated ideal of what constituted the "art of living." She had early been drawn to a possible career in science, a natural outgrowth of her father's work in physics and electricity and her mother's mathematics teaching, but her father's warning against preparing herself for something in which she could find no career openings turned her to the humanities and economics in her undergraduate work at Vassar from 1903 to 1908. Upon graduation she began teaching high school in Kansas City, a career that ran uninterrupted until 1956 except for an early break of 5 years during which she studied schools in Europe, earned a master's degree in rhetoric at the University of Michigan, and taught briefly in two private schools. Because women, not as yet enfranchised, were not seen as adequately prepared to teach in the social sciences, her teaching field became English, and she embraced it fully, becoming an aspiring poet and literary critic. It was, however, the breadth of her education that permeated her leadership (Byers, 1991).

Although the NCTE presidency had traditionally been largely ceremonial, the actual workings of the organization being in the hands of Executive Secretary W. Wilbur Hatfield, Weeks's predecessor had challenged that arrangement and thus set a precedent for real presidential authority, which Weeks followed (Mason, [1961]). She personally laid out the Curriculum Commission's structure and led in the selection of its 175 members (Hook, 1979). Weeks's vision was that a comprehensive study of curricula in place would provide the cumulative wisdom for drafting a course of study in English from the primary grades through the university that would be a model, not in the sense of "rigid universal applicability," but "model in being planned as a whole from top to bottom—model in integration, in elimination of waste and duplication, in scientific grade placement of different types of material, and in implication of useful aims and effective methods" (1931, p. 9). In one sentence she combined the language of those advocating curriculum integration; those who had been seeking greater efficiency in schooling through the factory model; those who, using the language of efficiency, sought to vitalize a plodding and repetitive curriculum for the sake of children; those who were attempting to establish curriculum decisions on a scientific footing; and the full range of those who spoke in terms of the child's interest and aims.

AN EXPERIENCE CURRICULUM IN ENGLISH

Once underway, the direction of the Curriculum Commission was determined by chairman Hatfield, who now joined this work to his editorship of the *English Journal* and his position as secretary-treasurer of the NCTE. As a way of discovering "the general attitude of the committee toward curriculum problems," Hatfield asked in September 1930 that each member of the commission react to the proposed principles laid out as "Foundations of Curriculum Making" in the *Twenty-Sixth Yearbook* of the National Society for the Study of Education (NSSE, 1927). He then presented a set of proposals for members to react to, among which was the suggestion that members engage in a critique of the 1917 report, *Reorganization of English in Secondary Schools* (Hosic, 1917), as a first step toward determining what their own study might contain (Mason, 1961). Hatfield's assessment of the prospects for the commission was enthusiastic, based upon the "splendid energy"and "wonderfully progressive attitude" evident from the replies to the NSSE principles, as he reported to the 1930 annual meeting, and he looked forward to "a formulation of aims, activities, and materials" that might provide a departure point for local curriculum makers, as well as recommendations for "scientific experiments and for subjectively judged tryouts of proposed procedures" (Hatfield, 1930, pp. 57–58).

Hatfield foresaw the Curriculum Commission study as a potential contribution toward a science of teaching, focusing on the possibility of recommendations for scientific experiments and testing of procedures toward determining universal applicability. He was thus working squarely within the "scientific curriculum-making" context of Franklin Bobbitt and W. W. Charters, a fact made even clearer by a perusal of his final report. *An Experience Curriculum in English* is built firmly on the premise that "an ideal curriculum consists of well-selected experiences," the determination of which was to be made by surveying life, "noting what experiences most people have and what desirable possible experiences they miss," from which the curriculum builder would then select typical examples as well distributed as possible and arrange them in an orderly fashion (Hatfield, 1935, p. 3). Each major field of English—literature, readings, creative expression, and communication—was subdivided into "experience strands," from each of which at least one unit was to be covered each year. Literature at the secondary level (grades 7–12) included the greatest number of strands, identified as the following nine topics: Enjoying Action, Exploring the Physical World, Exploring the Social World, Studying Human Nature, Sharing Lyric Emotion, Giving Fancy Rein,

Solving Puzzles, Listening to Radio Broadcasts, and Enjoying Photoplays. For each strand, several "primary objectives" were given, each followed by "enabling objectives" and typical materials for instruction. For example, the primary objectives of the strand, Giving Fancy Rein, were:

1. To enjoy humorous fantasy in which exaggeration is a principal element
2. To enjoy relatively simple fantasies which are vehicles for ideas
3. To enjoy relatively simple fantastic plays
4. To enjoy fantasies in which the usual story interests, suspense, characters, humor, and theme are fairly well balanced
5. To enjoy allegories
6. To become acquainted with the more important myths, especially Greek and Norse
7. To read epic poems with satisfaction
8. To enjoy more difficult fantasies which are primarily intellectual
9. To enjoy poetic fantasies, in which beauty and mysticism predominate (Hatfield, 1935, pp. 60–62)

Although perusal of the literary works to be used might tempt one to interpret such an approach as merely clothing the traditional curriculum in the garb of "scientific curriculum-making," to at least some extent there appears to have been a circumscribing of the realm of possibilities for learning. The enabling objectives for enjoying "more difficult fantasies which are primarily intellectual," for instance, were merely "to recall the information assumed by the authors" and "to be sensitive to both atmosphere and slight specific hints as clues to the theme of each work" (Hatfield, 1935, p. 62), which would indicate a fairly superficial approach to major literary works such as Mary Shelley's *Frankenstein*. It was an approach perhaps consonant with enjoyment but apparently not concerned with greater understanding. The subdivision of secondary-level writing experiences—an element of the communication field—into the five strands of Social Letters, Business Letters, News Stories, Reports, and Opinions reinforces the impression that personal, intellectual, and spiritual growth were not among even the unarticulated goals of *An Experience Curriculum in English*.

Hatfield's report was in a sense a logical successor to the 1917 report, *Reorganization of English in Secondary Schools*, which fed into the Cardinal Principles Report (U.S. Bureau of Education, 1918). Produced by representatives of the NCTE working with the National Education Association (NEA) Commission on the Reorganization of Secondary Education that was responsible for the Cardinal Principles Report, the 1917 report had taken as a basic premise that "the course in English should be organized with reference to basic personal and social needs rather than with reference to college-entrance requirements" (Hosic, 1917, p. 26). At the same time, however, the aims of the English teacher were expressed as "first, to quicken the spirit and kindle the imagination of his pupils, open up to them the potential significance and beauty of life, and develop habits of weighing and judging human conduct and of turning to books for entertainment, instruction, and inspiration as the hours of leisure may permit"; and then second, "to supply the pupils with an effective tool of thought and of expression for use in their public and private life" (p. 30). Hatfield's *An Experience Curriculum in English* addressed the second aim but not the first.

A CORRELATED CURRICULUM

Weeks's *A Correlated Curriculum* (1936) traced its legacy back to the 1917 report's loftier goals. Its opening lines made the contrast clear: "The purpose of education is to give students an understanding of life and the character, information, and skill needed to meet its problems. Without such understanding, no man can apply the best learned skills appropriately" (p. 1). For Weeks, the path to that understanding lay through correlation of the subjects, which were "the pieces in a great picture puzzle which, if assembled, will reveal the image of the world" (p. 1). Rather than leaving it to students to solve that puzzle themselves, a task made more difficult by the increasing diversity and size of the student population, educators were duty-bound to develop ways to guide them toward that solution through an integrated curriculum. In addition to the forces toward fragmentation in modern life, the findings of Gestalt psychology argued for paralleling in the curriculum the integration toward which individual students naturally move in their development. Noting that "this methodology has supposedly been the theme of a previous Council publication, *An Experience Curriculum in English*," Weeks asserted that an integrated curriculum, with its implied project method of instruction and practice in problem solving, provided the only adequate material for training students not only to "mere adjustment to life as it is but for building a new and better world" (p. 4).

Weeks's reference to *An Experience Curriculum in English* may well have been sardonic, as Hatfield attended only briefly to the idea of integrated curriculum, then asserted that it was generally inadequate to remedying the real evil, which was "the divorce of all school study and drill from dynamic experience" and the offering of only intellectual activity as a preparation for "future successful living" (Hatfield,

1935, p. 11). As he put it, "normal living is a composite of dynamic experiences in which the will, the feelings, memory, and reason are all exercised as a single organism. Such typical life experiences as running an errand for mother, organizing a baseball team, giving a party, producing a play, conducting an election campaign or a community drive, all have other elements quite as prominent as the intellectual. It is chiefly of such materials that the warp of life is composed." It was therefore the school's job to achieve "a functional combination of the dynamic experiences of active life and the intellectual activities which have been teachers' chief concern" (Hatfield, 1935, pp. 11–12), but that integration would be determined by the nature of the experiences identified without reference to the insights that might be offered by those pursuing an understanding of life at a higher level.

Weeks may well have realized in establishing the Curriculum Commission that a professional organization of English teachers would not contain an abundance of members who were willing to subordinate their particular subject-area interests to a more comprehensive vision of the unity of the disciplines. Equally likely, however, is that organizational politics played a role. Weeks, like all NCTE presidents, had had presidential authority for only one year, and despite the confrontations she and her predecessor had found necessary in order to untangle some questionable business practices by Executive Secretary Hatfield (Mason, 1961), he had remained the key to continuity in any extended effort. Presumably for that reason, he had been appointed chair of the Curriculum Commission, thus ensuring its continuation beyond Weeks's term. Weeks herself, however, had chosen to chair the separate Committee on Correlation, which, according to a historian of the NCTE, became essentially independent (Hook, 1979). It had begun work in 1931 and, according to Weeks's account upon publication of its report, followed a path of trying to discover

> first, which schools were trying to weld the whole of education into a meaningful pattern; second, what subject-patterns, life-patterns, and growth patterns these schools proposed to use; third, by what tests such integrated educational patterns could be judged; and, fourth, whether the patterns proposed could stand the applications of these tests. (Weeks, 1937b, pp. 189–190)

"Subject patterns" referred to the organization of the subjects into something meaningful, "life patterns" referred to life as students would someday live it, and "growth patterns" referred to the pattern of development of the child. What the committee had discovered was a wide variety of correlations which could be categorized on a spectrum from incidental to radical, the last of which would

> transcend subject divisions, abandon a fixed body of subject matter, and attempt to integrate education with the world, on the one hand, and with the child's experience on the other, by a series of student-initiated but teacher-guided investigations which answer student questions by leading out into all the widening circles of social and subject-matter ramifications entailed in completing the original investigation. (p. 190)

This method, said Weeks, "might be described as 'the flower in the crannied wall' procedure" and concluded that, "when the student has solved his original questions, he will know what God and man is!" (p. 190).

The bulk of *A Correlated Curriculum* consisted of examples from classroom practice of each possible type of correlation of English with other subjects of instruction collected by the 43 researchers and 3 central committee members, embedded in synthesizing commentary. None of these was offered without qualification, and in fact tests of their value were suggested in both a prefatory chapter and in the introductions to each section. Revised and cut drastically because of space limitations, the report progressed from a short chapter on "Correlation of English with Other Fields through Incidental References and Isolated Projects" through a minimum of four illustrative examples each for other types of correlation—that is, an English course based on correlation but without changes in courses in any other subject, fusion of English with one other subject, fusion of groups of subjects, and a curriculum based on integration of all subjects. With rare exceptions, examples were taken from the secondary and college level, in keeping with Weeks's desire to maintain continuity through the first 2 years of college work.

The examples were not offered piecemeal. Rather, there was a serious attempt to provide criteria for critique and conceptual grounding. The report offered eight "tests of the value of correlation," three dealing with feasibility in terms of administration, teacher abilities, and materials and supplies, but the other five aimed toward testing any correlation effort in terms of academic integrity. First was the question of whether it was genuine correlation, that is, based upon synthesis. Discerning the same governing principles in several arts and sciences (e.g., universal grammatical principles), using material from one subject to explain another (such as the impact of the French Revolution on English romantic poetry), "pursuing the same theme through several media of expression," and "employing several arts and sciences in the execution of a single project or in answering some significant question" were the four ways in which genuine correlation could be achieved (Weeks, 1936, p. 6). The second test asked whether there were values gained through the proposed integration that could not be gained through a nonintegrated curriculum. Those values include a "more nearly complete and comprehensible picture of the world," more immediate connection with student experience, and stimulation and utilization of all the students' faculties (p. 7). The third test asked whether, on the other hand, tried-and-true values were lost by integrating the curriculum. The peculiar values of, for instance, the nonutilitarian aspects of the English curriculum, or of the fine arts, should be protected or at least compensated for by the new values that replaced them. The fourth test asked if the program was well-balanced. The goal should be a program which can "yield the highest returns in intellectual stimulus, in understanding of life, in enrichment of personality, in deepening of culture, and in future efficiency." It should "enlarge student experience beyond what he can gain from life at first hand," and it should be designed so that "all sides of the student's nature and all types of human being" can find expression in it, rather than "forcing upon all a single approach to life" (p. 8). Finally, the program must command student interest, not only meeting current interests, but commanding and enlarging them.

Notable in Weeks's report was the participation of 21 advisory experts from fields of knowledge and the arts as represented at the university level. Wary of correlation that only became a vehicle for leaving aside some materials in favor of others, Weeks contended that integrating curriculum made it all the more crucial "that these core topics be such that the student may through them approach the world by every significant avenue of human thought and experience, and that education may in turn approach this student along avenues calculated to bring into play every faculty of his nature" (1936, p. 13). Thus she addressed to those advisory experts the question, "What are the four or five most significant facts, ideas, or points of view which your subject has to offer the modern world?" (p. 289). From their responses she culled 70 statements of significant concepts from the physical, biological, social, and "philosophical" sciences and from the fine arts which were to serve as the "seventy-eyed watchman" over the report as a whole to ensure that every alternative presented would be tested by this question: "Will the child, when he has passed through this course of study, have looked at life from all the angles which the cumulative thought of the race has found significant, and at all those major aspects of experience which are in the picture from each significant angle?" (p. 13).

THE RECEPTION OF *A CORRELATED CURRICULUM*

Although overshadowed in historical accounts by *An Experience Curriculum*, the appearance of *A Correlated Curriculum* did not go unnoticed. The announcement in the *English Journal* of its publication described it as containing "widely divergent opinions held by leading teachers of English, as well as eminent educators in other fields" and "striking experiments in integration which have been going on all over the country," with "every possible form of correlation or of integration" described in detail and "actual samples given in full." It was a "pioneer work in the direction of a greater unity of purpose and of design in the high-school curriculum" (Hatfield, 1937, p. 70). An article on the work of the council's first 25 years commented that the report "should stimulate natural fusions and integrations and discourage some of the ill-considered attempts at correlation made merely because it is in fashion. The report attempts to lift the veil of the future a little for us, but its visions are always restrained by common sense" (Hatfield, 1936, p. 823). Less sympathetic views reveal more about its reception and may in fact shed light on why it has remained obscure in educational history. L. Thomas Hopkins (1937) of Teachers College read the report as written by English teachers for English teachers, although he noted that it would be of service to others "interested in curriculum reconstructions in the secondary and college fields," but he objected to what he saw as "no fundamental change in the process of learning" and to the interchangeable use of "correlation," "fusion," and "integration," despite the fact that "they have different psychological and philosophical antecedents" (p. 418). Further, he questioned whether "synthesizing parts or elements into a complex whole will satisfy the needs of pupils for wholeness or unity in their experiences . . . since a closer synergism among the parts can occur only when the wholeness or the unity appears first, and the parts are differentiated therefrom" (p. 418). That it was precisely that prior wholeness or unity that Weeks and the Committee on Correlation were striving to develop in the minds of teachers seems to have escaped him.

Franklin Bobbitt's (1937) review was similarly ambivalent, although his focus was, predictably, upon the absence of clear objectives. He judged favorably the consultation with specialists in the various disciplines as an attempt to "correlate the objectives of the English with the objectives of all other portions of education . . . to combine them at the source," which would lead to a result that was "entirely organic and not an artificial conjunction of disparate and never entirely fusible things" (p. 419). The committee had merely suggested the nature of this, although he thought it might be fruitfully built upon. He felt, like Hopkins, that there was a strong departmental bias in the report. But his main criticism was that the objectives of that department had not been formulated "with sufficient exactness. As a result, the reviewer reads this careful report, in spite of its terminology here and there, with a certain sense of academic unreality and remoteness from the throbbing life that is today driving forward in boys and girls and in men and women" (p. 420). Bobbitt noted that this failure to first formulate objectives was, however, characteristic of all levels of the educational profession "because of the latter's propensity to do the thing which fashion pronounces timely rather than that which scientific effectiveness pronounces needful" (p. 420). He seemed, however, to be somewhat confused with regard to the thrust of the report. Enumerating the types of correlation described in it, he remarked, inaccurately, that "the fusion of subject matter reaches its most extreme and, in the judgment of the Committee, most questionable form in the integration of all subjects or of content materials without regard to departmental sources" (p. 419). Contrary to his contention, the committee did not question the desirability of complete curriculum integration but was only articulating in some detail the barriers to and dangers inherent in it. Besides the necessity of casting aside traditional subject matter organization and of increasing both knowledge and the repertoire of methods, complete integration demanded "that educators develop a philosophy of education and of life, that they formulate a social program, that they commit themselves to some scale of values" (Weeks, 1936, p. 196). The report acknowledged that educators, "pledged always to please the public," found such commitment a risky business, as indeed it had proven to be in some trial programs of integrated curriculum (p. 196).

MAINTAINING A VOICE IN AN ERA OF CHANGE

The apparent failure of *A Correlated Curriculum* to achieve a greater impact may have been due to the fact that it was simply speaking a foreign language. It sounded like child-centered, experience curriculum thinking to some, while it echoed traditional English teacher thinking to the ears of others. What apparently could not be heard was a distinctive voice that did not fit the dominant trends of the time but drew strengths from them and projected a fuller, more intellectual and spiritual notion of life as its educational goal. Yet that voice permeated the report. According to the report, the goal to be achieved by education was "an intelligent understanding of life as a whole and of the place of its major elements in this whole" (Weeks, 1936, p. 1). To attempt to achieve this through individual subjects, "the pieces in a great picture puzzle," without attending to their connections was to leave the students with no means "by which to pick out a pattern from the educational pieces rattling in the puzzle box of the curriculum" (p. 1), particularly in the face of pressures in modern life which militated against synthesis. The "hyper-specialization" permeating commercial and professional activity, the mobility of the population, the "noise, confusion, and distraction of urban life," the "dead weight of civic and political indifference" (p. 2) on the part of citizens all pointed to the need for a curriculum which could provide a sense of wholeness. Even more, the multiplication of new knowledge, much of which seemed to undermine traditional moral and religious sanctions, necessitated an integration of "the scientific, esthetic, philosophical, and ethical branches of the curriculum" in order "to prevent students from viewing the world with purposeless despair" (p. 3).

In view of such language throughout *A Correlated Curriculum*, it is somewhat remarkable that Weeks could be viewed, as she was by historian Edward Krug (1972), as a supporter of the activity or experience curriculum who felt "that modern developments were inevitable and that it was up to her and other English teachers to make the required adjustments" (pp. 270–271). A closer reading of her writing reveals that she had a great deal more than adjustment in mind. Her remark, "educationally we are going to swap horses, and I intend to ride the new horse," quoted by Krug (p. 271), was made following the publication of *A Correlated Curriculum* in response to a somewhat deprecating newspaper comment that "it was the business of teachers, at any rate, to drown fighting" (Weeks, 1937a, p. 296). Weeks did not plan to drown. She responded, "I have no intention of being futile. I intend to throw my force into seeing that the thing which is going to happen produces the most possible good or the least possible misery!" (p. 296). For herself and those who shared her views, she pointed the way: "We may not like this new philosophy which we see forming about us, but, whether we like it or not, if we expect to make any mark upon our time we shall have to work through it. No quicker avenue to futility exists than to set one's self against the time spirit of one's age" (p. 296). Her response was thus to speak in the language of her age, yet to express in that language her own vision of a life lived through the pursuit of intellectual, spiritual, and creative fulfillment. By bringing together what appeared to be opposite poles, she sought a greater synthesis.

BRIDGING THE ABYSS: THE ACADEMIC DISCIPLINES
AND THE PUBLIC SCHOOL CURRICULUM

What is remarkable about *A Correlated Curriculum*, therefore, is the emphasis that it places upon the integrity of the intellectual pursuits embodied in particular disciplines at the same time that it recommends a disregarding of discipline lines. The selection of core topics around which to organize a correlated curriculum is, of course, crucial, as such topics can be superficial or merely an excuse for placing one's own favored material at center stage. What must be borne in mind is

> that special subjects arose from the need of man to view life from many angles, that each of these angles is significant, and that the educational picture of life gained from a series of core centers drawn from one mode of viewing the world may turn out to be as false and flat as the pictures of a one-eyed camera now seem to those who have compared them with the products of two-eyed camera photography. (Weeks, 1936, p. 13)

The standard by which to test the program thus becomes whether "the child, when he has passed through this course of study, [will] have looked at life from all the angles which the cumulative thought of the race has found significant, and at all those major aspects of experience which are in the picture from each significant angle" (p. 13). It was to that end that the statements were solicited from the internationally recognized thinkers in each of the disciplines, describing the most significant ideas, points of view, or facts that each discipline could offer to students exploring "the many-colored dome of life," as the section of the report containing the statements was called (p. 289).

As an attempt to involve college and university disciplinary scholars in public school curriculum making, the solicitation of those statements could perhaps be seen as only a variant of the earlier work embodied in the Committee of Ten Report (U.S. Bureau of Education, 1893) or of later efforts in the 1960s to implement curriculum developed at the university level. What is noteworthy, however, is the attempt to elicit from these scholars the ideas or principles of their disciplines which might then be used to develop correlated curricula. In other words, what Weeks and the Committee on Correlation appeared to be seeking were principles of such scope that they would provide a framework for a curricular vision across disciplines. The report itself states what they—or at least the author of the report—felt was the question to be addressed: "How to assemble the arts and sciences into a bold and colorful picture of the living world; how to set it glowing before our students in all its radiance till they cry out, 'This is the life we want and mean to live'" (1936, p. 286).

The assistance they received from their experts, however, was widely variable. Some interpreted the request as seeking a list of interesting topics, while others offered the main ideas emanating from their fields. Still others seem to have seen the request as a challenge to justify their fields in terms of value to students. Surprisingly few focused primarily on a broader substantive contribution of their disciplines to furthering the life of the mind through larger ideas. Those who did offered pregnant possibilities; for example, the imaginative appeal of astronomy and its exploration of humanity's place in the natural world and "the power and habit of bringing to bear on the problems of life in organized society a knowledge of the relationships between man and his natural environment" (Weeks, 1936, p. 296), as well as "the psychological aspect of religious attitudes and the attempt at adjustment with the universe by the utilization of social and personal experience" (pp. 306–307). The link of the human and natural worlds was also reflected in contributions advocating a sense of the "dependence of man on earth conditions and earth resources as the material bases of social development" (p. 297), of the interdependence of inhabitants of different regions of the earth, and of "the inherent unity of Man with the rest of living nature" and thus his subjection to the same fundamental laws, but at the same time his progressive "humanization," moving toward a higher state (p. 301). A broader vision of the arts was expressed in the hope of instilling the notion that human beings "experience a fundamental human need for . . . setting forth their inner life in an external form" (p. 310) that manifests itself in dance, among other arts, and that that form has a significance, aside from what it represents, and a recognition of "the unity of form in all of the arts of a given epoch, and the close relation of this to the underlying intellectual atmosphere or world-conception of the epoch" (p. 308).

On the whole, however, the separate lenses appear to have been more intact than any sense of a shared enterprise. Few seemed to see the task articulated by the report. Weeks wrote:

> We cannot cling either to our accustomed subject-matter, or our accustomed course divisions, or our accustomed methods. We must abandon all these things and start at the other end by asking, "What is the meaning of life? What must a young man know to understand this meaning? What sort of life will he then wish to live? And what tastes and skills must

he have to live this meaningful existence?" Then turning back to our fund of familiar subject-matter, we shall pick out the things needed for this educational synthesis and reject all else as slag from which the ore has been extracted. (Weeks, 1936, p. 287)

This meant "recasting the whole educational program in the mold of a central purpose, so that not only the parts but the whole will have a meaning" (p. 10). This was by no means an easy task, as the extensive treatment of problems in specific correlated curricula pointed out. The demands upon a correlated program were many:

> Does it meet immediate student needs? Does it have the highest possible ultimate significance? Does it multiply interests and values? Does it permit every approach to life of which the human mind is capable—every mode of thinking, every field of living? Does it integrate experience as well as knowledge? And does it lead through joy to understanding? If you cannot answer these questions in the affirmative, your program is only an arc and not a circumference, a segment and not a synthesis. (Weeks, 1936, p. 285).

Correlation was "a complicated problem of readjustment and compromise, of division of subject-matter and abandonment of subjects" (p. 286); it was not an easy solution, nor even a safe one. Weeks saw that it was entirely possible to replace a discipline-based program with one characterized by forced or artificial correlations or one which was a more blatant example of "educational fascism" than would have been possible under departmentalization (p. 199). The report warned clearly of the dangers of cavalierly discarding the subject matter divisions without creating a synthesis which could give the knowledge contained within them greater meaning. The new knowledge of the natural and social sciences, far from representing a new knowledge to replace the old, merely provided a "larger view of the truths which previous ages could only glimpse," a new lens on the "eternal verities" that old formulae sought to express (pp. 2–3). In order to give students the vision needed to develop toward a full unfolding of their potential, the curriculum must integrate its scientific, aesthetic, philosophical, and ethical branches. As the report concluded,

> May our eyes be keen, our hands cunning, and our vision wide! For a social pattern once broken, can never be remade. It would be indeed tragic to shatter our great educational dome of many-colored glass not to let in the white radiance of blended knowledge but to replace its rainbow glory by the dull grays of partial peering. (p. 287)

That blended knowledge was integrated but firmly rooted in the disciplines.

Thus Weeks represents at one and the same time a participant in the spirit of her age and a force working against it. From within the increasingly popular integrated curriculum discourse, she sought to shed light on the essential connections of the disciplines to the development of the human spirit. Through that curriculum she hoped to redefine what "education for life" really meant, namely gaining access to a vision of the unlimited possibilities of being human. While her vision connects her in some way to Dewey's vision of the unfolding of possibilities as the essence of education, it connects her equally to contemporary efforts to move beyond a view of academic disciplines as the tools to bolster national economic or technological aims or to achieve individual material advantage. Those who support a redefinition of curricular goals in terms of understanding, who speak of overarching goals, essential questions, and enduring understandings are, like Weeks, seeing in the academic disciplines far more than an accumulation of information and, like her, they see the greater potential of an interdisciplinary approach to the development of human understanding. Though not strictly "humanists" in Kliebard's (1995) sense of the term, they represent a line of continuity that draws upon the discourse and tools of the movements of their times to further a vision of the fullest human potential through interdisciplinary pursuit of the academic disciplines.

REFERENCES

Beane, J. A. (1995). Curriculum integration and the disciplines of knowledge. *Phi Delta Kappan, 76,* 616–622.

Beane, J. A. (1997). *Curriculum integration: Designing the core of democratic education.* New York: Teachers College Press.

Blythe, T., & Associates. (1998). *The teaching for understanding guide.* San Francisco: Jossey-Bass.

Bobbitt, F. (1937). *A Correlated Curriculum* evaluated. *English Journal, 26*(5), 418–420.

Brady, M. (1989). *What's worth teaching? Selecting, organizing, and integrating knowledge.* Albany: State University of New York Press.

Byers, J. P. (1991). Ruth Mary Weeks: Teaching the art of living. In J. M. Gerlach & V. R. Monseau (Eds.), *Missing chapters: Ten pioneering women in NCTE and English education* (pp. 30–48). Urbana, IL: National Council of Teachers of English.

Clapp, J. M. (1926). The place and function of English in American life. *English Journal, 15*(2), 110–134.

Clarke, J. H., & Agne, R. M. (1997). *Interdisciplinary high school teaching; Strategies for integrated learning.* Boston: Allyn and Bacon.

Dewey, J. (1990). *The school and society; and, The child and the curriculum.* Chicago: University of Chicago Press. (Original works published 1902)

Fay, R. S. (1979). The reorganization movement in secondary English teaching. *English Journal, 68*(4), 46–53.

Hatfield, W. W. (1930). Report of the Curriculum Commission, Minutes of the Board of Directors, November 1930, *President's Book*, NCTE Archives, Urbana, IL [unpaginated typescript].

Hatfield, W. W. (1932). The Curriculum Commission. *English Journal, 21*(5), 407–413.

Hatfield, W. W. (Ed.). (1935). *An experience curriculum in English: A report of the Curriculum Commission of the National Council of Teachers of English.* New York: Appleton-Century.

Hatfield, W. W. (1936). The National Council, 1911–36. *English Journal, 25*(10), 805–829.

Hatfield, W. W. (1937). *A correlated curriculum*—English Monograph No. 5. *English Journal, 26*(1), 70.

Hook, J. N. (1979). *A long way together: A personal view of NCTE's first sixty-seven years.* Urbana, IL: National Council of Teachers of English.

Hopkins, L. T. (1937). *A correlated curriculum* evaluated. *English Journal, 26*(5), 417–418.

Hosic, J. F. (comp.). (1917). *Reorganization of English in secondary schools.* Report by the National Joint Committee on English Representing the Commission on the Reorganization of Secondary Education of the National Education Association and the National Council of Teachers of English. (U.S. Bureau of Education, *Bulletin*, 1917, No. 2.)

Kliebard, H. M. (1995). *The struggle for the American curriculum, 1893–1958* (2nd ed.). London: Routledge.

Krug, E. (1972). *The shaping of the American high school* (Vol. 2). Madison: University of Wisconsin Press.

Mason, J. H. (1961). The National Council of Teachers of English 1927–1936. Typescript, NCTE Archives, Urbana, IL.

National Society for the Study of Education. (1927). The foundations of curriculum-making. In *Twenty-Sixth Yearbook: The foundations and technique of curriculum construction, Part II: The foundations of curriculum-making* (pp. 11–28). Chicago: University of Chicago Press.

U.S. Bureau of Education. (1893). *Report of the Committee [of Ten] on Secondary School Studies.* . . . Washington, DC: U.S. Government Printing Office.

U.S. Bureau of Education. (1918). *Cardinal Principles of Secondary Education; A report of the Commission on the Reorganization of Secondary Education, appointed by the National Education Association.* (U.S. Bureau of Education *Bulletin* 1918, No. 35). Washington, DC: U.S. Government Printing Office.

Weeks, R. M. (1931). Teaching the whole child. *English Journal, 20*(1), 9–17.
Weeks, R. M. (Ed.). (1936). *A correlated curriculum; A report of the Committee on Correlation of the National Council of Teachers of English.* New York: Appleton-Century.
Weeks, R. M. (1937a). Content for composition. *English Journal, 26*(4), 294–301.
Weeks, R. M. (1937b). Pattern-making in education. *English Journal, 26*(3), 187–194.
Wiggins, G., & McTighe, J. (1998). *Understanding by design.* Alexandria, VA: Association for Supervision and Curriculum Development.
Wiske, M. (Ed.). (1998). *Teaching for understanding; Linking research with practice.* San Francisco: Jossey-Bass.

Afterword

Schools as "Dangerous Outposts of a Humane Civilization"

Herbert M. Kliebard

For once, I am at a loss for words. Or nearly so. I am eternally grateful to my friends and colleagues for undertaking this venture and for contributing their precious time and considerable talent to bringing it to fruition. It is a great honor not just to have this volume appear, but to be associated with scholars of such eminence and with friends who have meant so much to me over the years. Theirs is a gift I shall always treasure. Special thanks, of course, needs to be accorded to Barry Franklin, who conceived of the project and, by dint of his dedication and resourcefulness, was able to bring it to a successful conclusion. I have valued his friendship enormously ever since he was a graduate student at the University of Wisconsin-Madison. I honor him as a human being as well as a scholar. I am also especially grateful to Arno Bellack, my former mentor and dear friend over a great many years, for agreeing to write the Foreword.

Mine is not the task of commenting on the individual essays (although I read them with great care and genuine admiration); Professor Franklin has already commented on them so splendidly in the Introduction. I was struck, however, by the themes that Franklin had singled out as the central ones in my work; perhaps I can say a few words about them. As so often is the case with me, I learn about myself by what others say rather than by conscious introspection and self-examination. I have learned a great deal about myself, for example, from reviews of my books as well as through the sometimes casual comments of colleagues and students. Had someone asked me to discern the most persistent themes in my work, I don't know what I would

have said, but once Franklin identified the themes of democracy and
liberal education, I realized he had something there.

Democracy, as John Dewey argued, is not just a political system
but a way of life. It does not consist simply of formal political structures, of elections and candidates, or of a judicial system; it is something that infuses our social relations and our sense of community and
belonging. The great enemies of democracy as I see it are social schisms
and invidious distinctions. That this country is a country of different
peoples with different cultures is something we need to not just toler-
ate but to honor. But out of the differences of race, class, gender, and
a host of other identifiable characteristics also come wrenching conflicts that divide us as a people and thereby undermine our democracy.
Formal schooling did not create these divisions, but it has needlessly
served to exaggerate and to exacerbate them. This occurs, for example,
not only when we provide grossly unequal opportunity for our children in terms of resources and advantages, but through the formal structures of the curriculum that serve to bifurcate school populations and
limit rather than broaden the horizons of the very children and youth
that schools are supposed to serve. All this has made me deeply suspicious of the kind of curriculum that attends too closely to alleged differences in children, whether they be differences of talent, condition,
or probable destination. Too often these differences turn out to be
imaginary or contrived and too often the mechanisms that are developed to deal with them become obstacles to our students' growth as
human beings. Democracy does not mean that everyone is the same,
but it can mean that people from all walks of life and whatever their
special circumstances can be initiated into the great intellectual resources of our culture. To me, this implies much more of a common
curriculum than a specialized one. By providing for such an initiation,
we minimize the risk of denying to certain groups the power to gain
control over their lives and destinies.

To raise the issue of a common curriculum is to allude to the other
theme that Franklin singled out: liberal education. To my great regret,
liberal education is now often identified with a stodgy and shopworn
tradition. It is associated with subjects of study that are remote from
those things that give meaning to our existence. To some extent, that
association is the outgrowth of the position of some advocates of a liberal education, who claim for its province a preordained domain of
knowledge and a ritualistic allegiance to what is past. My own allegiance
is to the *ideal* of a liberal education, that is, the notion that education
can indeed be liberating. It is not a possession; it is power. A truly liberal education supplies the power to transcend one's own time and

circumstances and opens the way for human beings to gain a measure of control over the many forces that impinge on their lives. It is the antidote to ignorance born of parochialism. As I envision it, a liberal education enlarges the tiny world into which we happen to have been born and invites us into a world that is, for all intents and purposes, geographically, temporally, and conceptually without boundaries.

For all its association with the past and with tradition, a liberal education is a supremely radical idea, particularly when it is associated with universal education. It is actually radical in two senses: On the one hand, it conveys the humanistic notion that human beings can indeed become masters of their own fate and are not simply the pawns of those social structures and abstract forces that confine and constrict our destinies. It reminds us, in other words, of the ever-present power of human agency. On the other hand, under the right circumstances, it reflects the supreme faith that such power is not simply the legacy of a select few, but, potentially at least, is within the grasp of nearly everyone.

One can hardly claim great success for our system of education in these respects. Just as the great disciplines of knowledge are inevitably in a constant state of flux, so must the subjects of study that reflect them become much more open to reexamination and reformulation. The school curriculum cannot afford to remain static in a world where knowledge itself is forever reinventing itself. Without constant renewal, a liberal education can at best be conveyed only to a lucky and select few. The task that lies ahead, it seems to me, is to make its values and meanings available to all. This is obviously a monumental task, but a beginning can be found by finding within the child's own experience those elements that give the most promise of eventuating in the kind of organized and systematic knowledge that the disciplines of knowledge reflect.[1] This is a process that cannot be rushed.

Bringing disciplined intelligence within the scope of ordinary people is a truly radical idea and teachers, not just the curriculum, are instrumental in this regard. Dewey was particularly eloquent on that point:

> What will happen if teachers become sufficiently courageous and emancipated to insist that education means the creation of a discriminating mind, a mind that prefers not to dupe itself or be the dupe of others? Clearly, they will have to cultivate the habit of suspended judgment, of skepticism, of desire for evidence, of appeal to observation rather than sentiment, discussion rather than bias, inquiry rather than conventional idealizations. When this happens, schools will be the dangerous outposts of a humane civilization. (Dewey, 1922, p. 141).

The qualities of mind that Dewey enumerates are precisely those that can make democracy work. It is at these points that democracy and the ideal of a liberal education intersect, and it is my fond hope that in the century ahead a truly democratic liberal education will emerge to help fulfill the tremendous promise of schooling. Apart from democracy itself, universal public schooling is America's greatest experiment. If schooling can help forge the "discriminating mind" that Dewey speaks of so admiringly, then education can take its proper place as the linchpin of an authentic democracy.

NOTE

1. I am obviously drawing on John Dewey at this point.

REFERENCE

Dewey, J. (1922, October 4). Education as politics. *New Republic, 32,* 139–141.

Index

About the Editor and the Contributors

Michael W. Apple is the John Bascom Professor of Curriculum and Instruction and Educational Policy Studies at the University of Wisconsin-Madison.

Kathleen Cruikshank is an Assistant Professor of Education at Indiana University-Bloomington.

Barry M. Franklin is a Professor of Education and Public Administration and Assistant to the Dean of the School of Education and Human Services at the University of Michigan-Flint.

Herbert M. Kliebard is Profssor Emeritus of Curriculum and Instruction and Educational Policy Studies at the University of Wisconsin-Madison.

Reba N. Page is a Professor of Education at the University of California-Riverside.

Daniel Pekarsky is a Professor of Educational Policy Studies at the University of Wisconsin-Madison.

Thomas S. Popkewitz is a Professor of Curriculum and Instruction at the University of Wisconsin-Madison.

William J. Reese is a Professor of Educational Policy Studies, Chair of the Department of Educational Policy Studies, and Professor of History at the University of Wisconsin-Madison.

José R. Rosario is a Professor of Education and Director of the Center for Urban and Multicultural Education at Indiana University-Purdue University-Indianapolis.